Managing Small
NetWare 4.11
Networks

Managing Small
NetWare® 4.11
Networks

Douglas Wade Jones

NETWORK PRESS®
SYBEX

San Francisco ▪ Paris ▪ Düsseldorf ▪ Soest

Associate Publisher: Steve Sayre
Acquisitions Manager: Kristine Plachy
Acquisitions & Developmental Editor: Guy Hart-Davis
Editor: Carol Henry
Project Editor: Alison Moncrieff
Technical Editor: Jim Huggans
Book Designer: Seventeenth Street Studios
Graphic Illustrator: Patrick Dintino
Desktop Publisher: Susan Glinert Stevens
Production Coordinator: Alexa Riggs
Indexer: Nancy Guenther
Cover Designer: Archer Design
Cover Photograph: IFA/West Stock, Inc.

Screen reproductions produced with Collage Complete.

Collage Complete is a trademark of Inner Media Inc.

SYBEX is a registered trademark of SYBEX Inc.
Network Press and the Network Press logo are trademarks of SYBEX Inc.

TRADEMARKS: SYBEX has attempted throughout this book to distinguish proprietary trademarks from descriptive terms by following the capitalization style used by the manufacturer.

Netscape Communications, the Netscape Communications logo, Netscape, and Netscape Navigator are trademarks of Netscape Communications Corporation.

The author and publisher have made their best efforts to prepare this book, and the content is based upon final release software whenever possible. Portions of the manuscript may be based upon pre-release versions supplied by software manufacturer(s). The author and the publisher make no representation or warranties of any kind with regard to the completeness or accuracy of the contents herein and accept no liability of any kind including but not limited to performance, merchantability, fitness for any particular purpose, or any losses or damages of any kind caused or alleged to be caused directly or indirectly from this book.

Library of Congress Card Number: 96-70746
ISBN: 0-7821-1963-8

Manufactured in the United States of America

10 9 8 7 6 5 4 3 2 1

To Dr. Suess, who wrote, "Oh, the THINKS you can think up, if only you try!" And to my kids who made me read it. Over and over.

Acknowledgments

I WOULD LIKE TO THANK GATEWAY 2000 for loaning me a speedy P5-166 for the duration of the project. I originally intended to use it as a test machine in the lab, but the computer's speed and graphics capabilities made it my favorite for writing instead.

Thanks to Kelley Lindberg, who suggested I write the book.

Guy Hart-Davis and Alison Moncrieff also deserve special recognition for suffering with my inability to meet deadlines, and for their kind, tactful way of saying, "Get it in gear, slow poke."

Thanks also to the following people at Sybex: Production Coordinator Alexa Riggs, Desktop Publisher Susan Glinert Stevens, Graphic Artist Patrick Dintino and Technical Editor Jim Huggans.

Perhaps I owe the greatest debt to my editor, Carol Henry, who showed through her thoughtful edits that she actually read every word. Now, that's dedication.

Contents at a Glance

Table of Contents

Introduction

I F YOU ONLY RECENTLY GOT THE JOB of running a network, you might not know yet that you have the best job in the world. It might take a few months. At first there's that awkward time, when you're trying to figure out how the last administrator set things up and why he or she didn't document anything. After that, if you're reasonably well organized, it's fun.

You see, we all watched too much TV when we were little. Every few seconds we were treated to a chase scene, a violent thwack, or a song. Every few minutes we got a commercial that sold us some sizzle, whether or not there was any substance to it.

When in school, we got a new teacher and a new subject at least every hour. Now that we've "grown up" we spend our time channel surfing or Web surfing at the rate of a channel or site per minute.

We have acquired, in short, an attention deficit disorder. Big surprise.

Well, now there's a job for people like us called NETWORK ADMINISTRATION. In this job, you get to change your focus every few seconds, from PC hardware, to applications, to routers, to network operating systems, to hubs, to cables.

Most of the time, there's an employee that needs help with a problem we can easily (and quickly) fix. For long-range stimulation, there's always that nagging intermittent hardware problem (believe me, all nagging intermittent problems are hardware problems).

For tactile stimulation, there's making cables whether you actually need them or not. ("Honest, Ms. Manager, you really can't have too many patch cables around.")

For slow times, you can read trade magazines. For creative times, you can write in your logs. For sleepy times, you can read the logs.

Without taking the fun out of it, this book attempts to: (1) get you through that preliminary awkward time when you're setting up the network or figuring out an existing one; (2) help you keep the network reliable; and (3) help you get credit for your work, so you can keep your great job.

What This Book Covers

Perhaps reading this book is a bit much to expect—only the truly self-destructive actually read technical books cover-to-cover. Accordingly, I've tried to include both casual reading material for background understanding and reference material for on-demand answers.

You should read Chapter 1, the introduction to small networks. That'll give you an overview of the most common networking terms, with a focus on Novell's idea of small networks.

And certainly Chapter 2 provides stimulating entertainment while explaining NetWare Directory Services, along with tips for setting up the physical network and the file system.

Read Chapter 3 only if you're upgrading an existing network, including a NetWare 4.*x* network. Read Chapter 4 only if you're installing a new network.

Chapter 5 is a good "read," since it covers the most common day-to-day activities of a network administrator. It also gives you some great tips for automating routine tasks. This chapter should work well as reference material, too. Just look up the task you want to accomplish, and perform the steps.

You might not want to read Chapter 6, Documenting the Network, but I implore you to do it. No matter how boring it sounds, your own documentation can save your hide in countless ways. I've included worksheets you can copy to make the task easier.

Use Chapter 7 as a reference chapter when you work on login scripts. It also has a section on NetWare Application Launcher, which is a way to make network applications appear magically for your MS-Windows users.

Chapter 8 covers printing. If you're not familiar with NetWare printing, you'll want to read it to get oriented. If you already have a working print setup, then you can use this chapter just for reference.

Read Chapter 9, at least the sections on server maintenance and statistics. The last section in that chapter covers detailed statistics, which you'll only need in certain situations.

Chapter 10, Backing Up and Restoring Data, has an overview of NetWare's tape backup capabilities. Beyond that, it's a reference chapter.

Look at Chapter 11 on time synchronization only if you have questions or problems. Time synchronization sets itself up automatically and normally runs fine without intervention on a small network.

Read Chapter 12 only if you bought and need to use IntranetWare, Novell's new product suite for Internet and intranet functions.

Read Chapter 13. It covers some theory and practice regarding troubleshooting that you'll need in the back of your mind when something goes wrong.

Appendixes A and B can be used as references for utilities to be run from DOS and OS/2 command lines and training resources. In the Glossary, you will find specialized terms and their meanings.

Who Should Read This Book

This book is written especially for the administrator who gets the job and isn't sure where to start. To help you get started, the book has plenty of practical advice on how to sort out an existing network or create one from scratch.

Once you have the network figured out, set up, and documented, this book helps you settle down to a daily routine that includes a healthy dose of preventive maintenance.

This book is for managers of small NetWare 4.*x* networks. This means a network with fewer than four servers and without wide-area links to other networks. The actual number of users is not part of the equation here, since you can have thousands of users in this definition of a small network, and that's okay.

Conventions Used in This Book

I have used the following conventions in this book to make it easier for you to follow along:

- Text in **boldface** is information you type in.

- *Italics* are used to call attention to new terms or to identify variables.

Notes give you useful information or cross-references about the topic at hand.

Tips are hints, shortcuts, or bits of advice to help you accomplish your task more easily.

Warnings alert you to common pitfalls or problems you might encounter.

Introduction to Small Networks

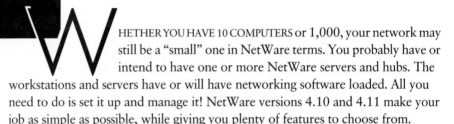

HETHER YOU HAVE 10 COMPUTERS or 1,000, your network may still be a "small" one in NetWare terms. You probably have or intend to have one or more NetWare servers and hubs. The workstations and servers have or will have networking software loaded. All you need to do is set it up and manage it! NetWare versions 4.10 and 4.11 make your job as simple as possible, while giving you plenty of features to choose from.

First and foremost of NetWare's features are file and printer sharing, the reasons that networking came to be in the first place. These services are typically part of a business's infrastructure, so you want them to be fast, reliable, and simple to manage. Beyond these basic features of any network, NetWare 4 adds some great bonuses.

- Intelligent file compression gives you more disk storage—and it works at night, so you don't even know it's there.

- Web Server gives you intranet functionality.

- Security features protect your data from unauthorized access.

- NetWare 4 allows your network to grow to gargantuan proportions without your having to change operating systems.

- You, the network administrator, can manage and troubleshoot the network from the server, from a workstation, or from your home.

In addition, you can count on the fact that the best third-party networking software and hardware will work with NetWare 4, the most popular network operating system on earth.

This book will help you learn and master the intricacies of NetWare 4 administration, from installing the server to writing login scripts, to troubleshooting.

Did you inherit a NetWare 3 network? Here you'll see how to upgrade to NetWare 4 and understand the new concept of NetWare Directory Services (NDS). It's not so hard as you may have heard.

Are you responsible for setting up the network? Don't worry. This book will introduce you to the basic hardware and software components of the network, give you tips on choosing hardware, help you select a cable installer, and guide you through your first login as ADMIN, the network administrator.

What Is a "Small" Network?

NETWARE 4 WAS DESIGNED to handle a large company's networking needs better than any other operating system to date. For such a company, NetWare 4 has some great features that make the system fast and easy to manage. A "large" network requires configuration of its more complicated features, such as directory partitioning, replica management, and time synchronization. There are good books available to explain these features, but this isn't one of them. This book is for the administrators of "small" networks that don't have all that complexity.

NetWare 4 was designed to work well for small networks. That means it is easy to install and manage if you accept Novell's defaults and forgo the fancier features. So what is a small NetWare 4 network? It has *all* of the following:

- Fewer than four NetWare servers

- Only one site (no wide-area links to NetWare servers at other sites)

- Fewer than 3,000 users

In these first sections, we'll look at what hardware and software components make up a typical small network.

Typical Hardware Components

WHETHER YOU ALREADY HAVE a network to manage or you are preparing to install one, you will benefit from a general knowledge of typical hardware components before you start. Figure 1.1 shows the hardware components of a typical small network.

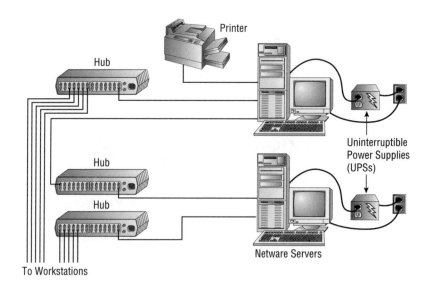

NetWare Servers

Your network has one or more (up to three) NetWare servers. Each server runs NetWare, and does some very basic jobs:

- It holds the shared files on its hard drives.

- It manages communication (such as messages and e-mail) among the workstations.

- It coordinates printing to shared printers.

In addition to these three fundamental duties, your NetWare server can do much more for you, if you know how to configure it. For example:

- It can hold CD-ROMs that are available to network users.

- It can hold a tape drive or other drive used for backing up its hard drive and/or the hard drives on workstations.

- With additional software and hardware, it can also route e-mail to and from the Internet. It can route faxes to and from fax machines outside the company. In fact, it can perform almost any job that involves the transfer of data.

Look at the typical server shown in Figure 1.2. A NetWare server has one or more network adapters, often called *network interface cards* (NICs), to connect it to the cabling system. The server's case should plug into an uninterruptible power supply (UPS). The server's monitor doesn't typically display fancy graphics. The server needs a keyboard but doesn't need a mouse.

FIGURE 1.2
A typical NetWare server connects to the network via network interface cards (NICs), also called network adapters.

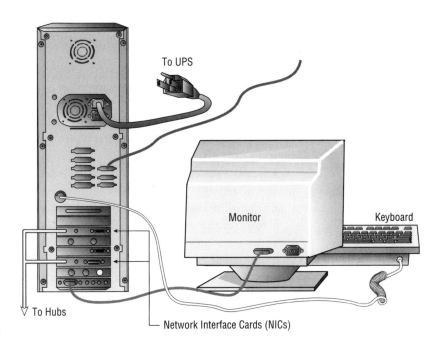

To UPS

Monitor

Keyboard

To Hubs

Network Interface Cards (NICs)

Workstations

In Novell NetWare circles, a *workstation* is a network computer that a user uses. In some other circles, the term workstation applies to high-end computers, often RISC processor- and UNIX-based, and often made by Sun or DEC. But for the purposes of this book, it's any old network computer where somebody works.

Workstations all have two things in common: (1) They have a network adapter that connects them to the network. And (2) they have software that gives the user access to network resources such as shared files and printers. On a NetWare 4 network, this software is called the NetWare Requester, or client.

With additional software and/or hardware, a workstation can also be a fax server, a print server, or a mail server. The concept of a workstation also being a server may be somewhat confusing. Think of it this way: As a general rule, a *NetWare* server is not a workstation; and a workstation is not a *NetWare* server.

*Although any computer on the network can be a server of some kind, in this book the term **NetWare server** refers to a computer running the NetWare operating system. Workstations that function as fax servers, print servers, or mail servers are not considered NetWare servers.*

Workstations have access to shared files by means of *mapped drives* to the NetWare server's file system. For a typical DOS/Windows workstation, this means additional drives are created beyond A, B, C, D, and E. Network drives, usually beginning with F and ending with Z, become as accessible as the workstation's own drives.

Similarly, workstations have access to shared printers by *capturing* printer ports to a network printer. After capturing a printer port, a user can print to that network printer as easily as to a printer attached to the workstation.

A workstation can be of the DOS/Windows variety, or it can run OS/2, Macintosh System 7, Windows 95, Windows NT, or UNIX. Each workstation architecture has its own NetWare Requester. The requester allows a workstation to use network resources in a way that is native to the workstation's architecture.

Hubs

The most popular cabling system for Ethernet networks uses unshielded twisted pairs of wires with telephone-style connectors. It's called 10BaseT. For each network adapter on each server or workstation, one of these cables connects to a hub.

Figure 1.3 shows a typical 10BaseT hub. The hub conditions the electronic signals, making them clear and strong. The hub can shut down (partition) ports connected to bad network adapters that generate numerous collisions.

FIGURE 1.3
A typical 10BaseT hub

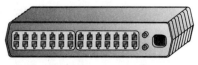

Stackable Ethernet Workgroup Hub

10BaseT hubs come in a wide variety of sizes, from 5-port to 48-port models. *Stackable* hubs can be attached to each other to add more ports to your network. A logical hub can be made from a stack of smaller hubs, giving one cable segment hundreds of possible ports. A *manageable* hub has a means of attaching a terminal. From that terminal, you run special management software to control and monitor the hub.

10BaseT cabling has a limit to its usable length, but you can put a hub on the remote end of a cable to extend its length and allow more workstations to connect.

Switching hubs are enhancements to typical hubs. 10BaseT is a 10 megabit-per-second (Mbps) technology, but switching hubs offer separate 10Mbps channels and often a faster port for the server. They may offer a fiber distributed data interface (FDDI), which operates in a fiber-optic ring topology at 100Mbps. Or they may offer one or more 100BaseT or 100BaseVG ports operating at 100Mbps. Switching hubs also offer the advantage of filtering packets, which means each port only receives the packets it needs. Thus, switched hubs eliminate the need for bridges (see upcoming section).

Prices and capabilities of hubs vary widely. Whatever hub you choose, make sure you're not wasting money on features you won't use. Also make sure the hub matches your cabling and network adapters. Switching hubs are a rapidly-changing technology, so check the latest reviews in magazines such as *Network Computing* to get cost and value comparisons.

Bridges, Routers, and Gateways

As technology advances, the differences between bridge and router operations have become blurred. This is because vendors, in their efforts to provide more functionality in their hardware, have put more intelligence into their devices.

Bridges link two networks together by transferring data between them. For instance, a bridge can connect a cable segment of Token Ring architecture with one running Ethernet, or two Ethernet segments together. A bridge cuts down on traffic by passing only data that is meant for a destination on the other side. Intelligent bridges can go one better by filtering, or passing only certain packets to the other side.

A *router* generally provides more control over network traffic. Routers also are used to connect dissimilar networks, such as one running (Novell's) IPX/SPX protocol and one running TCP/IP.

A *gateway* provides a sophisticated connection between a local network and a mainframe computer or a packet-switched network.

NetWare servers have built-in, limited routing capabilities. For instance, you can install two network adapters in a file server and connect each to a different hub. The server then transfers the appropriate packets between each network. A network cable segment with network adapter may be Token Ring; another such segment may be Ethernet.

Thus, the server can act as a router to connect any number of different topologies, only limited by the number of network adapters you can install. It's not as fast as a dedicated hardware router, but it gets the job done. In a small network, your NetWare server can probably do all the routing you need.

Wireless Networking

Wireless communications is a fairly new and broadly interpreted aspect of networking. Companies looking for wireless solutions have encountered trouble because of a lack of applications, no standards, unrealistic expectations, and a market without clear technology leaders. Therefore, company managers and network administrators should not expect wireless networking to approach the speed or reliability of cabled networks.

Wireless networking generally occurs over infrared, radio, or microwave frequencies. Infrared products cannot penetrate walls or floors and are therefore already falling out of favor. Radio frequency products are most popular, most using a spread-spectrum technology that was developed for secure, interference-tolerant military communications.

Following are summaries of the available wireless concepts.

Wireless Point-to-Point

One option for wireless networking is point-to-point microwave (see Figure 1.4). This technology gives you a connection bridge between two buildings up to 3 miles apart. Southwest Microwave of Tempe, Arizona, sells a system that operates in the 23GHz band and transfers data at up to 20Mbps—a very respectable LAN speed.

Radio frequency point-to-point solutions carry data at one-tenth the speed of wireless point-to-point, but this may be sufficient for your particular network.

Cellular Wireless

Pick up a technology magazine these days, and you might very well see an article on wireless data. Don't get this confused with wireless LANs. It's just another name for cellular phone service. Sure, the service can carry data, too. Nevertheless, it's just an implementation of dial-up phone line communication over modems.

It's possible to get your laptop to dial up a NetWare server via cellular data transmissions, but the cellular wireless technology currently lends itself more to paging and e-mail. Phone lines can give you 28.8Kbps; wireless generally provides only 4.8Kbps or 9.6Kbps.

If this an area that interests you, you'll need to know something about Cellular Digital Packet Data (CDPD). Peter Dyson's *Network Press Dictionary of Networking* (Sybex, 1995) defines CDPD as "a method used in cellular communications and wireless modems for sending data more efficiently by using any available cellular channel." CDPD uses voice channels, but it can switch to a new frequency if a voice transmission begins in the cell currently in use.

Cellular service providers began promoting CDPD as a way to sandwich data in with voice transmission. There is hope that new, higher-frequency cellular networks will give this industry a boost. Currently, though, the costs are several times those of cabled phone lines and the "speed" is thousands of times slower than a LAN.

FIGURE 1.4
Microwave point-to-point hardware can connect LAN segments up to 3 miles apart.

Wireless Network Adapters for Workstations

You can get PC-card wireless network adapters for notebook workstations, or ISA cards for desktops, that transmit data to a back link attached to your wired network. The price for the PC cards is currently about $400 or more; the network access point costs another $400 plus. The number of access points you need depends on the geographic area of the network and the amount of traffic. The range of the radio transmitter runs from a few hundred to a few thousand feet.

Again, this is another rapidly expanding market with technology that is improving every month. The various vendors are seeking interoperability with the IEEE 802.11 standard under development. If your users need freedom from cable, my advice again is to do some shopping.

Wireless Handheld Devices

Grocery stores and other companies (Figure 1.5) are beginning to use wireless handheld computers for tracking inventory. The computers transmit the data to a server, which is most often UNIX-based. Look for NetWare solutions to be available by the time you read this book.

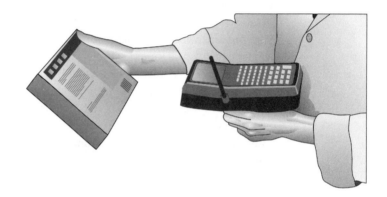

FIGURE 1.5
A retail employee relays inventory data using a handheld computer.

Uninterruptible Power Supplies (UPSs)

Certainly, a UPS is not used exclusively by networks: You can use one on any alternating-circuit power device. (After losing two VCRs to power surges, I installed one on my stereo and TV equipment.) But the UPS is a crucial piece of equipment for a company that uses computers in its critical money-making path and can't afford to lose data or employee computing time. In every case that I can imagine, a UPS is worth the investment of a couple hundred dollars for every workstation, hub, and server on the network.

Since most power outages last less than 15 minutes, a simple UPS (Figure 1.6) can save your company money most of the time.

For protection against extended outages, or outages when nobody is around to gracefully shut down the server, a UPS with intelligence can help. An intelligent UPS provides some or all of the following benefits:

- A UPS on the server can quietly shut the server down if the power goes down.

FIGURE 1.6
A typical UPS

- Many UPSs record power characteristics over time, giving you and the power company an idea of power problem trends. (Although such products may help you feel better by giving you concrete evidence of problems, don't expect to get improved electricity from the monopoly "grid." Just use it as a troubleshooting tool. "So, we started getting parity errors at the server console just after a major spike or brownout. Hmmm...")

- Some UPSs will page you if an unfavorable power event happens. Or they will send you a message over the network or e-mail.

- Some UPSs monitor temperature and humidity, alerting you when the climate is unfavorable for electronics.

- Many UPSs provide information to network management software by way of Simple Network Management Protocol (SNMP). SNMP applications give you a management console, from which you can monitor and control many network devices at once. Adding your UPSs to SNMP management gives you another network device at your command.

Experienced network administrators always recommend evaluating UPS options and buying the ones that are right for your network. And for the sake of your company's profitability and your own job security, you really should do so.

Printers and Other Peripherals

Printers, of course, are one of the main reasons networks exist. Since the average printer doesn't get used much by any one user, it makes economical sense to share. A printer can be cabled directly to a workstation or to a server. Hewlett-Packard, Castelle, and other third parties manufacture "black boxes" with multiple parallel and serial ports that connect directly to the hub via the same cabling that connects workstations. In addition, these companies also manufacture boards that fit directly into HP printers and connect to the hub.

You can also attach scanners, CD-ROM "jukeboxes," and other useful devices for sharing on the network. Like everything else, it just takes the right software and hardware to do so.

Typical Software Components

NETWORKING INVOLVES NETWORK SOFTWARE at every computer. Networks use software for some important fundamental tasks. *Networking software drives the hardware.* For instance, a NetWare server has special software modules to access its drive controllers, network adapters, and other adapters. Software modules used to drive hardware are called *drivers*. In workstations, the network adapter is controlled by a driver and other networking software.

Networking software enables other software. In a workstation, for instance, you can load a software module that allows the server to back up the workstation.

Networking software takes care of business. Networking software brings all the benefits of networking to the users. It routes print jobs to the printer; it makes files on the server work like files on the workstation; and it allows the administrator to view and control the day-to-day workings of the network.

Following are summaries of the networking software used in NetWare 4 environments.

NetWare Server Software

A NetWare 4 server has at least two disk partitions: a DOS partition and a NetWare partition.

DOS Partition

The NetWare server boots up on the DOS partition. The DOS partition should be at least 15MB to store the needed device drivers and disk repair utilities. It may take up an entire disk drive if the NetWare partition(s) are on another disk drive.

If the DOS partition takes up the entire disk drive, it is wasting space. You may want to rebuild it to avoid this. A good estimate for the size of the partition is 15MB as suggested by Novell, plus 1MB for every MB of memory in the machine. Allowing the additional space will let you do a memory dump to disk in the unlikely event that you experience problems and a "core dump" is requested. Without this space, the system dumps to floppies.

Like a DOS workstation, a NetWare server runs a CONFIG.SYS file and an AUTOEXEC.BAT file from the root of its DOS partition.

After the server boots up in DOS and runs CONFIG.SYS and AUTOEXEC .BAT, it runs the SERVER.EXE file to start the server. This program automatically loads the disk drivers, by default from the same directory on the DOS partition. The SERVER.EXE program is normally in the \NWSERVER directory if version 4.*x* is the first NetWare operating system on the computer. If the server has been upgraded from NetWare version 3.*x*, then SERVER.EXE is placed in the \NW410 or \NW411 directory. You can include SERVER.EXE in the AUTOEXEC.BAT file to automate the loading process.

Table 1.1 provides a list of files typically found in the server's boot directory.

TABLE 1.1 Server Boot Directory Files on the DOS Partition	**FILES**	**PURPOSE**
	SERVER.EXE	Starts the NetWare operating system.
	STARTUP.NCF	Works like the DOS CONFIG.SYS. A text script of NetWare commands that execute when you type SERVER.EXE. Contains such commands as LOAD IDE.DSK to load the disk driver. You can include commands to load patches to the NetWare operating system.
	*.DSK	These are disk driver files. They provide the software interface for your hard drives, CD-ROM drives, and disk controllers. In many cases, the functions of a DSK disk driver are better served by loading a HAM for each of your server's host adapters and a CDM for each of the drives.
	*.CDM	Device drivers for disk drives, CD-ROM drives, and tape drives. CDMs are not loaded if you use DSK files as drivers. Before a CDM can load, you must load a HAM to drive the adapter.

TABLE 1.1 (continued)
Server Boot
Directory Files on
the DOS Partition

FILES	PURPOSE
*.HAM	Host adapter modules that drive hardware such as a SCSI or IDE controller. If you use a DSK driver, you do not need to load a HAM. HAMs and CDMs work together.
*.NLM	Most files executed at the NetWare console are NetWare Loadable Modules (NLMs). Some NLMs stored on the DOS partition are patches to the operating system. Others are loaded to interface with or repair storage devices.
VREPAIR.*	NetWare utility used to repair corrupted volumes.
V_*.NLM	Special name-space modules used by VREPAIR. These may include V_LONG for support of long file names, V_MAC for Macintosh file support, V_OS2 for HPFS file support, and V_NFS for UNIX file support.

NetWare Partitions

The NetWare partitions include all the files available to workstations. After you run SERVER.EXE from the DOS partition, a batch file called STARTUP.NCF loads the device drivers for your hard drives, CD-ROM drives, and tape drives. In addition, STARTUP.NCF may also load patches to the operating system. (Patches are files loaded to fix bugs in the original software.)

When STARTUP.NCF has finished its work, the operating system mounts the required NetWare volume, SYS. After SYS is mounted, the operating system runs a file called AUTOEXEC.NCF from the \SYSTEM directory of SYS. This file generally mounts the remaining volumes if there are any, and loads LAN drivers (drivers for the network adapters).

Server Startup Process

Following is a summary of the sequence of events for starting a NetWare server.

1. You turn on the server power.

2. The computer runs its automatic hardware and firmware bootstrapping processes. This includes its BIOS reads and memory test.

3. The computer executes CONFIG.SYS from the root of its boot drive. The CONFIG.SYS must contain the following statements:

   ```
   Files = xx
   Buffers = xx
   ```

   It cannot load upper-memory managers such as QEMM or HIMEM.SYS.

4. The computer executes AUTOEXEC.BAT from the root of its boot drive.

5. You change directories to the server's NetWare boot directory. This directory is either \NW410, NW411, or \NWSERVER. You can automate this step in the AUTOEXEC.BAT or other batch file.

6. You type **SERVER <Enter>**. This step, too, can be automated in a batch file.

7. The NetWare operating system starts. It reads the STARTUP.NCF file from the same directory that holds SERVER.EXE.

8. The STARTUP.NCF file loads patches (optional) and disk drivers (.DSK files, or .HAM and .CDM files).

9. The operating system mounts the NetWare SYS volume. Another batch file, called AUTOEXEC.NCF, runs from the \SYSTEM directory of the SYS volume. This batch file establishes communication with the network via the network adapter, mounts all remaining volumes, and runs other executable files as necessary.

DOS/Windows Software

You have three options for networking your DOS/Windows workstations. The one that ships with NetWare 4.10 is the VLM version. The one that ships with NetWare 4.11 is called Client 32. The third is called the Netx client, an older bindery-only client. Netx is supplied for workstations that can't use VLM or Client 32.

For the following discussion of these options, you should be somewhat familiar with the operation of DOS/Windows computers and other computers on your network.

Netx

NETX.EXE is a bindery-only client supplied for compatibility with some older applications. These applications used "invalid" calls that only work with Netx and not with VLM or Client 32 software. Workstations that use Netx cannot access any of the features of NDS. Also, Netx workstations require your server to use bindery emulation. It is recommended that you upgrade applications that rely on Netx so your users can use NDS. (NDS, NetWare Directory Services, is described later in this chapter.)

DOS/Windows Workstation Using VLMs

Virtual loadable modules (VLMs) are software modules that the NetWare requester (VLM.EXE) loads. These modules handle the functions of a NetWare client, including those listed in Tables 1.2 and 1.3.

	MODULE NAME	FUNCTION
TABLE 1.2 Core Modules of a VLM Client	BIND.VLM	Implements the NetWare services using the bindery (not required for pure-NDS* clients).
	CONN.VLM	Manages connection tables.
	FIO.VLM	Handles file input and output.
	GENERAL.VLM	Handles miscellaneous functions for NETX.VLM and REDIR.VLM.
	IPXNCP.VLM	Provides IPX transport protocol functions.
	NDS.VLM	Provides NDS* functions.
	NETX.VLM	Makes VLM client compatible with older NETX clients.
	NWP.VLM	Allows multiple NetWare protocols.
	PNW.VLM	Provides Personal NetWare (peer-to-peer) networking.
	PRINT.VLM	Redirects printing to network printers.

TABLE 1.2 (continued) Core Modules of a VLM Client	**MODULE NAME**	**FUNCTION**
	REDIR.VLM	Coordinates the routing of workstation calls to DOS and NetWare.
	SECURITY.VLM	Provides enhanced security.
	TRAN.VLM	Coordinates multiple transport protocols.

* NDS is described in an upcoming section.

TABLE 1.3 Non-Core Modules of a NetWare VLM client	**MODULE NAME**	**FUNCTION**
	AUTO.VLM	Attempts automatic connection if the connection is lost during a networking session.
	MIB2IF.VLM	Supports Management Information Base II (MIB-II) interface groups.
	MIB2PROT.VLM	Supports MIB-II for the TCP/IP groups.
	NMR.VLM	Responds to NetWare management calls.
	RSA.VLM	Gives RSA encryption for NDS* authentication.
	WSASN1.VLM	Provides backwards compatibility to earlier SNMP versions.
	WSDRVPRN.VLM	Collects information about print mappings and captured printers.
	WSREG.VLM	Registers the SNMP MIB.
	WSSNMP.VLM	Provides support for MIB-II System and SNMP groups.
	WSTRAP.VLM	Trap SNMP information from the workstation.

* NDS is described in an upcoming section.

NetWare has a utility for installing the networking software components, which makes the following modifications to the computer's software:

- A LASTDRIVE parameter is added to the CONFIG.SYS file. This specifies the last drive letter that may be used on the workstation. The default is LASTDRIVE=Z.

- A DOS SET parameter is added to the AUTOEXEC.BAT file specifying the language of NetWare displays and help files. An example of this parameter is

  ```
  SET NWLANGUAGE=ENGLISH
  ```

- In the AUTOEXEC.BAT file, a line is added to call another batch file, STARTNET.BAT, in the \NWCLIENT directory.

- The \NWCLIENT directory is created.

- The networking files (see Table 1.4) are copied to the \NWCLIENT directory and its subdirectories.

- Windows applications, DLLs, and drivers needed for networking are copied to the default Windows and system directories. Modifications are made to the .INI files.

TABLE 1.4 Networking Files Copied to \NWCLIENT	**DIRECTORY/FILES**	**PURPOSE**
	\NWCLIENT\LSL.COM	Creates link support layer interface between the LAN driver and IPX, Novell's communications protocol.
	\NWCLIENT*LAN driver*	Establishes a connection with the network adapter. Specific for each model of adapter; sometimes called the multiple-link interface driver (MLID).
	\NWCLIENT\IPXODI.COM	Loads the IPX communications protocol (the default). In some cases you will need to load a TCP/IP module.
	\NWCLIENT\VLM.EXE	Launches virtual loadable modules (VLMs). By default, it loads all VLMs in the directory.

DIRECTORY/FILES	PURPOSE
TABLE 1.4 (continued) Networking Files Copied to \NWCLIENT		

DIRECTORY/FILES	PURPOSE
\NWCLIENT\NET.CFG	A text file used to list configuration parameters for the workstation's networking software.
\NWCLIENT\STARTNET.BAT	A batch file that runs LSL.COM, the LAN driver, IPXODI.COM, and VLM.EXE.
\NWCLIENT\NLS*Unicode files*	16-bit character sets for language support.
\NWCLIENT\NLS\ENGLISH*.MSG	Message files for NetWare command line utilities.
\NWCLIENT\NLS\ENGLISH\ TEXTUTIL.HEP	Help file for NetWare character-based menu utilities.

DOS/Windows Workstations Using Client 32

Novell's new Client 32 software is designed to utilize the full capabilities of 386 and later processors. Previous versions of DOS/Windows client software, such as VLMs and NETX, used only a 16-bit execution.

Client 32 software includes the files listed in Table 1.5.

If you bought NetWare 4.10 and don't have Client 32, you can get it by upgrading to NetWare 4.11. Or you can download Client 32 from Novell's NetWire forum on CompuServe (GO NETWIRE) or from Novell's Web site, http://NETWARE.NOVELL.COM/.

Macintosh Workstations

Novell's new NetWare Client for Mac OS gives Macintosh users full access to the NetWare network. You can install the client software from the NetWare 4.11 installation CD-ROM, or download it from http://netware.novell.com/.

TABLE 1.5	DIRECTORY/FILES	PURPOSE
Client 32 Files	\NOVELL\CLIENT32\STARTNET.BAT	A batch file that launches the other client software modules.
	\NOVELL\CLIENT32*LAN driver* (*.COM OR *.LAN)	Establishes a connection with the network adapter. Specific for each model of adapter; sometimes called the multiple-link interface driver (MLID). The LAN versions of these drivers are for 32-bit execution, and therefore perform faster.
	\NOVELL\CLIENT32\NIOS.EXE	Manages memory and establishes a software platform for other modules.
	\NOVELL\CLIENT32\LSLC32.NLM	Creates link support layer interface between LAN driver and communication protocol (IPX or TCP/IP).
	\NWCLIENT\IPX.NLM	Loads IPX communications protocol (the default). You can load TCPIP.NLM instead of or in addition to IPX.NLM
	\NOVELL\CLIENT32\CLIENT32.NLM	The 32-bit DOS Requester.
	\NOVELL\CLIENT32\CMSM.NLM	The client Media Support Module, which coordinates LAN driver interaction with LSL.
	\NOVELL\CLIENT32\ LOGINW31.EXE	Windows login utility.
	\NOVELL\CLIENT32\NAL.EXE	NetWare Application Launcher utility, which gives users improved access to network applications. Also allows administrator to manage that access.
	\NOVELL\CLIENT32\STARTNET.BAT	A batch file that runs the client software.
	\NOVELL\CLIENT32\NET.CFG	Configuration file for parameters of the Client 32 software.
	\NOVELL\CLIENT32*Unicode files*	16-bit character sets for language support.
	\NOVELL\CLIENT32*.MSG	Message files for NetWare command line utilities.
	\NOVELL\CLIENT32\NLS\ENGLISH\ TEXTUTIL.HEP	Help files for NetWare character-based menu utilities.

The installation program copies the following files to the workstation:

FILE	LOCATION
NetWare Client	Extensions folder
MacIPX	Control Panels folder
NetWare IP	Control Panels folder
NetWare UAM	Appleshare folder
MacIPX AppleTalk	Extensions folder
MacIPX Ethernet	Extensions folder
MacIPX Token Ring	Extensions folder
NetWare Object Assistant	Extensions folder
~NetWare Aliases	Extensions folder
File System Manager	Extensions folder
NetWare File Access	Extensions folder
NetWare Print Access	Extensions folder
Netware Client Utilities	New folder and contents at root of workstation startup volume

Windows 95 Workstations

You have two good options for your Windows 95 workstation software. You can either use Microsoft's Service for NetWare Directory Services, or Novell's Client 32 for Windows 95.

Comparison of Windows 95 Client Software

Microsoft's solution, Service for NetWare Directory Services, is about 700KB. Novell's Client 32 for Windows 95 is ten times as big. There are other major differences, as well.

- Microsoft's product adds NetWare Directory Services (NDS) access to the built-in Client for NetWare networks. Novell's product replaces it. So with the Microsoft add-on, you can still share files and printers via File and Printer Sharing for NetWare Networks. With the Novell software, you must use the Client 32 software for sharing local resources.

- Client 32 gives you a full-featured login utility, more options for LAN drivers, automated client updating, and NetWare Application Launcher (NAL). NAL gives the administrator greater control over network applications and how they are presented to users. NAL is discussed in Chapter 7, "Automating Access to Network Resources."

If your ambitions for Windows 95 are fairly modest, Microsoft's Service for NetWare Directory Services is your best bet. If you want more control and/or functionality with your Windows 95 workstations, Novell's Client 32 for Windows 95 is probably a better way to meet your demands.

Benefits of NetWare 4 for a Small Network

ALTHOUGH NOVELL IS PUTTING MOST of its effort these days into keeping NetWare dominant in the large-enterprise market, it is the small network that made Novell famous. Resellers, installers, and owners of small businesses cherish NetWare for its manageability, its stability, its support of diverse workstations, and its ability to grow with the business.

Over the last ten years, Novell has struggled with its identity. Its first real foray into the world of small business came with proprietary PC-based file servers. These were actual server hardware with networking software loaded. Novell emerged into the marketplace with its hardware, but to dominate the networking industry it had to get out of the hardware business and support industry-standard machines.

NetWare servers began to infiltrate the closets of large companies that used mainframes, providing better communication, improved file and printer sharing, and—most importantly—increased departmental control. Eventually, Information Services (IS) departments began implementing NetWare as a companywide solution, connecting and standardizing their departmental networks.

Novell went through a few dark years. Struggling to compete with Microsoft in the desktop applications market, the company bought WordPerfect. They released some shaky, unstable products during this time—namely, versions 4.0, 4.01, and 4.02 of NetWare. Novell has emerged from its problems, though, and has regained its focus. NetWare versions 4.10 and 4.11 are the company's premier networking products to date.

Because it is so dominant, NetWare commands first-rate attention from hardware and software manufacturers. Many of the benefits of NetWare 4 stem directly from its popularity in the networking market.

In this section you'll read a review of the features that make NetWare 4 the solution of choice for small networks, including

- File and printer sharing

- Intelligent disk compression

- Web Server

- Security

- Expansion capability

- Resource management

- Easy maintenance

- Remote troubleshooting

- Hardware and software support from other manufacturers

File and Printer Sharing

The heart and soul of any network operating system is the sharing of files and printers. Novell made its name because some geniuses in an elite brain trust called Superset devised the fastest, most reliable file-sharing around.

The NetWare File System

Novell takes advantage of speedy server RAM by using the maximum amount of file caching possible. When you open a file in the NetWare file system, the server keeps that file in RAM for quick response on its next access. In fact, you can expect that over 90% of the disk blocks accessed on the server are delivered from RAM rather than from the disk. This makes your file system response time very fast.

Directory entries are also indexed and cached, making the lookup time very fast. Read requests are buffered (queued in RAM), write requests are buffered, and multiple processing threads are created as needed to service the file-system requests.

When a server does access the hard disk, it does so very efficiently. Disk reads and writes are coordinated so that the drive heads move as little as possible, sweeping across the disks in a deliberate fashion rather than zigzagging back and forth like the drive heads on most workstations. Physical disk writes and reads disturb servicing from cache as little as possible.

LARGE BLOCK SIZE AND SUBALLOCATION Disk blocks are large, normally 32KB or 64KB. This improves performance by allowing more data to move to and from the disk in one request. To minimize waste of partially used blocks, a background block suballocation feature breaks up a large block if necessary. Then a background "garbage collection" process frees up the unused portions, reassembles them, and makes them available.

SALVAGE When you delete a file, NetWare normally keeps it salvageable if disk space allows. This feature is available in most contemporary file systems, but NetWare makes the process of recovering files efficient and manageable. You can purge deleted files manually if you wish, or allow NetWare to do it automatically.

HOT FIX A feature called *hot fix* reserves a small percentage of disk space for redirecting bad disk blocks. When a drive has problems with a disk block, NetWare automatically marks that block as bad, copies the block to the hot fix area, and avoids using the bad block.

Intelligent Data Compression

You may already be familiar with disk compression, which works by replacing your normal disk volume with one that is completely compressed. Another implementation of compression is the file compression made famous by the PKZIP program. Compression is especially beneficial for those old .BMP files that are taking up space on workstation hard drives. These files, on average, can compress to half their original size.

Like file salvaging, disk compression in NetWare goes beyond the norm offered by other operating systems. NetWare's disk compression feature is really smart. And with the demand for storage nearly always exceeding projections, it's nice to have compression on your side.

HOW COMPRESSION WORKS Compression works by replacing commonly repeated sequences with short codes. When compressing a file, the operating system looks for these repeated byte sequences (such as the word *the* in most any language). It then replaces those sequences with a code (the number 1, for example) and lists the original sequence in the file header. When the file is unencoded, the 1s are replaced with the word *the*, and the file resumes its original size and content.

NetWare disk compression works on one of two levels. You can flag individual files with a compression attribute, which tells the operating system to compress those files only; or you can let NetWare decide which files to compress.

HOW NETWARE DECIDES WHICH FILES TO COMPRESS When you create a NetWare volume, you specify whether you want the volume enabled for compression. If you have enabled compression for a volume, any of three conditions can cause a file to be compressed:

- You have set the Immediate Compress (IC) flag on the file or on its directory.

- The file has been deleted but not yet purged from the file system. In other words, the file can still be salvaged.

- A nightly search by the operating system finds a file that hasn't been accessed for a while.

If you want, you can control compression parameters in great detail. But for most networks, the defaults work just fine.

Web Server

NetWare 4.11 comes with a World Wide Web server for publishing information on your company network and on the Internet. Web Server is implemented as a set of NLMs for publishing HyperText Markup Language (HTML) pages. You can publish Web documents whether your NetWare network is connected to the Internet or not.

Using Web Server, your company can market its products and services to Internet users if you have an Internet connection. Or you can use Web Server for internal company use only, and to communicate with customers, investors, and employees. Your internal workstations will need to load IP and use a browser such as Netscape Navigator.

NetWare Web Server supports the common features of the World Wide Web without a UNIX system. Web Server includes support for forms, the Remote Common Gateway Interface (R-CGI), access controls and logging, as well as BASIC and PERL script interpreters.

Security and Access

Even small companies have confidential information—salaries, employee performance reviews, and proprietary trade secrets, for example. With NetWare 4, such information is safe on the network.

The opposite of security is accessibility. Accessibility is also good, since the whole idea of a network is to make people more productive by allowing them to share. The trick for an administrator is to make sure that the *right* people have access to the *right* resources, and that others don't.

Security and access needs are different for every company and network. Administrators need to be proactively involved. Among other tasks, you may need to

- Create directories that have limited access

- Create groups of users with special privileges

- Create login scripts that give users easy access to needed network resources

- Enforce the use of passwords

- Take physical security measures to protect the server, such as locking it up in a closet and disabling the keyboard

Some of the security measures may seem harsh or rigid, and indeed a few administrators have been known to use security measures to bolster their esteem through control. The better administrators assume a posture of service, offering security as one way of providing what the company needs.

Whatever your attitude about security, you'll find NetWare's security and access features varied and powerful. The only problem is that you have to learn a fairly complex set of terms and tools to make it work as you want it to.

Ability to Grow

The first rule of networks is that they grow. NetWare 4's architecture allows your network to expand gracefully.

Growing with NDS

NetWare Directory Services (NDS) allows you to add NetWare servers, user accounts, printers, and other objects painlessly. Although adding a server does require an additional NetWare license, the job of integrating it into the Directory tree is virtually automatic. You can create a new branch of the tree for the server, either before installing it or during installation. Or you can put it in an existing branch. NetWare takes care of replicating the Directory onto the first three servers.

The administration utility for Windows, called NetWare Administrator, is very intuitive. It allows you to add objects such as user accounts, printers, and new container objects (branches), with just a few mouse clicks. NetWare Administrator's status and error messages are more informative than most Windows programs, and it includes plenty of online help.

Adding Disk Space

Unless you are using a Redundant Array of Inexpensive Disks (RAID), you have to bring the server down to add disk space. Once you've added a hard disk, you can easily add it to existing volumes, create new volumes, or use it to mirror an existing disk.

Adding Workstations

Your NetWare license allows only a limited number of users, so you need to be aware of the number of users on the system. Otherwise, with NDS you just add a user account for each new user and you're done. NDS accommodates virtually unlimited users on the network. The only hitch comes when the total number of objects grows to a few thousand; then you need to partition the Directory. It's not hard, but it takes more savvy on your part.

If you need to add a hub for new workstations on a 10BaseT network, you have several options. You can chain the hub via one of the ports on the existing hub. Or you can "stack" the hub via a special port on the existing hub. Yet another way is to create a new cable segment by installing a new network adapter to the server and cabling the new hub to it. This option offers better performance over the others, but it costs you a new adapter.

Resource Management

The NetWare Administrator is a useful tool for managing all your network resources. Some common tasks you can complete with NetWare Administrator areas follows:

- You can easily edit login scripts.

- You can change rights for users or groups simply by dragging one object onto another and filling in a checklist.

- You can navigate the file system, create directories, and modify rights and attributes.

Remote Troubleshooting

NetWare's remote console utility allows you to work at the server's console from home. This means you can check on the server's status when you get a late-night call from your company's accountant, complaining that the printer doesn't work.

Logging in remotely to the server's console requires a phone line to the server. Once you set up the remote connection, you can do almost any of the routine maintenance tasks, including

- Monitoring the server's status, including disk space, file caching, processor utilization, and memory usage

- Changing SET parameters

- Loading/unloading NetWare Loadable Modules (NLMs)

- Rebooting the server

Since you can also perform these tasks from your workstation on the network, the remote console utility is particularly useful if you're workstation is not very close to the server.

Support from Other Manufacturers

Due to NetWare's popularity, third-party manufacturers find it profitable to make their products compatible with NetWare. This means most off-the-shelf hardware and software will work on your network. This support from manufacturers is critical, because everything in your network besides NetWare—the computers that work as your servers and workstations, all the infrastructure, peripherals, and software that make your business run—come from third parties.

Hardware and software that are certified to work on your NetWare network have the "Yes! It runs with NetWare" logo on their advertising. While this improves your chance of compatibility, it still doesn't guarantee anything. Especially with disk controllers and network adapters, you need to go beyond the "Yes!..." program and take further precautions. Namely, you should take care to buy from retailers who offer product support. Also, be sure you establish contact with the manufacturer. Find out about their bulletin board or Web page. This often gives you access to updated drivers and "workarounds" for common problems.

Here are just a few of the many optional add-ons for your network that are available from third-party manufacturers:

- Diagnostic hardware and software

- Inventory software

- Network planning utilities

- Application licensing and management utilities

- Print servers

- Fax servers

- CD-ROM jukeboxes

- Virus scanners and cleaners

- Time synchronizers

- Modem-sharing hardware and software

- Protocol analyzers

- Internet access and e-mail

- Groupware

- Server automation and scheduling software

- Backup software and hardware

Summary

WHAT IS A "SMALL" NETWORK? You might consider it an infrastructure that allows the employees of your organization to work smarter and faster. It includes workstations running client software, at least one but no more than three servers, and all the cabling and hubs needed to tie everybody together.

Novell NetWare makes your network administration job as simple as possible. The file and print services are fast and reliable, yet they require very little management on your part.

Add to these basic services the bonuses of e-mail, enhanced security, expansion capabilities, resource management, remote troubleshooting, and support from other manufacturers, and you have a real investment in productivity.

Planning the
Network

CHAPTER

2

THIS CHAPTER HELPS YOU prepare to install a new NetWare 4.1*x* network. A large portion of the material in this chapter focuses on planning the Directory tree, and is for those of you unfamiliar with NetWare Directory Services (NDS). You'll learn how *objects* represent physical entities such as users and printers. Also, some objects simply contain other objects, just as DOS directories contain files.

You can usually take the NetWare defaults during installation and do just fine. But it does help to become acquainted with the more commonly used object classes and their salient properties. Unique among the object classes is the Volume object, which assumes twin personalities—one for the Directory and one for the file system.

Also covered in this chapter is another topic that will help you as an administrator: designing a naming scheme for objects and properties. If you name objects consistently from the start, you and your users will have less confusion later.

Perhaps the most critical part of this chapter deals with Directory context, which means an object's position in the Directory tree. You will need a good grasp of context to do your work as an administrator. Related to context are the concepts of *distinguished* and *relative naming,* and the so-called *typeless* and *typeful* names.

The Directory and the Directory Tree

WHAT IS THE DIRECTORY? In the NDS scheme of things, it's just a list of objects, with some information about each one. An object can be a user account or a printer or a pointer to a file system directory, or just about anything that you want to manage.

The View from the Top

Here is a preview of the steps required to plan your new NetWare 4.1 network.

1. Decide whether to accept the default Directory tree (with one Organization object) or to add Organizational Units (OUs) under the Organization.

   Multiple OUs are for larger networks with distinct workgroups. With multiple OUs, you'll need to maintain multiple login scripts.

2. Design the Directory tree.

   Decide on the placement of leaf objects such as Users, Groups, and Print Servers.

3. Decide whether to use bindery contexts.

   Bindery contexts allow NetWare to create a simulated bindery for compatibility with hardware and software made for NetWare 2 and NetWare 3.

4. Devise a naming scheme.

   Used for giving consistency to object names and other properties.

5. Plan the file systems.

   Decide on the server's DOS partition size, NetWare partitions, volumes, and fault-tolerant features.

6. Select a topology and communications architecture.

   Primary options are Ethernet, Token Ring, FDDI, ATM, and wireless. Ethernet leads in popularity and price.

7. Select a protocol suite.

   IPX/SPX or TCP/IP. IPX/SPX is the standard and default. TCP/IP gives you Internet, WAN, and UNIX compatibility.

8. Determine the physical layout.

   Includes the power sources, network cabling, and physical security of the servers.

9. Plan the selection and placement of hubs and network adapters.

   Select standard or high-speed hubs, switches, and network adapters. Make sure your cabling matches your selection.

Figure 2.1 shows a Directory tree. The list is organized in tree form, starting with an object called the [Root], which you will always see written with the brackets. The [Root] is a container object, meaning it holds other objects.

Other container objects are the Organization object and Organizational Unit (OU) objects. In Figure 2.1, OURCO is the name of an Organization object. It contains the following objects:

- A Server object named SERVER1

- Three OU objects named ACCT-DEPT, PROD-DEPT, and SALES-DEPT

- A User object named ADMIN

- A Volume object named SERVER1_SYS

This graphical representation of the Directory tree is what you see when using NetWare Administrator, the Windows utility you'll use to manage the network.

FIGURE 2.1
The Directory tree, displayed in the NetWare Administrator utility

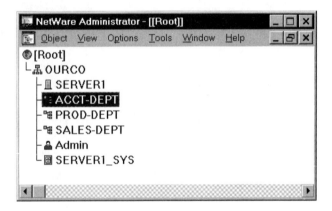

Objects

FIGURE 2.2 LISTS THE VARIOUS OBJECT CLASSES you can create in the Directory. The [Root] and Organization objects aren't shown; these objects are created automatically when you install your first server.

You probably won't use all of the available object classes. In fact, most networks do just fine with five or six of them. A few of the most useful are explained in the following sections.

FIGURE 2.2

You can create objects in
any of these classes.

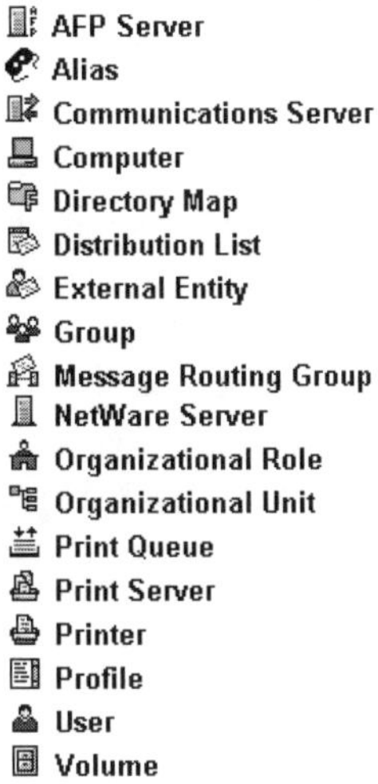

- AFP Server
- Alias
- Communications Server
- Computer
- Directory Map
- Distribution List
- External Entity
- Group
- Message Routing Group
- NetWare Server
- Organizational Role
- Organizational Unit
- Print Queue
- Print Server
- Printer
- Profile
- User
- Volume

[Root]

The [Root] object, as mentioned, is created automatically when you create your first Server in the tree. [Root] is actually an object class, and its name is the tree name you specify when creating that first Server. But in NetWare Administrator, you just see the word [Root] next to the globe icon.

NDS limits what you can create under the [Root] container object; or, put another way, NDS limits what a [Root] can contain. These objects are as follows:

- *Organization,* normally the name of your company

- *Country,* another container object (seldom used)

- *Alias,* a pointer to another object

Organization Objects

The Organization object is a container object. You can only create it under the [Root]. (You can also create it under a Country object, although use of the Country object is not recommended.)

The Country object class was originally created to comply with the X.500 specification, which may someday govern the infrastructure of global networks. For now, use of this object adds unneeded complexity. If future developments make it more meaningful, you can always add a Country object to your tree later.

When you install a NetWare server, the installation program prompts you to specify your company name. This name becomes the Organization object under which the other objects in the tree are created.

Thus, the simplest Directory tree contains two container objects: [Root] and an Organization object named after your company.

Objects that represent your users and other network resources are commonly called *leaf objects*. The leaf objects created by your first server installation include your NetWare Server, a User object ADMIN, and Volume objects. If you accept the default Directory tree, all these leaf objects are created under the Organization object.

The Organization object has a *login script* property, in which you define login parameters for all users directly under the Organization. This login script can define the default drive mappings and printer captures for those users, as well as set up a consistent environment for users. If all your User objects are in the Organization container, its login script will execute for all users. (Login scripts are discussed in Chapter 7.)

Organizational Unit Objects

You can create Organizational Unit objects to further divide your Directory tree. Organizational Unit objects can be under an Organization object, or under other Organizational Unit objects. Most administrators call Organizational Unit objects OUs for short.

Why divide the Directory tree with OUs? The best reason is to make your job easier when your company has distinct divisions or departments. When your network resources are used only by a certain set of users (such as a department), separating those users and resources into their own OU can help you set up their *rights* and *login scripts*.

The default rights for objects in the same container allow proper access to those objects. This means User objects in a container can access Printer objects in the same container; but User objects in a separate container cannot. You can work around this limitation in a single-container tree, but creating separate OUs saves you the trouble.

All User objects in the same container execute the same login script when logging in. This happens because the login script is a property of the OU object. Therefore, when you create separate OUs, you need to manually create separate login scripts. When a user logs in to the system, the following login scripts will be executed:

1. The container login script, in which the user exists.

2. The user profile login script, if the user is a member of a profile. Assigning a member to a profile is optional.

3. The user's personal login script. If there is none, a default login script will be executed instead.

Let's look at an example of when separate OUs are needed. The imaginary company OURCO has three departments: Production, Sales, and Accounting. Each department uses its own printer and accesses different files and applications on the NetWare server. You might create these three OUs: ACCT-DEPT, PROD-DEPT, and SALES-DEPT, as shown in Figure 2.3.

With these OUs in place, you can administer rights by the container objects, rather than by individual users. The users in PROD automatically have rights to the printer in the PROD container, but not to the ACCT or SALES printers. You can also grant file-system rights to the container PROD that only apply to objects in PROD, not to those in ACCT or SALES.

FIGURE 2.3
Creating separate OUs allows you to administer rights and login scripts separately.

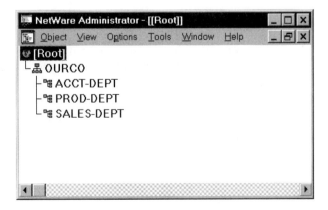

This division also allows you to administer separate login scripts for the three departments, since the login script is a property of the Organizational Unit object. User objects in PROD execute the PROD login script, while User objects in ACCT execute the ACCT login script and User objects in SALES execute the SALES login script.

NetWare Server Objects

The NetWare server object is created automatically when you install the NetWare 4.*x* operating system on a computer. The default installation process puts the NetWare Server object directly under your Organization object. If you do a custom installation, you can specify a different context for the server, meaning its position in the Directory tree. We'll be exploring context in more detail later in this chapter.

Volume Objects

When you create a physical volume, you also create a Volume object in the Directory. This distinction between physical volumes and Volume objects is important, since you must administer trustee rights for the two entities separately.

A volume is really a set of twins, each twin having a distinct nature. Each volume has its physical side and its Directory object side. Though Volume objects are truly Directory objects, the physical disk partitions are not; nor are the files and directories.

For instance, you can make the User object Amy a trustee of the Volume object, granting her the Read right to all the object properties. Amy, however, can't read files in the volume until you grant her rights to the Volume object's twin, the physical file system volume.

Furthermore, when you create a physical volume and give it a name, that name is changed for NDS purposes. Let's say you create the volume VOL1 on server SERVER1. The physical volume's name is VOL1, but the Volume object's name is SERVER1_VOL1. You can also change the Volume object's name without changing the physical volume's name.

Physical Volumes

Physically, a volume is simply a component of the NetWare file system, similar to a DOS volume. When you format a DOS partition, the FORMAT command prompts you to give it a "volume label." Similarly, when you create a NetWare volume, you give it a volume name.

A NetWare volume, however, is more flexible than a DOS volume. A NetWare volume may be a part of a disk drive, may span multiple disk drives, or may be simply an entire disk drive. A NetWare volume can also be very large, spanning up to 32 volume segments. A NetWare server can have up to 64 volumes.

CREATING AND MOUNTING PHYSICAL VOLUMES You create a volume from the NetWare server console using the INSTALL NLM. Before creating a volume, you must first identify the component disk sections as NetWare partitions (also using the INSTALL NLM). You create the volume SYS, a required volume, when you create a NetWare server. You can also create a volume from a CD-ROM on the server.

After you create a volume, you need to mount it to make it available to the network. Normally this is done with a MOUNT command in the server's STARTUP.NCF file or AUTOEXEC.NCF file. For CD-ROMs, you use a CD MOUNT command. Mounting a volume performs these tasks:

- It makes the volume available to the operating system.

- It makes the volume available to workstations on the network.

- It loads the volume's file allocation table (FAT) into server memory.

- It loads the volume's directory entry table (DET) into server memory.

Of course, since mounting volumes means loading FATs and DETs into memory, your volume size directly increases the amount of RAM needed by your server.

Volume Objects

You can see both Volume objects and the physical volumes from NetWare Administrator. OURCO's twins are shown in the Volume object identification screen in Figure 2.4, and Figure 2.5 shows how you can view Volume objects and their files and directories from NetWare Administrator. Notice that its name is SERVER1_SYS, but it refers to a "host volume" called simply SYS.

FIGURE 2.4
The twin identities
of the volume

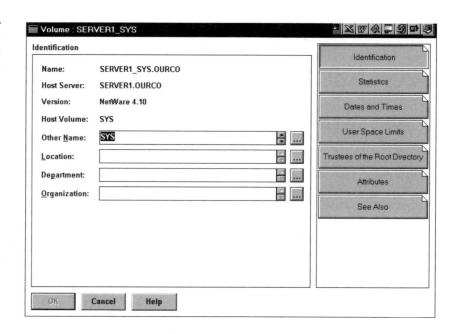

FIGURE 2.5
The Volume objects,
their files and directories,
shown in NetWare
Administrator

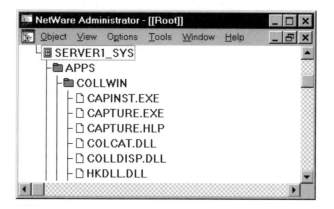

User Objects

The User object represents the network account. When users log in, they employ the name of a User object. Through a process called *authentication*, NetWare then determines the user's rights to access the Directory.

User objects have over 80 properties, the most notable of which are listed in Table 2.1.

TABLE 2.1 User Object Properties	USER OBJECT PROPERTY	FUNCTION
	Login Name	User objects require a login name. This is the name used to log in and the name shown in NetWare Administrator.
	Last Name	NetWare requires a Last Name for each user account.
	Language	The language needed for NetWare messages.
	Default Server	Normally, this is the NetWare Server closest to the user's workstation. This server delivers messages addressed to the user with SEND commands.
	Network Addresses	The address of each workstation from which the user is logged in.
	Home Directory	A directory on the NetWare Server created especially for the user's benefit.
	Rights to Files and Directories	Specific trustee assignments made for this User object that apply to a file or directory.
	Group Membership	A list of groups to which you have assigned this User. (See "Group Objects" section.)
	Login Time Restrictions	You can use this property to set times when the user may or may not log in to the network.
	Network Address Restrictions	You can use this property to specify from which workstations a user may log in to the network.
	Login Script	The User object's personal login script. When the user logs in, the container login script executes first. Then a Profile login script runs if the User has been assigned to one. if any data exists in this property; otherwise, a default user login script executes.
	Limit Concurrent Connections	Limits the number of network sessions a User object can have at once.
	Last Login	A system-generated property showing the User object's last login time and date.

USER OBJECT PROPERTY	FUNCTION
Account Expiration Date	Allows you to disable a User object after a certain date.
Account Disabled	System-generated property that indicates a User object's login account has been disabled.
Force Periodic Password Changes	Allows you to require password changes when a password reaches a specified age.
Require a Password	Allows you to require passwords for the User object.
PROFILE	Allows you to assign a user to a profile.

Using trustee rights, you can allow users to modify their own User object properties, or you can restrict modifications. The default rights work well for most circumstances.

Group Objects

Group objects are very useful for managing network users. You can create a Group object and add users from different OUs, and then administer rights for the Group rather than the individual users. For instance, you could create a Programmers group for users Amy and Doug as shown in Figure 2.6. Then you could give that group access to a special programming directory in the file system (Figure 2.7). The rights will apply automatically to both Amy and Doug.

Group objects are also helpful in login scripts. Figure 2.8 shows a command in a login script to map a drive K for the Programmers to the CODE directory. This "IF MEMBER OF..." syntax is quite easy to test and maintain, and it takes advantage of the Group object. As you'd expect, the drive mapping occurs for both Amy and Doug automatically when they log in.

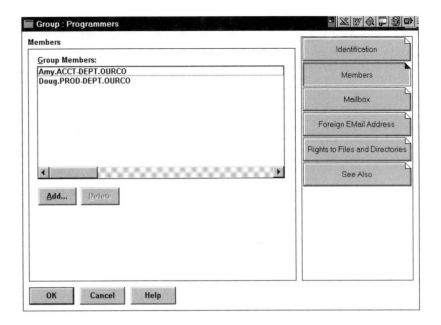

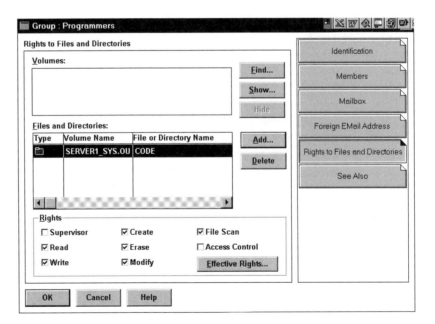

FIGURE 2.8
Using a Group object
in a login script

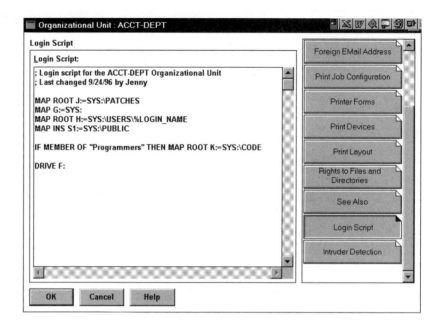

Printer Objects

Printer objects represent a physical printer on the network. You associate a Printer object with a Print Queue object on a server, and with a Print Server object.

When a user sends a print job to the printer, the job actually goes to a Print Queue, which is a place on the NetWare volume. From there, a NetWare Server running a PSERVER NLM watches the queue and the printer, transferring print jobs to the printer as it comes available.

The printer may be physically attached to a NetWare server or to a workstation. To activate network printing, the server or workstation runs a port driver (NPRINTER.EXE for workstations and NPRINTER.NLM for servers). The Printer object contains information about how the physical printer works, the workstation or server it is attached to, and which queues it services. The Printer object also contains information about the Print Server from which it receives print jobs.

Print Server Object

A Print Server object represents a service, rather than a physical entity. The service is provided by a NetWare server running PSERVER.NLM or a network device such as an HP JetDirect print server. A Print Server is associated with both Printer objects and Print Queue objects. Its job is to watch over the Print Queues and Printers, sending print jobs from queues to available printers.

Print Queue Objects

The job of a Print Queue object is to point to a position in the file system where print jobs are temporarily stored on their way to printers. For instance, when you create a Print Queue, you are required to select a Volume object that will store the print jobs. Other notable associations for the Print Queue object are the Print Server that services the queue, and the Printer for which the queue stores print jobs.

   You can define a Print Queue operator, who has power to rearrange print jobs in the queue and delete them if necessary. You can also select which User or Group objects have the power to submit print jobs to the queue.

If you use bindery-style printing as a holdover from pre-NetWare 4 printing configurations, you can create a Print Queue object in the Directory. The Print Queue object is then associated with the bindery queue and refers to that queue when NDS actions are performed on the Print Queue object.

Alias Objects

An Alias object is simply a pointer to another object. It is most useful when you rename a container object. For instance, you might want to change the ACCT-DEPT Organizational Unit name to Accounting. If you leave an Alias object named ACCT-DEPT, services will be able to find the objects in the container with the new name. Figure 2.9 shows the Rename dialog, with the check box option for leaving an Alias when you rename a container.

   Alias objects aren't just for renamed containers; you can create Alias objects for any purpose you want. Remember that the Alias object only points to another object. It doesn't carry trustee rights or other properties of its own. Actions you perform on the Alias are actually performed on the object it refers to.

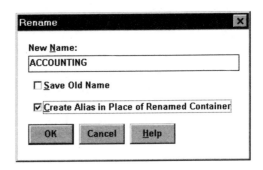

Directory Map Objects

A Directory Map object is a pointer to a place in the file system. It makes creating and maintaining drive mappings easier. For instance, say you have the following line in a login script to set up a word processing application:

```
MAP INS S2:=SERVER_SYS.OURCORP:\APPS\WORDPROC\WORD
```

In terms of typing it correctly and maintaining it, this is a somewhat complex line. Also, when you change the location of the word processor, you'll need to revise and troubleshoot the login script(s) that refer to it.

The alternative is to create a Directory Map object that points to the application. Then the login script line will look like this:

```
MAP INS S2:=WORD
```

Figure 2.10 shows the dialog in NetWare Administrator in which you create the pointer for a Directory Map object.

Object and Current Context

P ROBABLY THE MOST DIFFICULT THING for new NetWare 4 administrators to get used to is the idea of *context*. The concept is extremely important, because you often need to specify an object's context and know your workstation's current context when using utilities.

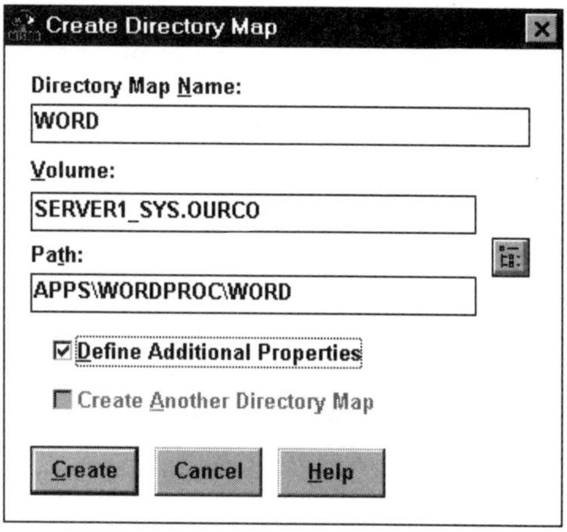

FIGURE 2.10
Creating the pointer for a
Directory Map object

FIGURE 2.10

Creating the pointer for a
Directory Map object

Like the concept of the current directory in a file system, context is the current position of the object in the Directory tree. Just as you specify the current directory with a path, you also specify context with a path.

But that's where the similarity ends; everything else about the current directory and the current context is different. When compared to a file system directory, a context appears backwards: Where a file system path is listed from most general to most specific, the context path is listed from most specific to most general. (If you are familiar with the conventions of Uniform Resource Locator (URL) naming used in the Internet, you'll have an easier time with context.)

The following sections explain the following topics:

- The definition of current context

- Distinguished object names

- Relative object names

- Typeful versus typeless naming

- Bindery context

- Using the CX command

Current Context

A workstation that is logged in to the network has a current context, just as it has a pointer to the current directory in the file system. If you type **CD** at the

DOS command line, you see your current directory. Similarly, if you type **CX** from a workstation's command line, you see the current context, like this:

```
C:\WINDOWS> CX
PROD-DEPT.OURCO
```

The current context lists container objects, starting from your workstation's current setting, up to but not including the [Root] object. The container objects are separated by periods. For instance, if you typed **CX** and got the response shown above, your workstation would be set to the PROD-DEPT container, which is in the OURCO container.

One way to understand the current context is to substitute the phrase *which is in* for the periods that separate container objects. Thus

```
R-AND-D.ENGINEERING.HOUSTON.INC
```

would mean "the R-AND-D container, which is in ENGINEERING, which is in HOUSTON, which is in INC."

Distinguished Object Names

If you add a context specification to an object name and put a period in front of it, you get a *distinguished name*.

A distinguished name is analogous to a complete path in a file system name. For instance, the complete path to the COMM.DRV file in the C:\WINDOWS\SYSTEM directory would be

```
C:\WINDOWS\SYSTEM\COMM.DRV
```

Using a DOS program, you could type in the complete path and file name to specify the file, no matter what your current directory is.

Now consider context. Appending the PROD-DEPT.OURCO context to a Printer object called OKIDAT and then putting a period at the beginning would yield a distinguished name of

```
.OKIDAT.PROD-DEPT.OURCO
```

The full distinguished name would identify the object no matter what your current context is.

Remember: The beginning period identifies the name as a distinguished name.

Relative Object Names

You've learned that the period at the beginning of an object name means it's a distinguished name. If you add a path to the object name and *don't* begin with a period, you specify a *relative object name*. This is also called (confusingly) a *relative distinguished name*.

For instance, assume your workstation's current context is OURCO and you want to specify the Printer OKIDAT in the PROD-DEPT.OURCO container. As stated earlier, the Printer object's distinguished name is .OKIDAT.PROD-DEPT.OURCO. Its relative name, however, would be

```
OKIDAT.PROD-DEPT.
```

Notice that the relative object name loses the leading period and the current context.

How NetWare Resolves a Relative Name to Get a Distinguished Name

Here's a simplified version of the steps NetWare takes to read a relative name and derive a distinguished name from it:

1. NetWare recognizes the name as a relative name by the absence of the leading period.

2. NetWare starts with your workstation's current context. Then, for each period at the end of a relative name, it subtracts the lowest container.

3. NetWare then adds the relative name to result of step 2, to get the distinguished name of the object.

This process is illustrated in Figure 2.11.

Now let's put the OURCO relative names through NetWare's process. Figure 2.12 shows a Directory tree example, with relative object names. Table 2.2 shows the steps for getting to the distinguished names.

FIGURE 2.11
How NetWare gets from
a relative name to a
distinguished name

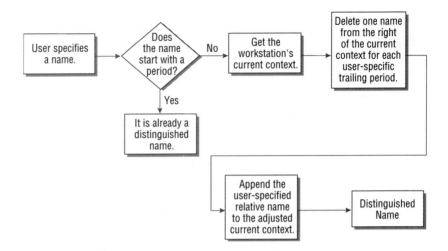

FIGURE 2.12
Object names relative
to the workstation's
current context of
PROD-DEPT.OURCO

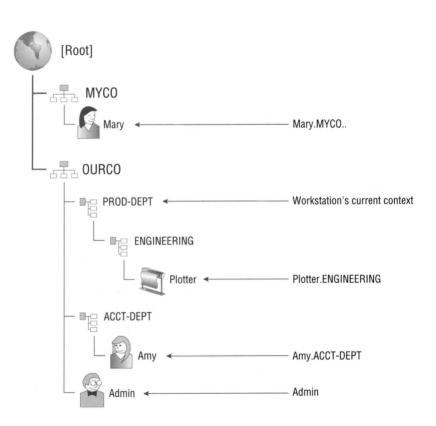

TABLE 2.2 From Relative Object Name to Distinguished Name	STEP 1: RELATIVE NAME	STEP 2: WORK-STATION'S CURRENT CONTEXT	STEP 2: SUBTRACT ONE CON-TAINER FOR EACH TRAILING PERIOD	STEP 3: ADD THE RELATIVE NAME TO GET THE RESULT
	Mary.MYCO.	PROD-DEPT.OURCO	(nothing)	.Mary.MYCO
	Plotter .ENGINEERING	PROD-DEPT.OURCO	PROD-DEPT .OURCO	.Plotter .ENGINEERING. PROD-DEPT. OURCO
	Amy.ACCT-DEPT.	PROD-DEPT.OURCO	OURCO	.Amy.ACCT-DEPT. OURCO
	Admin.	PROD-DEPT.OURCO	OURCO	.Admin.OURCO

Creating a Relative Object Name by Climbing and Hopping

To form a relative object name, follow these steps. (See Figure 2.13 for an example.)

1. Picture the Directory tree. Use NetWare Administrator's view to help.

2. List the object's name.

3. List all the containers the object needs to *climb through* in order to reach a container in common with the workstation's current context. Insert a period to separate all the containers climbed through.

Don't include the common container in the list!

4. From the container in common, hop down to the workstation's current context. How many hops did you make? Add that many periods to the end of the result of Step 3. You now have the relative name.

Typeful and Typeless Naming

Thus far we have only studied *typeless* object names, which are sufficient for most administrative tasks. Some NetWare utilities, however, require that you include the object *types* in the distinguished name. Requiring an object type is

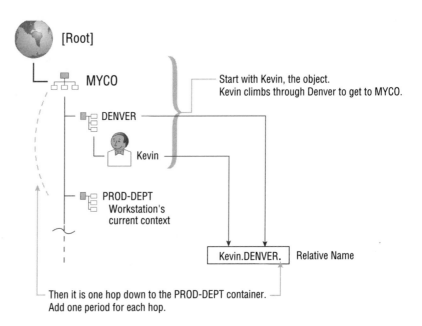

FIGURE 2.13
Devising a relative object
name by climbing and
hopping in the tree

an inconsistency that Novell will hopefully remedy at some point, although there are cases in which stating the object type is necessary.

Typeful naming simply means adding CN= for each leaf object in the name, and either OU= or O= for each container object, depending on the object's class. CN stands for common name. Here are some examples of typeful naming:

.CN=Amy.OU=ACCT-DEPT.O=OURCO (a distinguished name)

CN=LaserQ.OU=PROD-DEPT. (a relative name)

CN=Admin

These examples, stated in typeless form, look like this:

.Amy.ACCT-DEPT.OURCO

LaserQ.PROD-DEPT.

Admin

The Server's Bindery Context

NetWare operating systems before version 4 didn't use the Directory. They used a list of objects that was specific to one server called the Bindery. If you wanted to use objects relating to a server, such as one of its volumes, you would log in to that server. If you wanted to use a volume on another server, you would attach separately to that server, using a login name in its Bindery.

NDS has a way of making the Directory look like a server-specific Bindery, for those applications that require it. Each server can specify a container or a number of containers as its *bindery contexts*. All objects in all the server's bindery contexts then appear as a flat list of objects.

A server's bindery context is set by default to the container where you install the server. You can easily change the bindery context, however, using a SET command at the server's console.

Figure 2.14 shows where you might set a server's bindery contexts, and the objects that would appear in the server's bindery.

FIGURE 2.14

Setting the server's bindery contexts at MYCO and ACCT-DEPT causes the objects to become part of an emulated bindery.

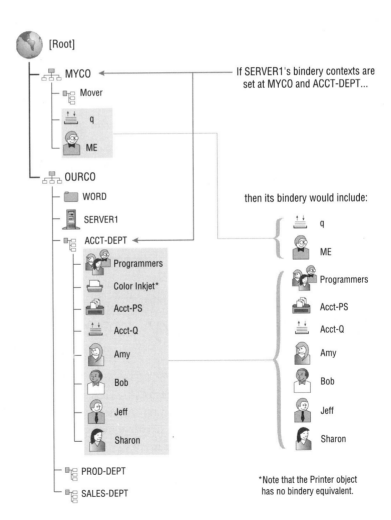

If SERVER1's bindery contexts are set at MYCO and ACCT-DEPT...

then its bindery would include:

*Note that the Printer object has no bindery equivalent.

Note that many of the object classes you see in the Directory tree are new with NetWare 4, so there are no bindery equivalents. These new objects include Directory Map and Printer.

The CX Command

Since this is the chapter on planning, we won't go into the exact syntax of the commands you'll learn later in the book. But while we are on the subject of context, here are some of the options for using the context command CX:

- View and set current context

- View all container objects below the current or specified context

- View container objects at the current or specified level

- Modify or view all objects at or below the context

- Change context or view objects relative to the [Root]

- View directory tree below the current context

- View containers within a specific context

Notice the similarities between the CX command and the DOS command CD. A context can be entered relative to your current context, or as a distinguished name relative to the directory root. You can use trailing periods to change context to a higher level than your workstation's current context. Example:

        CX ..

Planning the Directory Tree

ALTHOUGH THE DEFAULT TREE works for most small networks, planning your Directory tree can save you administrative work later. Included in this planning task is creating a naming standard for objects in the tree. First you need to decide whether to accept NetWare's default tree, which is minimal, or go for a more expanded version. See Figure 2.15.

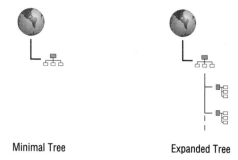

FIGURE 2.15
NetWare's minimal
default tree vs.
expanded tree

Minimal Tree   Expanded Tree

There is much to be said for keeping your Directory tree simple, putting all users and other objects in one Organization object. With such a tree you can still create Group objects for administering subsets of your users. You can also use "IF MEMBER OF..." statements in login scripts to run a variety of login commands for those Groups.

The drawback of the minimal tree comes into play if you are viewing many hundreds of users, or if you have departments that are very distinct in their resource usage. It may be easier in these cases to distribute users using separate OUs for specific departments or divisions, as described next for the expanded tree.

Let's assume you're planning a network for a small college, which will have 300 workstations and three servers. Often in such circumstances the network is already nicely divided. Consider the following example:

- The 70-member faculty has its NetWare 3.12 server, used for e-mail and general data storage. Another 100 student workstations are tied to this server.

- The administration has a NetWare 2.2 server and 80 workstations for its accounting and student records.

- You are planning to upgrade the two servers to NetWare 4 and add a third NetWare 4 server with 150 workstations for student use.

You can assume that the administration does not want the faculty to have access to the accounting and historical student records. The faculty feels just as protective about its own data and high-speed printer. And nobody wants the students to have access to any faculty or administration data (except the students, of course).

Here you have three distinctly separate management arenas. The three user types only need access to their local resources, and they are guarded about sharing those resources with the other groups. You might plan the Directory tree shown in Figure 2.16.

FIGURE 2.16
Directory tree for distinct resource needs

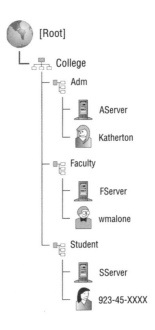

Rather than grouping User objects by their physical location on the network, put User objects in the same container as the resources they will use, such as Volumes and Printers.

The main issue in planning a Directory tree for your company is whether or not to accept the default, with its single Organization object and no Organizational Units. Carefully consider the number of User objects and the amount of resource sharing. Figure 2.17 gives you a workable procedure for making the decision.

Planning a Consistent Naming Scheme

No matter the size of the network, your users will benefit from a design that includes a consistent naming scheme for objects. For instance, imagine that you're trying to send another user, Kim Wilson, a message. You have used a consistent naming scheme in your network, giving users a login name that begins with the

FIGURE 2.17
How to plan a
Directory tree

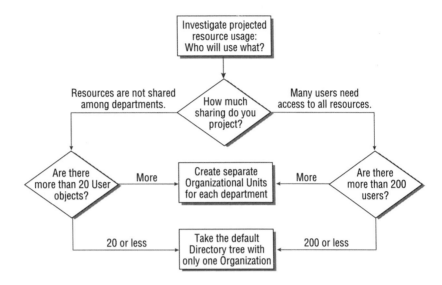

first letter of the first name and ends with the last name. Therefore, you know immediately that Kim's login name is kwilson. Without the naming consistency, you won't know whether to send the message to Kim, to Wilson, to KimW, or to kw. And your other users will have the same problem.

Since you'll be typing object names in utilities, it will save you time and trouble if you keep the names short, memorable, and easy to type. Thus ACCT is better than Accountg_Depart^.

Take a little time in the planning stage to standardize your naming and write down your standard. You can use the sample shown in Table 2.3 as a starting point.

Planning the File Systems

I F YOU'VE INHERITED AN EXISTING NETWORK, you already have the partitions and volumes defined. Still, you might want to read this section to get some ideas for improving your system.

TABLE 2.3	OBJECT CLASS	PROPERTY	STANDARD	EXAMPLES
A Sample Naming Standard	User	login name	First letter of first name plus last name. Add middle initial for duplicate login names. Truncate to 8 characters. Hyphenate multiple-word last names. Lowercase.	djones, klharris, mworthin, ksaint-m
	User	last name	Full last name, capitalized as preferred by user.	Jones, Harris, Worthington, Saint Marie, van Winkle
	User	middle initial	Initial only, capitalized, no period.	W
	User	telephone	Local extension only.	3978
	User	given name	User-preferred first name.	K.C., Wilma, Thunder Cloud
	User	department	As listed on official organization chart. Title case.	Accounting, Assembly, Mail Room
	Server	name	"SERVER*n*" (all caps), replacing *n* with integer.	SERVER1, SERVER2, SERVER3
	Server	location	Building, room number, and direction, separated by hyphens.	Main-110-SW
	Volume	name	Server name, underscore, volume name. All caps. Volume names: First: SYS Second: VOL1 Third: VOL2 CD-ROM volumes named by their purpose.	SERVER1_SYS, SERVER2_VOL1, SERVER3_VOL2, WPOFFICE

	OBJECT CLASS	PROPERTY	STANDARD	EXAMPLES
TABLE 2.3 (cont.) A Sample Naming Standard	Directory Map	name	Short word, all caps, representing purpose of directory.	DATA, APPS, WP6, PATCHES
	Printer	name	"P-*name*" where *name* is easily recognized by users.	P-inkjet, P-checks, P-Harvey, P-laser
	Print Server	name	"PS-*server*" where *server* is the name of the NetWare server that runs the Print Server.	PS-SERVER1
	Print Queue	name	"Q-*name*" where *name* is easily recognized by users.	Q-invoice, Q-Okidata

DOS Partitions and NetWare Partitions

Each server needs a DOS partition on the server's boot drive. This is the partition that holds SERVER.EXE, the drivers for the server hard drives, and some of the NetWare operating system patches.

Novell recommends a 15MB or larger DOS partition, plus 1MB for every MB of server RAM. For example, if your server has 32MB of RAM, you might want to create a DOS partition of 47MB. A good rule of thumb for the DOS partition size is 50 MB. (See the discussion on typical software components in Chapter 1 for a more thorough listing of files and directories on the DOS partition.)

Your server's NetWare partitions occupy the remaining space on the boot drive and the space on additional drives.

How Much Drive Space Do You Need?

The easy answer is, "As much as your company can afford." Intelligent disk compression can maximize your disk efficiency on NetWare volumes, making them more efficient than your workstations' hard drives. Thus it makes sense to put much of the data you might normally have on a workstation's hard drive on the server. Also, putting the data on the server allows you to monitor, control, and back up the data more easily.

Bear in mind, however, the following limitations to the amount of data you want on the server:

- For every increase in the size of NetWare volumes, the server needs more RAM. For instance, an average system with 2GB of disk space requires 20MB of RAM. Double the disk space to 4GB, and you need 30MB or so of RAM. A very loose rule of thumb is 5MB of memory for each additional G of hard drive space—but don't be taken by surprise. Go through the calculations that Novell recommends.

A complete process for calculating disk space requirements is included in Appendix A of the NetWare Installation Manual.

- If you have hundreds of users accessing all their data from a server, the bandwidth limitations of the network channel will slow data transfers for these users.

- "Mobile" users with laptop computers will want their data on the workstations, so they can work even when not connected to the network.

Following is a rule-of-thumb list for deciding how much network disk space you need:

- 200MB for NetWare files on each server.

- Space for e-mail applications and mailboxes. (See your e-mail documentation for this calculation.)

- Space for all shared data, including databases, artwork, documents, applications, and files being transferred between users.

- Space for a home (personal) directory for each user, of the size you specify.

- Space for future growth in the needs of your users.

Here are a couple of other considerations.

- If you will mirror drives to increase the reliability of the network, You'll need an additional drive for each one mirrored. Mirroring is discussed in an upcoming section.

■ Enabling compression on your volumes will give you about 30% to 50% more disk space. You'll probably need it, to offset demands you don't anticipate now.

Volumes on the NetWare Partitions

NetWare requires only one volume: SYS. The SYS volume, or any volume, can span multiple disk drives.

Before you install NetWare on a server, decide whether to add long name support for Macintosh, OS/2's High Performance File System (HPFS), or UNIX's Network File System (NFS). This support is necessary if you have corresponding workstation users who will want to use the capability to have longer file names associated with these operating systems. Addition of long name support to volumes will mean a small increase in the RAM needed by your server, and a small amount of disk space will be needed to hold the additional information that is required.

You can add the additional name space to the SYS volume, or create a separate volume for files with long file names.

If most of your users have DOS/Windows workstations, you can keep the normal DOS file system for the SYS volume, and then create a separate volume for storing MAC, OS/2, and NFS files as required.

Mirroring and Duplexing Hard Drives

Mirroring hard drives means telling NetWare to duplicate the data from one hard drive to another on the same controller. *Duplexing* means duplicating drives on separate controllers. You may mirror or duplex two drives to each other, or you may add even more drives to the mirrored group.

Advantages of mirroring and duplexing include faster reads from the disk. For instance, when NetWare does a read from a mirrored pair of drives, it reads from the drive that can provide the data first.

More important than speed, however, is the redundancy of data. Since all disk drives eventually fail, data redundancy gives you the opportunity to remove and replace a failed drive without loss of data. Mirroring protects you if a hard disk fails; duplexing protects you if either a hard disk or a controller fails.

Before installing a NetWare server, decide whether you want your drives mirrored, duplexed, or neither. If the drives are not of the same capacity, the smallest drive in the group limits the size available to NetWare.

Using RAID

RAID stands for Redundant Array of Inexpensive Disks. It is another scheme, similar to mirroring, for providing increased speed and/or fault tolerance in your server. There are at least six levels of RAID, with proprietary controllers available for many of the levels.

Contact your Novell reseller for a RAID solution that is Novell tested and approved. Rather than purchasing only drives, you can also purchase entire disk subsystems that include fans, redundant power supplies, and slide mounts for easy replacement.

Planning the Physical Network

PLANNING THE PHYSICAL LAYOUT includes selecting a topology and protocol, and planning the physical layout of your cabling. If you have inherited an existing network and it is working fine, you may not have much planning to do and can skip to the next section.

Selecting a Topology

Topology, according to Peter Dyson's *Dictionary of Networking*, is defined as the "map of a network. Physical topology describes where the cables are run and where the workstations, nodes, routers, and gateways are located. Networks are usually configured in bus, ring, star, or mesh topologies. Logical topology refers to the paths that messages take to get from one user on the network to another."

Cabling schemes have evolved significantly since networking began a few years ago. Once upon a time, there was the star topology, the ring topology, and the bus topology. The star was used mostly for ARCnet, the ring for Token Ring, and the bus for Ethernet. Now let's see where we are today.

The Star Topology and ARCnet

At one time the star topology did in fact describe the physical layout of ARCnet. As shown in Figure 2.18, there was a hub in the middle feeding workstations and servers. But electrically, it worked like a token-passing ring on a bus. Confused? Well, it gets worse.

Modern ARCnet, though much improved over the original 2.5Mbps speed, has effectively dropped out of the race for network dominance. For that reason alone, I recommend sticking with Ethernet or Token Ring. Those two topologies give you a variety of hardware and software options, along with the most comprehensive expertise among installers and support personnel.

FIGURE 2.18
ARCnet's physical topology looks like a bus and star, but works like a token-passing ring.

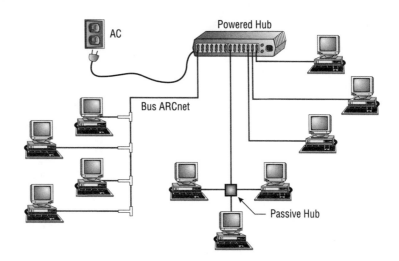

The Ring Topology and Token Ring

Token Ring networks function like a ring, with ring-in and ring-out connections for each workstation and server (Figure 2.19). Each station waits for an empty token to transmit. But physically, a Token Ring looks like a star, with a multistation access unit (MAU) in the middle, handling the exchange (Figure 2.20).

FIGURE 2.19
Token Ring passes tokens
around the ring.

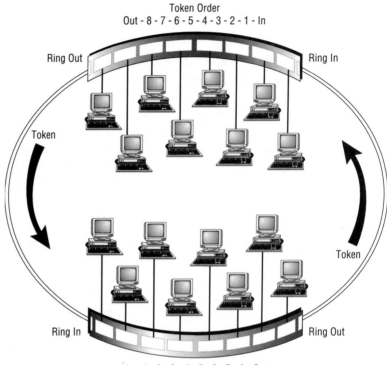

FIGURE 2.19
Token Ring passes tokens
around the ring.

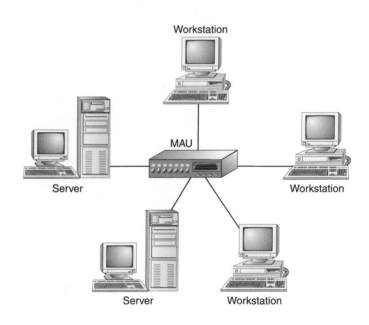

FIGURE 2.20
Token Ring looks
physically more
like a star.

The Bus Topology and Ethernet

Ethernet at one time looked like a bus (Figure 2.21). It worked over coaxial cable connections between all workstations and servers on the network. All the stations got all the electrical signals. The network adapters at each station only worried about the signals labeled with that workstation's address. Today coaxial cable has given way to—you guessed it—a more starlike layout, with a hub in the middle and all stations connected to the hub (Figure 2.22).

FIGURE 2.21
Ethernet on a coaxial bus

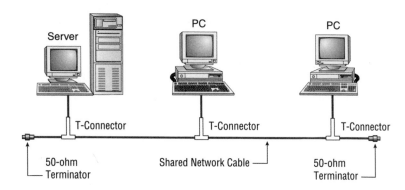

FIGURE 2.22
Ethernet hub layout

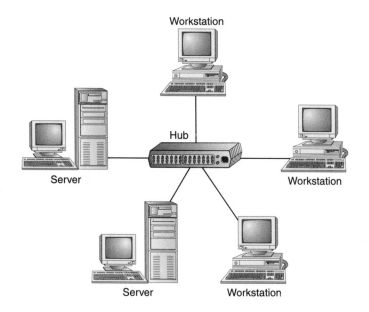

FDDI

Fiber Distributed Data Interface (FDDI) is another ring technology, unique for its high speed (100Mbps) and its long run-length. FDDI uses fiber-optic cable, a fairly expensive hardware solution for small networks. Figure 2.23 illustrates the dual, counter-rotating, token-ring topology of FDDI.

If you have workstations in separate buildings more than a few hundred yards apart, FDDI may be your answer. An FDDI network using multimode fiber-optic cable can connect as many as 500 stations more than a mile apart. A version of the FDDI standard, FDDI II, is designed for networks transmitting video, a form of data that can't tolerate any delays.

FIGURE 2.23
FDDI's dual, counter-rotating token rings

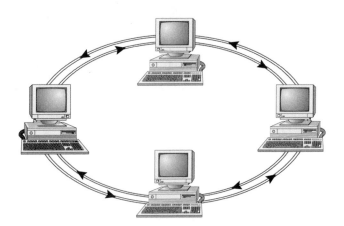

Fiber Distributed Data Interface

ATM

Asynchronous Transfer Mode (ATM) networking has been rather long on promise but short on products. Lately, though, ATM switches have become available for NetWare networks. The ATM switches can provide up to 2.4Gbps transmission, with sixteen 155Mbps full-duplex ports per switch.

A great advantage of ATM is its guaranteed bandwidth allocation, which prevents jitter in video over the network. *Jitter* is a momentary pause in the video motion, caused by a pause in the data flow. Other network technologies (except FDDI II) are considered too "bursty" for video, since a workstation is allowed to monopolize the wire. Ethernet, for example, can deliver data at high speeds but cannot guarantee a constant stream.

Considering the high cost and overkill in bandwidth, ATM technology is probably not in the immediate future of your small NetWare network.

Wireless

Wireless networking has about one-fourth the speed of the average Ethernet LAN, at a higher price. It does, however, offer some advantages. First of all, you can obviously skip the cabling step in your network setup. Second, your laptop users will enjoy the freedom of networking without a tether on their computers. If you're in a situation where you don't want to run wires on the floor and can't get into the walls, perhaps wireless is the answer for you.

Choosing between Ethernet and Token Ring

Ethernet and Token Ring have long been the two most popular LAN topologies, with Ethernet in the lead. Both have their loyal supporters; both have extensive hardware, software, and "mind share" in the marketplace.

My advice is to go with the technology you know. If you're familiar with Token Ring, it makes no sense to learn a new style. Expertise being equal, I'd go with Ethernet because of the high-speed, low-cost products becoming available now. Two lines of products—switching hubs and fast Ethernet hubs and adapters— are worth consideration in planning your network.

Ethernet Switching Hubs

Imagine that your network is a freeway, with workstations and servers sending data around in cars. The server is an office building that has a ramp allowing 10 cars per minute (comparable to 10Mbps). Let's say there are 24 workstations, each with its own ramp that can also handle 10 cars per minute. The freeway itself can handle 10 cars per minute, too.

Almost all network traffic goes to and from the server. If an average of 6 users are employing the network at any given time, each of the workstations can therefore average only 1.7 cars per minute, via the 10-car-per-minute highway and server ramp. You get a bottleneck at the on-ramps that keeps the workstations at one-sixth their capacity.

One solution is a switching hub that gives each workstation dedicated 10Mbps access, with a special 100Mbps port for the server. That's like increasing the server's ramp to 100 cars per minute and giving each workstation its own highway, which eliminates the bottleneck.

Today's cost for such an Ethernet switching hub is about $200 per node for 12 ports, or about $135 per node for 24 ports. You'll need to pay an extra $50 for a 100Mbps network adapter in the server. The workstations stay with their 10Mbps adapters.

A note about prices: The prices discussed in this section as "today's cost" are the prices that are current as of this writing.

Fast Ethernet Hubs and Adapters

Another solution that is almost as inexpensive as a switching hub is to increase all connections to 100Mbps with Fast Ethernet. Very few applications can actually use the bandwidth now, but your users will appreciate your foresight. And your bottleneck at the server will be eliminated.

Today's cost for a Fast Ethernet hub is about $150 per port, with network adapters running about $50 more for Fast Ethernet over regular Ethernet.

If you have an existing 10Mbps Ethernet network, you can start replacing network adapters with 10/100 cards that automatically sense the hub speed and operate at that same speed. Later, when your adapters are upgraded and budget allows, you can change your 10Mbps hub for 100Mbps.

Protocol Suites: IPX/SPX vs. TCP/IP

First a few acronym definitions are in order: Internet Packet Exchange (IPX) has nothing to do with *the* Internet. IPX and Sequenced Packet Exchange (SPX) together form Novell's default rules for network communication. NetWare also supports Transmission Control Protocol/Internet Protocol (TCP/IP), which is *the* Internet protocol. It is also the preferred networking protocol of UNIX.

In choosing between IPX/SPX and TCP/IP, you need to ask two key questions:

- Does your company do extensive business over the Internet?

- Does your company's business revolve around UNIX, requiring UNIX-style file transfer, data storage, and printing?

Your company has probably already made these decisions, and if the answer is "Yes" to either question, it's your job to implement the decision by using TCP/IP on the network.

TCP/IP with NetWare/IP

TCP/IP is a set of protocols that define the following aspects of internetwork communication: media access, packet transport, session communications, file transfer, e-mail, and terminal emulation.

If you're moving to an IP infrastructure, integrating into an existing one, or creating a mixed environment, you can do so with NetWare/IP. The product is available with NetWare 4.11 and free to all NetWare customers, via the following options:

- World Wide Web (http://netware.novell.com)

- CompuServe (GO NOVFF, files NIPF22.EXE and NIPW22.EXE)

You can also get the NetWare/IP files from Novell Fulfillment for a fee. In the United States and Canada, phone 800-395-7135, or fax 510-657-0182. In other countries, phone 353-1703-8910, or fax 353-1703-8955.

NetWare/IP manages IP addresses with the following features:

- *Dynamic Host Configuration Protocol (DHCP)* uses the addresses of your network adapters to allocate IP addresses. It allocates these addresses automatically from an address pool.

- *Boot Program (BootP) Protocol* permits the assignment of IP addresses to diskless machines.

Using NetWare/IP can speed up NetWare over wide-area links. It also expands users' printing options to include UNIX and other IP-based printers. NetWare/IP also enables you to manage a NetWare 4.1*x* network from any UNIX management console via standard Management Information Bases (MIBs) and the XCONSOLE interface.

With NetWare/IP and some expertise in the TCP/IP protocol suite, you can set up wide-area links using Internet circuits. This lets you link up networks that are geographically dispersed, for file sharing and remote management. Mobile users with a connection to an Internet service provider can access your NetWare servers from anywhere in the world.

NetWare/IP also allows Windows NT workstations to access NT services via IP, and supports Microsoft's 32-bit TCP/IP stack used in NetWare, Windows 95, and NT workstations. You can use NetWare/IP on SFT III servers for fault-tolerant IP networking.

IPX/SPX

You don't have to do anything special to use IPX/SPX on your Novell network. It works behind the scenes, all the time, to manage network communication.

IPX is a fast, reliable LAN protocol that does not set up a connection before communicating. When it is important to set up a connection between source and destination workstations before data can be transmitted, NetWare uses SPX. SPX guarantees packet delivery by having the receiving station verify that the data has been received correctly. All packets are sent in sequence, and all packets take the same route to the destination station.

Remember, if all you need is Internet e-mail, you don't need TCP/IP for your entire network. You can use an e-mail server such as Pegasus or Mercury for that. An e-mail server makes a TCP/IP connection to an Internet Post Office Protocol (POP) server on the Internet. They exchange messages, and then the e-mail server delivers the messages over the LAN.

Planning the Physical Layout

I F YOU ALREADY HAVE a network to manage, there's probably not much you can do about the physical layout of the cabling. Nor can you change the type of cabling in the walls. But you can still have a significant impact on the speed of the network by selecting and arranging hubs and network cards on the servers.

If you have the luxury of planning the physical layout, too, then you might consider the advice that follows.

Physical Security

Plan to put your servers in a secure place. This means a room or closet that you can keep locked, with keys only for yourself, your backup administrator, and your manager. (Be sure to provide adequate clean power, and sufficient cooling and clean air for the server.)

This security measure not only protects against the notorious and malicious "disgruntled employee." It also guards against the innocent cleaning person who might plug the vacuum cleaner into the server's outlet, trip the fuse, and bring down the network. Or the conscientious employee who turns off the server to save power. Or the local network experimenter, who wants to "try some things" at the server console.

Power

Plan to have the server closet on its own circuit breaker at the main breaker box. You don't want your network down because someone powered up their blow dryer in the restroom. Make sure to avoid sharing a circuit with heavy, motor driven loads such as air conditioners, refrigerators, copiers, and industrial machinery.

Don't plug printers into a UPS, or into the same circuit as the server. Use a surge suppressor for your laser printers.

Plan to have an electrician verify that all your server closet outlets are properly wired. Even when equipment appears to operate properly, if it's running from improperly wired outlets it can become a shock hazard.

Make sure to use three-wire grounded outlets. If the site has outlets with only two holes (no center ground hole), have an electrician upgrade the building wiring. Do not attempt to add auxiliary ground conductors to your equipment or building. Many UPSs have a wiring fault indicator that warns of improper building wiring, including lack of a safety ground.

UPSs

Plan UPSs for your servers and hubs. Besides providing backup power in case of power outages, the UPS protects against surges, brownouts, and other events that are common in public power circuits.

To calculate the UPS size you need, use the following procedure:

1. Check the back panels of the computers, hubs, and monitors that will be plugged into a UPS. Write down the load rating.

2. Convert the load rating to volt-amps (VA). If the rating is given in watts, multiply it by 1.4 to get VA. If it is stated in amps, multiply it by 120.

3. Sum the VA requirements of equipment that will plug into one UPS.

4. When purchasing the UPS, select one that will give you 15 minutes or more of power at the required VA.

Most computer manufacturers overrate the power requirements of their equipment, to be conservative and to cover the extra power demand of user-added expansion boards. That's all right. If you get more UPS than you need, you'll just extend the time it can run without power.

Most UPSs have an optional serial link that you can attach to the server. This allows you to run software on the server to monitor the UPS status. In case of an extended power outage, this software can log out users and shut down the server gracefully. This is, of course, much preferred over draining the battery and letting the server shut down for lack of power.

Intersystem Ground Noise

Intersystem ground noise can wreak havoc on your network. This phenomenon occurs when the computers are connected to separate ground wiring, causing electricity to flow through the ground wire.

For instance, suppose your company has two buildings. The electrical system of each building, including the computer equipment, is tied to the building's ground circuit. The ground noise problem occurs when there is a difference in the electrical potential of each system's ground circuit. When you connect the two buildings with communication cables that are grounded, the difference in the two ground circuits causes electricity to flow over the ground wires.

10Base-T Ethernet is one system this is completely isolated and safe from intersystem ground noise. RS-232 connections are susceptible, however.

To avoid inter-system ground noise on your RS-232 connections, avoid running links between equipment in separate buildings. You can use modems for this purpose.

Planning for 100Mbps Speed

If your network demands high speed, your options include two fairly new 100Mbps Ethernet architectures: 100VG-AnyLAN and Fast Ethernet.

100VG-AnyLAN

100VG-AnyLAN comes from two well-respected technology leaders, AT&T and Hewlett-Packard. It is governed by the IEEE 802.12 standard.

100VG-AnyLAN uses a configurable access method called *demand priority*. This method eliminates collisions prevalent in other Ethernet architectures by letting only one station transmit at a time. To supervise this transmission activity, the hub monitors requests to transmit and grants only one station the wire. Demand priority also ensures that all packets arrive in sequence.

With demand priority, you can also configure specific nodes for special priority. For instance, you can set up your file server so that it never has to wait for workstations.

Fast Ethernet

Fast Ethernet was developed by Intel and a consortium of vendors under the old 10Base-T standard, IEEE 802.3. The standard is used for normal 10Mbps Ethernet with its Carrier-Sense, Multiple-Access/Collision Detection (CSMA/CD). For Fast Ethernet, they just cranked up the speed to 100Mbps.

CSMA/CD is the ultimate in electronic democracy. With no demand priority, any station can transmit when it senses that the wire is free. If two stations transmit at once, a collision occurs that is immediately detected. The stations back off and try again after a waiting period of random length.

Fast Ethernet is the most popular 100Mbps solution for high-speed networks. As such, it commands the most vendor support and the lowest hardware prices.

100Base-TX and 100Base-T4 are two Fast Ethernet implementations. 100Base-TX is the most popular, with low-cost adapters and hubs from various vendors competing in the marketplace. It carries the disadvantage of requiring Category 5 cable (see "Network Cabling" section just below). 100Base-T4 can work over Category 3 or better.

Network Cabling

If you have the option of selecting the cabling for your network, you'll probably want to stick with standard unshielded twisted pair (UTP) cables. The older coaxial cabling schemes do not provide the reliability and maintainability of UTP.

You have a number of options for UTP cabling, with Category 3 and Category 5 being the most commonly used. Since Category 5 supports many of the emerging high-speed network options, select this option if you're having new cable installed.

From the wall jacks for each workstation to the wiring closet where the servers and hubs will be, you'll want to have the cables installed in the walls. If you're using direct-connect printers, remember to add a jack for each of them. An extra jack for each room wouldn't hurt. You'll also need patch cables for connecting your workstations to the wall jacks. See Figure 2.24 for a sample wiring diagram.

FIGURE 2.24
This wiring diagram shows the locations of jacks and spare connections for one room.

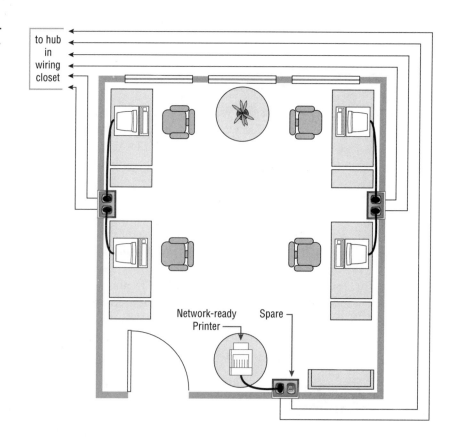

Planning Hub Connections

This section offers five scenarios to help you plan the use of hubs and network adapters. All scenarios use Ethernet components with 24 workstations; similar configurations should be generally available for Token Ring. The configurations can also be expanded, using multiple hubs, to support the number of workstations you have.

Scenario 1: Standard Hub with One Network Adapter in the Server

The configuration in Figure 2.25 shows one network adapter in the server and a single hub. This setup is quite sufficient for light network usage. It is inexpensive—the 24 network adapters in the workstations cost from $26 on up.

For the server, you will probably want a 32-bit multitasking adapter with DMA on a PCI or EISA bus. Replace all the adapters and hubs with a 100Mbps solution such as Hewlett-Packard's 100VG series, and you've got a lightning-fast architecture for an extra $4,000 (at today's cost).

FIGURE 2.25
A standard hub and one network adapter in the server make up an inexpensive network.

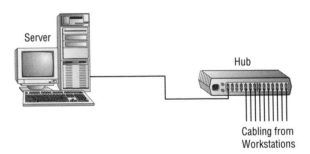

Scenario 2: Two Hubs with Two Network Adapters in the Server

Figure 2.26 shows a configuration with two network adapters in the server and two hubs. This entails the cost of an extra network adapter and hub but segments the LAN, so there are actually two cabling segments tied together by the server. The hubs you select will need only half as many ports as Scenario 1.

In this scenario, contention for the 10Mbps bus is cut in half, since each node is competing with half as many other stations. And because the server now has two 10Mbps ports, it can put twice as much data down on the wire.

F I G U R E 2.26

Double the throughput by adding an extra network adapter in the server and another hub.

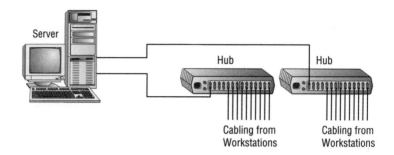

For this configuration, it is helpful to disperse your heavy users over the two segments, rather than keeping them on the same segment. Standing and watching the lights blink on your hub will give you an idea of who uses the network the most. Network printer ports will be primary candidates because they are shared resources.

You can further subdivide the network for as many network adapters as your server can hold, to increase throughput even more.

Scenario 3: An 8-Port Switch/Adapter in the Server

The network in Figure 2.27 has one 8-port switch/adapter in the server and 8 hubs. Matrox makes a switch/adapter like the one shown, called the Piranha.

This configuration effectively subdivides your network into eight cable segments. Three workstations each share the eight 10Mbps ports. On the server side, the adapter puts the bits down on the PCI bus at 80Mbps. Today's price of the switch/adapter is about $1,300.

Scenario 4: A 24-Port Switch with 10BASE-100TX Port

Figure 2.28 shows a network with one 24-port switch with a 100Mbps port for the server. If you're running 10Mbps on your workstations, this is about as fast as you can get. Each workstation has its own dedicated switch port, while the server gets a 10BASE-100TX port.

The only difficulty here lies in the cost of the switch: today's cost is $3,250 for a 3Com Linkswitch 1000. By the time you buy this book and get to this point in your network planning, you'll want to consult the trade magazines for the latest pricing.

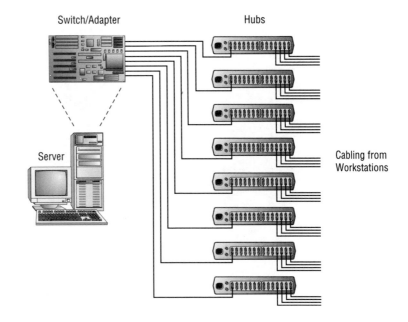

FIGURE 2.27
A switch/adapter combination segments the LAN and puts the data on the server's PCI bus at 80Mbps.

Switch/Adapter   Hubs

Server

Cabling from Workstations

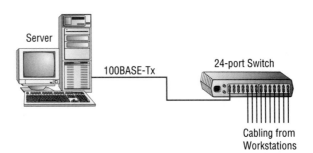

FIGURE 2.28
A very fast implementation of 10Mbps Ethernet on the workstation side.

Server

100BASE-Tx

24-port Switch

Cabling from Workstations

Scenario 5: Multiple Servers

Figure 2.29 shows a network with three servers and four hubs. One hub serves as the "backbone" for communication among servers only. The other three support workgroups.

The assumption here is that each of the servers primarily supports one workgroup. That is, the main traffic to and from each of the servers comes from its connected workgroup hub. All services are available to all workstations and servers, but packets routed between workgroups go through the server backbone to the proper destination. For instance, the three workgroups in our

FIGURE 2.29
Three workgroup
servers communicate on a
backbone cable segment
without workstations.

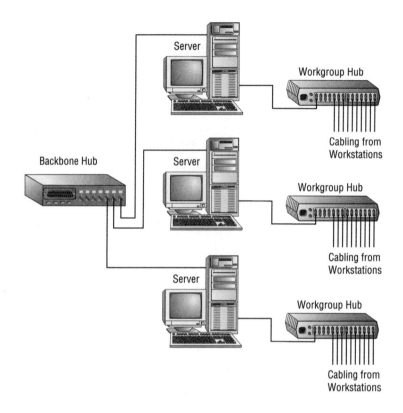

FIGURE 2.29
Three workgroup servers communicate on a backbone cable segment without workstations.

example could be Sales, Production, and Administration. The Sales people will normally print to the queue on the Sales server, which in turn routes the print jobs to the printer in the Sales group. Although the Sales people could print to the Production printer, this is not the nature of most traffic.

The three servers can synchronize time and Directory services, and route interworkgroup traffic quickly by way of the backbone. Like the other scenarios, you can increase the speed of any of the cable segments, including the backbone, by using switches or 100Mbps hubs and network adapters.

Summary

F YOU'RE CREATING YOUR company's network or expanding an existing one, each hour of planning you do will save you at least a day of trouble later—and probably much more.

For the Directory tree, you should carefully decide whether or not to accept the default tree. Larger networks, or networks with isolated departments (little resource sharing) should have additional OUs.

Document a standard for object names and other object properties.

For your servers' file systems, you need to do more detailed planning. How large will the DOS and NetWare partitions be? What volumes will occupy the NetWare partitions? What fault-tolerant options do you require, such as mirroring and RAID?

Most administrators need some consultant help with the physical network, including topologies and cabling. When working with these consultants, remember to avoid unpopular or outmoded standards, hire a qualified cabling professional, and document *everything*.

Upgrading an Existing NetWare Network

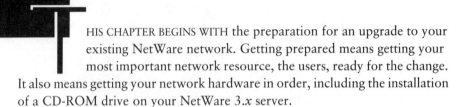

HIS CHAPTER BEGINS WITH the preparation for an upgrade to your existing NetWare network. Getting prepared means getting your most important network resource, the users, ready for the change. It also means getting your network hardware in order, including the installation of a CD-ROM drive on your NetWare 3.*x* server.

Another big part of upgrading is getting the right drivers and patches for NetWare 4. When you have updated LAN drivers, disk drivers, and operating system patches in place, you eliminate some problems that might plague your NOS upgrade later.

The next step is upgrading workstations. You can actually do this step at any time, since the newer client versions can access your older NetWare server just fine.

Last of all comes the NetWare Operating System (NOS) upgrade itself. It stands to reason that swapping in a new NOS strikes some fear in the hearts of administrators. Conscientious administrators want to be careful not to do something that may result in calamity. Your caution has proven to be wise with NetWare versions 4.0, 4.01, and 4.02. This new "Directory services thing" didn't work well, right?

Happily, version 4.1*x* is much more stable than 4.0*x*. Novell has also improved the migration and upgrade utilities, making the switch quite easy and safe. And Novell even gives you a *printed* manual for the upgrade!

As for your learning curve with NetWare 4.1, you've made a significant step in buying this book. Add the patches, your own experience in NetWare, and the new graphical NetWare Administrator utility, and your upgrade experience should be a pleasant surprise.

This chapter is intended to augment, not replace the NetWare Upgrade manual. Here you'll find some commonsense practices that may already be part of your standard procedures. The chapter also describes some of the traps to watch out for.

Preparing for the Upgrade

A N NOS UPGRADE OFTEN COINCIDES with a complex series of related upgrades. Perhaps you're adding some RAM, installing some new hard drives, or changing to a managed hub. You may be tempted to perform all your hardware and software upgrades in one weekend. ✓

But ignore that temptation—you probably already know better than to change everything at once. The upgrades might go faster, since you're downing the server and opening the box and unplugging everything anyway—but it's a trap. It won't work when you boot everything up, and then you'll be stuck doing fault isolation on the whole system instead of one thing at a time. You won't know where to start.

So take this advice to heart: Do your hardware and software upgrades one at a time.

Helping Users Through the Upgrade

A good practice when upgrading anything is to warn your users ahead of time. Users don't like surprises. At least one day before you do the work, you might send out a memo alerting them that something might not be the same next time they log in. Here's a sample:

To: Network Users in Accounting

From: Jeff Jeffries

Re: Tomorrow's Upgrade of Workstation Software

Happy Friday! Over the weekend we will be performing an upgrade of your workstation software to Novell's newer, faster, better Client 32. To help the upgrade go smoothly, please do the following:

****

* **If you have a power-on password on your computer,** *

* **please remove it, or call me.** *

************* **IMMEDIATELY** ****************

On Monday when you start your work you may notice a red bar scrolling up your screen. Do not be alarmed. It's only the new workstation software doing a little Novell advertising.

We'll test your workstation to make sure it runs right, but if there's any problem whatsoever, please let us know quickly.

Have a nice weekend.

Notice in the example memo that we have put asterisks around the important instruction about the password. If you want users to do anything, like turn off their hardware boot passwords, make sure your request is *highlighted* so it's not missed. We all tend to skim over memos rather than read them thoroughly these days.

On Monday, you might put fliers on the users' chairs with your phone number and a reminder of the upgrade. If they need to do something like create new passwords, remind them.

Lastly, if you're already busy and the upgrade is significant, you might arrange for some extra user support the day after the upgrade. If the upgrade goes well, then you'll just seem extra meticulous to both users and management. If there are problems to be handled, everyone will applaud your foresight and wisdom.

Hardware Upgrade Tips

As discussed earlier, you'll want to make any hardware upgrades either before or after the NOS upgrade, not at the same time. Following are some general suggestions for upgrading your hardware, as well as a procedure specifically for adding a CD-ROM drive to your NetWare 3 server.

General Suggestions

Prepare for server downtime. You can't upgrade a server while users are logged in. Depending on your situation, you may need to shut it down, bring it up, and shut it down again for more changes. Make sure you otherwise accommodate your company's business as much as possible by working weekends and nights on the upgrade. Also make sure you get management approval for the downtime and schedule it well in advance.

Add memory. If you're upgrading your server's hard drives to get more space for NetWare volumes, you may need to add memory first. The same goes for adding a CD-ROM drive. Check out the formula for calculating memory requirements in Appendix A of the NetWare 4.1 Installation manual.

And be sure to take your RAM to a computer shop to have it tested *before* bringing down the server to add it. Add the memory; then restart the server and let it run a day or more (an hour or so if you have a production server). NetWare exercises memory quite thoroughly, so any problems should show up soon. If the memory checks out fine, then you can proceed to upgrade your drives and mount the new volumes (or add the disk space to an existing volume).

Get new controller/adapter drivers. Before you upgrade a controller or network adapter, get the latest driver from the hardware manufacturer. By the time you buy the controller or adapter, its manufacturer has probably found the bugs in the driver and posted a new driver for you to download. Virtually every manufacturer maintains a bulletin board, a Web site, an FTP site, or a CompuServe library for this purpose.

Don't throw away the old settings. When configuring the new hardware, use the old hardware's interrupt and memory settings if possible. That way, if the old settings have been working fine but the new hardware doesn't, then you know a memory or interrupt conflict is not the cause of the problem.

Using an IDE CD-ROM Drive on a NetWare 3.12 Server

Read the Upgrade manual that came with the NetWare 4 software. You may be surprised at all the options you have for getting a NetWare 3.12 server up to NetWare 4. These options include the generic installation program, the across-the-wire migration, and the same-server migration.

Your NetWare 4 software comes on CD-ROM. If you have more than one server, you can access the CD-ROM with one of the following methods:

- If you have 170MB extra disk space on a server, you can put the NetWare 4 CD-ROM in a workstation and then copy the installation files to a hard drive volume on a server. Instructions for this procedure are found in the Installation manual.

- Use a CD-ROM drive as a DOS device attached to the server you're upgrading. This works most reliably if you have the CD-ROM on a controller *separate* from the hard drives.

■ Mount the NetWare 4 CD-ROM on another server. Then, from the DOS partition on the server you're upgrading, you can map a drive to the CD-ROM and run the installation.

NetWare supports both IDE and SCSI CD-ROM drives. SCSI controllers and drives tend to conform better to standards, and therefore work more consistently. You will have the best success using a separate controller for your CD-ROM drive, rather than running it off the same controller as your hard drives.

The NetWare 4.10 manuals do not give instructions for mounting an IDE CD-ROM. If you want to upgrade using the third option above, using an IDE CD-ROM drive, here's how to do it.

First, you need to obtain the latest CDROM.NLM and support files. These files contain important enhancements that allow you to use IDE CD-ROM drives and controllers. More importantly for this chapter, they also fix problems with file transfers when doing installations across the network.

Novell provides the CDROM.NLM and support files in a self-extracting executable file named CDUP*n*.EXE, where *n* is the latest revision. At the time of this writing, CDUP3.EXE is the most recent.

You can download CDUP*n*.EXE from CompuServe using the GO NOVFF command to access the Novell File Finder application. Novell's Web page at `http://netware.novell.com/` also gives instructions on downloading the file.

Once you've obtained the support files, follow these steps:

1. Delete any file named CDROM.MSG and replace it with the new CD-ROM message file, as follows:

   A. Change your current directory to the root of SYS.

   B. Type the command **FLAG CDROM.MSG N /S**. The FLAG utility removes the Read Only attribute so you can delete the file. It also lists all CDROM.MSG files found.

   C. Delete all files found by the FLAG command.

2. Create a directory, and copy CDUP*n*.EXE to that directory.

3. Change to the new directory, and type the command **CDUP*n*.EXE**, replacing *n* with the version of the file you have.

The file self-extracts, creating the files you need in the directory you created. These files are needed for CD-ROMs in NetWare 3.12 and NetWare 4. A subdirectory called NETWARE.312 is also created, with files needed specifically for NetWare 3.12.

4. Copy all files from the directory you created and from the NETWARE.312 subdirectory to a floppy disk. You will later copy the files from the floppy to the DOS partition of the NetWare 3.12 server.

5. Copy the same files to the SYS:SYSTEM directory of the server that will have a CD-ROM drive. This step ensures that the same versions of the CD-ROM files are on both the DOS partition and the SYS volume of the server.

6. Edit the AUTOEXEC.NCF file to include the following lines:

```
LOAD AFTER311
LOAD CDROM
```

7. Bring down the NetWare 3.12 server.

8. Install the CD-ROM drive as a DOS device according to the manufacturer's instructions. This allows you to test the device in DOS before using it in NetWare.

9. Run the CD-ROM drive as a DOS device, making sure you can access the files on a CD.

10. Edit the CONFIG.SYS file and AUTOEXEC.BAT file to remove the DOS drivers for the CD-ROM drive. This makes the drive unusable from DOS, but it solves some problems with mounting the drive under NetWare.

11. Restart the computer to load the revised CONFIG.SYS and AUTOEXEC .BAT files.

12. Copy the NetWare CD-ROM files from the floppy (where you copied them in step 7) to the directory with SERVER.EXE.

13. Edit the STARTUP.NCF file, adding the following line as the *first* line in the file:

```
LOAD NPAPATCH
```

NPAPATCH.NLM auto-loads PM312.NLM. Failure to load this patch to the operating system's media manager may cause the server to abend. Do not unload this patch.

14. Remove the command to load any IDE disk drivers, such as IDE.DSK or ISA.DSK. The new IDEATA.HAM and its .CDM drivers replace IDE.DSK and ISA.DSK.

15. Add the following command to load the IDE controller driver. Supply the proper port and interrupt values for the controller.

```
LOAD IDEATA.HAM PORT=1F0 INT=14
```

If the HAM finds an IDE hard drive attached to the controller, the HAM loads the IDEHD.CDM. If it finds an IDE CD-ROM drive, it loads IDECD .CDM. These CDM files replace the old .DSK drivers.

16. Start the server by typing **SERVER** and pressing Enter.

17. Type **LOAD CDROM**. The new CDROM.NLM auto-loads the NWPALOAD.NLM, which in turn loads NWPA.NLM. Then the NWPALOAD .NLM unloads itself.

18. To mount the NetWare 4.11 CD-ROM, use the following command from the console:

```
CD MOUNT NW411
```

To get information on all the CD commands, use the CD HELP command.

At this point the CD volume is available to the network. You can now bring down another server to be upgraded, and map a drive from the DOS partition of that server to the NW410 CD-ROM volume. Then run the installation or migration program. Make sure you read and follow the instructions in the Upgrade manual.

Getting Patches and Drivers

A VERY IMPORTANT PART of any upgrade is getting the latest software. I suggest having all possible updates available *before* you perform an NOS installation or upgrade.

Novell and your hardware vendors are generally quite responsible about fixing the known flaws in their software, so all you have to do is get the fixes and use them. These software fixes fall into three categories:

- Patches to the NetWare operating system and upgrades to the corresponding support modules and utilities

- Improved disk drivers and other storage-device drivers

- Improved network adapter (LAN) drivers

Since the NetWare fixes are regularly updated and you have so many hardware driver options, the following examples won't fit your situation. The scenarios are presented merely as examples, from which you can deviate as necessary according to your circumstances.

Example of Updating NetWare Software

This procedure gets a list of important file updates for NetWare from CompuServe. The steps may change along with Novell's evolving presence on CompuServe.

1. Use the CompuServe GO NWOSFI command to get to the NetWare Operating System File Updates forum.

2. Click on the Notices icon. The Notices window appears.

3. Select News Flash from the Notices window. The following message appears:

MINIMUM OS & NLM UPDATES

```
For a listing of Minimum OS & NLM Updates download
PATLST.TXT from the NWOSFILES forum. PATLST.TXT is a brief
listing of minimum OS & NLM update files. Novell Technical
Support recommends applying all of these updates as a
baseline. This file will be updated as needed.
```

```
NETWARE CLIENT 32 FOR DOS/WINDOWS AVAILABLE

The NetWare Client 32 for DOS/Windows (Open Beta) is
available. To download GO NWCLIENT.
```

4. When you're prompted, click on the Libraries icon. The Library Sections window appears.

5. Select Minimum OS, NLM, & File Updates.

6. Click on the Description button to get the following message:

```
PATLST.TXT is a brief listing of OS, NLM, & Utility update
files. Novell Technical Support recommends applying all
of these updates as a baseline. This file will be updated
as needed.
```

7. Click on the Retrieve button, select a directory, and click on OK.

A text file listing the required update files (patches) is downloaded to your hard drive. The file also includes information on where you can download the patches.

Example of Updating Disk Driver Software

Before you upgrade your server to NetWare 4.1, you should check to see if there is a new driver for your disk controller. Let's say you have an Adaptec 2940 controller. The following steps would get the latest disk driver, AIC7870.DSK.

1. In the documentation that came with the drive, look for a bulletin board number, Web URL, or CompuServe GO word.

2. For this example, we'll use the Adaptec bulletin board (BBS). The telephone number of the BBS is (408) 945-7727. Dial the BBS number using your modem software.

3. Supply your customer information and access file area 4, shown as the NetWare files area.

4. List the available files by typing the L command.

5. Browse through the files until you find the NetWare 4.*x* drivers. The file name you need to download is NW4X.EXE.

6. Download the file as instructed.

7. Create a separate directory for NW4X.EXE and move the file to that directory.

8. Change to the new directory and type **NW4X.EXE**; press Enter.

   The self-extracting archive file creates a number of files, including the AIC7870 driver required by your controller. This driver is less than two months old yet is more than a year newer than the one you received with your controller! Also included in the download is a bonus two-page list of tips for using the controller with NetWare.

9. Print AIC7870.TXT and file it for later reference.

10. Copy the AIC7870.DDI and AIC7870.DSK files to floppy disk, for use when you upgrade the server to NetWare 4.1.

Example of Updating LAN Driver Software

Before you upgrade your server to NetWare 4.1 there's another task to complete. You need to see if there is an updated driver for the network adapter. In this example, the adapter is a pair of Microdyne NE5500s. Microdyne has an FTP site, a Web site, a CompuServe forum, and a bulletin board.

   Here's how you'd get the latest LAN driver, PCNTNW.LAN, via CompuServe.

1. Using CompuServe's Search feature, look for the word *Microdyne*. CompuServe responds with the Novell Vendor B forum.

2. Select the GO button to access the Novell Vendor B forum.

3. Click the Library Sections icon.

4. Select the Microdyne library.

5. Browsing through the library files, you see "ODI Drivers for NE2500/5500."

6. Click on the Retrieve button to download the file, named E25-5O.ZIP.

7. Once the file is downloaded, create a directory for the new drivers and change to that directory.

8. Unzip the file; for example, enter

    ```
    PKUNZIP H:\E25-50.ZIP -d
    ```

    The file is unzipped, creating subdirectories for 3.XX and 4.XX.

9. Copy the contents of the 4.XX subdirectory to a floppy disk, to use in the upgrade to NetWare 4.1.

10. A 29-page supplement to your manual is included as MANUAL.TXT, created in the directory where you unzipped the E25-5O.ZIP file. Print the MANUAL.TXT file to use as a supplement to the manual that came with the network adapter.

Upgrading Workstation Software

BEFORE YOU UPGRADE THE SERVER, you should upgrade all the workstations' networking software to the version you will use with NetWare 4.1. The new client software is compatible with your older servers and will work well through the server upgrade. For DOS or Windows workstations, your options include Virtual Loadable Module (VLM) software and Client 32 software.

To use NDS and the other features of NetWare 4, it is important to update DOS/ Windows workstations to either the VLM client or Client 32 software.

VLMs

Assuming that you already have client software of some kind working on your workstations, you can load VLM installation software on the server. Then you can run an installation program from each workstation to update the VLMs and Windows networking support files.

The following procedure sets up a directory and files on an existing server for installing the latest VLM clients:

1. Using a workstation with a CD-ROM drive, insert the NetWare 4 Operating System CD-ROM in the drive.

2. Change your current drive and directory to the \CLIENT\DOSWIN directory of the CD-ROM. For NetWare 4.11, this directory is \PRODUCTS\VLM\IBM_6. For instance, type

   ```
   D:
   CD \CLIENT\DOSWIN
   ```

3. Create corresponding subdirectories of SYS:PUBLIC. Type

   ```
   MD Z:\PUBLIC\CLIENT
   MD Z:\PUBLIC\CLIENT\DOSWIN
   ```

4. Map a drive to the new subdirectory, with the command

   ```
   MAP I:=SYS:PUBLIC\CLIENT\DOSWIN
   ```

5. Copy files and subdirectories from the CD-ROM to the new subdirectory. Type

   ```
   NCOPY *.* I: /s /e /v
   ```

If you are using the newer NetWare 4.11 software, you should stop here. For NetWare 4.10, continue with steps 6 through 18.

6. At this point, you could run the VLM installation from each of your workstations to get the NetWare 4.1 version of the software. However, significant improvements have been made since the original release. To update your installation files to the latest versions, do the following:

   A. Create a directory for the downloaded update file. For this example, we use VLMUP4 as the update file.

      ```
      MD \VLMUP4
      ```

   B. Download the VLM update files from CompuServe or Novell's Web site.

   C. Change to the directory you created and execute the update file. In this example, you would type

      ```
      CD \VLMUP4
      VLMUP4
      ```

The self-extracting VLMUP4.EXE creates documentation files for the update.

7. Follow the instructions included in the update you obtain—for this example, VLMUP4. Copy all files from the VLM subdirectory created by VLMUP4 to the SYS:PUBLIC\CLIENT\DOSWIN directory.

8. You now have the compressed versions ending in an underscore, and new uncompressed versions of many of the files. For example, you have both VLM.EX_ and VLM.EXE. Flag the compressed files as normal so you can delete them. Type

```
FLAG *.??_ N /S
```

9. View the files in Windows File Manager. Make sure the files are sorted by file name.

10. Delete the compressed versions (ending in underscores) of those files that exist in both compressed and uncompressed form. Hold down the Ctrl key while selecting all the compressed files that have uncompressed counterparts; then press Delete. Now when the client installation utility runs, it will automatically select the uncompressed version of the files if the compressed version is missing.

11. Copy the .MSG files to the SYS:PUBLIC\CLIENT\DOSWIN\NLS\ENGLISH directory. You can do this in File Manager, or change to the SYS:PUBLIC\CLIENT\DOSWIN\ directory in DOS and type

```
NCOPY *.MSG NLS\ENGLISH
```

12. Using File Manager again, delete the compressed version (*.MS_) of the message files in SYS:PUBLIC\CLIENT\DOSWIN\NLS\ENGLISH for those files that have an uncompressed version (*.MSG).

If you don't delete the old compressed versions, the installation program will select them instead of the newer files.

13. Copy all files from the ODIDRV directory to the SYS:PUBLIC\CLIENT\DOSWIN\DOS directory.

14. Using File Manager again, delete the compressed files in SYS:PUBLIC\CLIENT\DOSWIN\DOS where an uncompressed file of the same name exists.

15. Update other files in the DOSWIN directory as needed.

For instance, a Windows driver update is currently available, called WINDR3.EXE. This file contains NETWARE.DRV, VIPX.386, and other files that can improve the stability and performance of your Windows workstations. (Make sure you read the documentation for any updates you apply.) Here is a simple procedure for checking versions of files in the DOS/WIN directory.

A. Unpack the compressed file in question using the NWUNPACK utility. The compressed version of the file will *not* be deleted. For instance, you could type

```
NWUNPACK NETWARE.DR_
```

B. Compare the date of the file to the one created by the update package (e.g. WINDR3.EXE).

C. Put the newer file in the DOSWIN directory.

D. Delete the packed version of the file (e.g. NETWARE.DR_).

16. Test a workstation with the new installation files by running INSTALL.EXE from the SYS:PUBLIC\CLIENT\DOSWIN directory.

17. Flag the installation files as Read Only and Sharable. Type

```
FLAG SYS:\PUBLIC\CLIENT\DOSWIN\*.* RO S /S
```

18. Run the client installation. For example, from each DOS workstation on your network, type

```
MAP I:=SYS:PUBLIC\CLIENT\DOSWIN
I:
INSTALL
```

Client 32

If you have used or installed VLM software before, you will find Client 32 a welcome relief. Here are the simple instructions to load the installation files onto the server and run the DOS installation or Windows setup from a workstation.

1. Obtain the Client 32 software and any updates. You can download the software from NetWire on CompuServe (GO NetWire) or from Novell's Web site (http://netware.novell.com/). The Client 32 installation files are in \PRODUCTS\DOSWIN32\IBM_6 on the Netware 4.11 CD.

2. Create an installation directory on the server. For this example we will use SYS:PUBLIC\CLIENT\CLIENT32.

3. Copy the downloaded Client 32 file (in this case DW32NA.EXE) to the installation directory you created in step 2.

4. Run the self-extracting DW32NA.EXE file to create the installation files and directories.

5. Apply any updates (patches) as directed in the update's README file.

6. For each workstation on your network, obtain the latest 32-bit (server) LAN driver and configuration file from the network adapter manufacturer. If you can't get the 32-bit LAN driver (.LAN) and configuration file (.LDI), you can use the 16-bit ODI driver (.COM or .EXE) and configuration file (.INS).

7. You may find it most convenient to copy the LAN drivers to the installation directory you created in step 2.

8. For each workstation, log into the network and run SYS:PUBLIC\CLIENT\CLIENT32\SETUP.EXE from Windows. INSTALL.EXE is available in the same directory for DOS workstations without Windows.

The CLIENT 32 setup program creates the Windows program group and program items shown in Figure 3.1.

The User Tools program lets you perform common tasks, such as mapping drives, sending messages, and capturing printer ports. The main screen is shown

FIGURE 3.1
Program group and program items created by the Client 32 setup

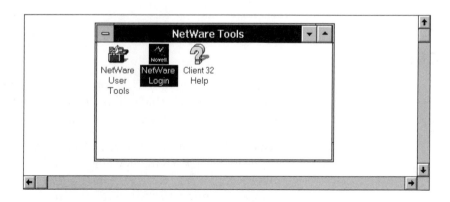

FIGURE 3.2
User Tools in Client 32
is similar to the program
that came with
NetWare 3.12 and 4.10.

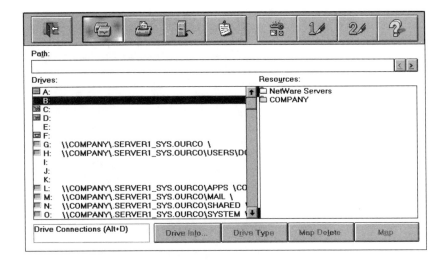

in Figure 3.2. You'll notice that the User Tools is similar to the program that originally shipped with NetWare 3.12 and 4.10.

Click on the Setup icon to view the new options, some of which are shown in Figure 3.3. Notice the new Windows login utility included in the program group. If your users' LOGIN command is already in the AUTOEXEC.BAT file, you won't need to use the Windows version. If you prefer that your users log in through Windows, you can copy the Windows login utility to the Startup group for an automated Windows login.

NOS Upgrades to NetWare 4.11

T HIS SECTION TELLS YOU how to upgrade your network operation system to NetWare 4.11. It covers upgrades from several earlier versions of NetWare. But before you do anything, read the following list of Notes, Warnings, and general reminders about prerequisites.

Do the footwork. Be sure you've already completed the planning exercises in Chapter 2. You should already have obtained the latest patches and drivers as described in the "Getting Patches and Drivers" section of this chapter. And

remember, it is best to perform the hardware upgrades, whenever possible, before installing a new NOS.

Add memory. NetWare 4.11 requires at least 16MB of RAM, a 15MB DOS partition, and a 120MB SYS volume. These are *minimums*. Novell recommends at least 20MB of RAM if you're upgrading from NetWare 3. Since the amount of RAM affects the performance of your server more than any other factor, you should always consider adding more.

See Appendix A of the NetWare Upgrade manual for a calculation of memory require-ments. If you are storing long or Mac file names on the server, you'll also need to look at Appendix B of that manual. Running out of RAM will cause poor performance, abnormal performance, and/or server crashes.

Do the hardware upgrade first. As mentioned earlier, if you're not creating a new server, make your hardware upgrades first if possible. After the hardware is configured and running under the current operating system, then upgrade the NOS.

If you are making a significant hardware upgrade, consider using one of the across-the-wire methods described in the following sections. This involves installing a new NetWare 4.11 server and transferring your old server data to the new server.

No matter which upgrade method you choose, do a complete backup of your server before starting. Also, since floppy disks are easily damaged, make a copy of the NetWare license disk.

Upgrading from NetWare 2

SINCE NOVELL HASN'T BEEN SELLING NetWare 2 for a few years, your server will probably benefit from a serious hardware upgrade before you step up to NetWare 4.11. Motherboards, CPUs, RAM, network adapters, controllers, and hard drives all offer considerably better performance for the cost than they did even two years ago.

You have two excellent options for upgrading a NetWare 2 server to NetWare 4.11: across-the-wire migration and same-server migration.

- *Across-the-wire migration* is actually a migration of your NetWare 2 server to a new computer that has NetWare 4.11 loaded. This is the upgrade method of choice if you're upgrading your hardware along with a NOS upgrade. This is also the safest method because the old server is left intact and you can always revert to it if the upgrade fails.

- *Same-server migration* involves a workstation that acts as an intermediate storage device. You must back up the server's volumes. The old server's bindery is copied to the workstation's hard drive. After the original server's NOS is deleted and 4.11 is installed, the bindery information is converted and transferred back to the upgraded server. The volume data is then restored.

If you have value-added processes (VAPs) running on your NetWare 2 server, you must get an NLM version of these processes for the NetWare 4.11 server. VAPs only run on NetWare 2.

Let's take a brief look at these two migration options.

Across-the-Wire Migration

This section only summarizes the migration steps. For more detailed instructions, see the NetWare Upgrade manual.

Across-the-wire migration transforms your NetWare 2.1x or 2.2 bindery information into an existing Directory. It begins with an activity that allows you to control how the bindery information will fit in the Directory tree. Then the files are migrated from the old server to the new. You accomplish the first phase using NetWare Administrator and the second phase using MIGRATE.EXE.

Before starting the migration, clean up the file system and rename files and directories as necessary to comply with 8.3 conventions. NetWare 2 allows file names up to 14 characters. Only files and directories that comply with 8.3 naming conventions will be migrated.

Transforming the Bindery Information and Migrating It to the Directory

DS Migrate converts your bindery users, groups, queues, and print servers into Directory objects.

1. Install NetWare 4.11 on the new computer.

2. Log in to a NetWare 4.11 server from a Windows 3.1 or Windows 95 workstation.

3. Attach to the NetWare 2 server.

4. Run SYSCON to create the User home directory on the new server.

5. Install and launch the DS Migrate option to NetWare Administrator.

6. Indicate the desired bindery server to "discover." The DS Migrate software generates a report that is displayed in a form like the Directory tree.

7. Modify the tree to your liking. In this stage it's only a model. You can also grant and delete trustee assignments in this step.

   All bindery objects are placed into an OU with the same name as the server being upgraded. You can rename, move, or modify these objects. You can also create new Directory objects and edit object properties and login scripts.

8. When you are satisfied with your modeling, the bindery information is integrated into the Directory.

Migrating the NetWare 2 File System

MIGRATE.EXE, a DOS text-based utility, transfers the file system to the new server. You run MIGRATE.EXE from a workstation that has a bindery connection to both servers. Therefore, make sure a bindery context is specified on the 4.11 server.

MIGRATE.EXE allows you to migrate more than files and directories, but the modeling exercise already handles the bindery information: Select only files and directories to migrate.

If a directory being migrated has the same name and path as a directory that already exists on the NetWare 4.11 server, the files from both directories are merged under the destination directory name. Any file on a source server that has the same name as one that exists on the NetWare 4.11 server is not copied to the NetWare 4.11 server.

The NetWare 2 user login script is a file called LOGIN in the user's MAIL directory. The LOGIN file is copied to the user's MAIL directory on the destination server. Likewise, the system login script is also copied.

It is recommended that you create new container login scripts and avoid the use of User login scripts. If that is not an option immediately users can log in using bindery mode. The bindery user and system login scripts will run. To convert the bindery login scripts to NDS User login scripts so users can log in using NDS, you can use the UIMPORT utility. The UIMPORT control and data files are created in the SYS:SYSTEM directory during the server migration.

1. Start MIGRATE.EXE from the NetWare 4.11 CD-ROM or from disks created using the CD-ROM.

2. Select Across-the-Wire migration.

3. Select a working directory on the workstation.

   The workstation must have 5MB of available disk space, 480KB of conventional memory, and FILES=20 in the CONFIG.SYS file. It should also have PROTICOL IPXODI and IPX RETRY COUNT=60 in the NET.CFG file.

4. Select the source server, the information to be migrated, and the source volumes to migrate.

5. Define the destination (new NetWare 4.11) server and volumes.

6. Migrate the server's information to the new NetWare 4.11 server.

7. Check the migration log and resolve any problems.

8. Test and troubleshoot the new server.

Same-Server Migration

This section only summarizes the migration steps. For more detailed instructions, see the NetWare Upgrade manual. Same-Server Migration uses the MIGRATE .EXE utility to convert an existing NetWare 2 server to NetWare 4.11.

Same-Server migration allows you to use only one server. For this reason, there is some risk to the data during the conversion process to NetWare 4.11. You must back up your data files, then restore them to the server after you install NetWare 4.11.

Before starting the migration, clean up the file system and rename files and directories as necessary to comply with 8.3 conventions. NetWare 2 allows file names up to 14 characters, but only files and directories that comply with 8.3 naming conventions will be migrated.

You run MIGRATE.EXE from a client workstation. Following is a summary of the steps required.

Using MIGRATE.EXE to Upgrade a NetWare 2 Server

1. Back up the server's file system.

2. Run BINDFIX on the NetWare 2 server.

3. Start MIGRATE.EXE from the NetWare 4.11 CD-ROM or from disks created using the CD-ROM.

4. Select Same Server migration.

5. Select a working directory on the workstation.

   The workstation must have 5MB of available disk space, 480KB of conventional memory, and FILES=20 in the CONFIG.SYS file. In the NET.CFG file, the settings should be PROTICOL IPXODI and IPX RETRY COUNT=60.

6. Select the source server, the information to be migrated (NetWare 2 bindery), and the source volumes to migrate.

7. Define the destination server and volumes. Specify whether the MIGRATE .EXE utility will assign random passwords or none at all.

8. Migrate the server's information to the working directory on the workstation and close MIGRATE.EXE.

9. Install NetWare 4.11 on the server.

10. Restore the file system to the new NetWare 4.11 server from the backup.

11. Start MIGRATE.EXE again and select the new NetWare 4.11 server.

12. Check the migration log and resolve any problems.

13. Edit login scripts for the new server.

14. Rebuild the printing environment.

15. Test and troubleshoot the new server.

Upgrading from NetWare 3

THE BEST WAY TO UPGRADE from NetWare 3 to NetWare 4 is with the INSTALL utility from the NetWare 4.11 CD-ROM. If you don't have a CD-ROM drive on your NetWare 3 server, see "Using an IDE CD-ROM Drive on a NetWare 3.12 Server" in this chapter.

Novell suggests a minimum of 20MB of RAM for this upgrade.

Once you have installed a CD-ROM drive, preferably on its own controller, access the CD-ROM from DOS. Then run INSTALL.BAT from the root of the NetWare 4.11 CD-ROM.

If you are upgrading several servers into the same NetWare Directory Services context, do the following first:

- Eliminate duplicate names for the same user. For example, user Amy Lassen might have an ALASSEN account and an AMY account on separate servers. If you upgraded both servers into the same context, two User objects would be created for Amy.

- Change names of users who have the same login name. For instance, you may have a KEVIN user on SERVER1 and a different KEVIN user on SERVER2. If you upgrade both servers into the same context, you'll have a conflict to sort out during the upgrade. It's better to sort the conflicts out beforehand.

Here's a summary of the upgrade process after you have started INSTALL.BAT.

1. Specify the country code, code page, and keyboard mapping.

   SERVER.EXE is then loaded and multiprocessors are auto-detected. If more than one processor is detected, you are prompted to load SMP (symmetrical multiprocessor) support. You are then prompted to load device drivers.

2. To load device drivers, select Load Device Drivers Manually if you have updated disk drivers (DSK, CDM, or HAM files) for your hardware. Otherwise, let the installation program auto-detect the hardware and load the appropriate drivers.

3. Verify that the settings (for interrupts, port values, DMA and the like) are correct.

4. If you have a separate controller for your CD-ROM drive, continue accessing the drive via DOS. If not, then attempt to mount it as a NetWare volume.

5. Supply a copy of the license disk when prompted.

6. Select Load LAN Drivers Manually if you have updated LAN drivers (LAN files) for your hardware. Otherwise, let the installation program auto-detect the hardware and load the appropriate drivers.

7. Verify the settings for your LAN drivers.

8. Install NDS. If there is an existing NetWare 4 server, the tree is discovered and you are prompted to install into this tree. If this is the first NetWare 4 server on the network, you are prompted to create a new tree. Name the tree and supply the time zone information.

If prompted for a type of time server, accept the default type.

9. Specify the server's context. (Use the planning you did in Chapter 2.)

10. Specify the administrator's name and password. Write them down.

11. You are presented with a suggested AUTOEXEC.NCF file. Accept it if the Ethernet frame type is okay. It should match the frame type used by your workstations.

If you need both 802.2 and 802.3 frame types, you can load both. However, standardizing your workstations and servers on a single frame type will reduce unnecessary network traffic.

12. When the main part of installation is complete, reboot your server and troubleshoot any problems.

13. Upgrade printing from NetWare 3 to NetWare 4.11 by loading and running PUPGRADE.NLM at the server console.

14. Log in using some dummy User objects you create to simulate real users. Make sure the login scripts work correctly. You may need to make modifications.

Upgrading from NetWare 4

NOVELL HAS MADE THE UPGRADE from other NetWare 4 versions to NetWare 4.11 especially painless. It's mostly a big file-copying process, with little intervention.

The one hitch occurs for those who have NetWare 4.0x servers. The older versions of NDS are somewhat foreign to the installation program. But there's hope! To remedy the problem, follow the steps in this upcoming section before you move on to your upgrade.

If You Have a NetWare 4.0x Server

Even if you don't fully upgrade all servers to NetWare 4.11, you should upgrade the version of Directory Services on your 4.0x servers. The newer version of Directory Services is required before installing NetWare 4.11.

Before you do anything, you need to run DSREPAIR version 2.23 on each and every 4.0x server on your network. The 2.23 version of DSREPAIR will run only on NetWare 4.0x servers and is not intended for NetWare 4.1 servers. You can download this version of DSREPAIR from NetWire. It's also in the \PRODUCTS\NW402\NLS\ENGLISH directory on the NetWare 4.11 Installation CD-ROM.

Here are the steps for running DSREPAIR 2.23:

1. Map a drive and change to the SYS:SYSTEM directory on your NetWare 4.0*x* server.

2. Flag DSREPAIR.NLM as normal. Type

   ```
   FLAG DSREPAIR.NLM N
   ```

3. Copy DSREPAIR.NLM version 2.23 from to the SYS:SYSTEM directory, replacing the older version.

4. At the NetWare 4.0*x* server console, type

   ```
   LOAD DSREPAIR
   ```

5. Select a full unattended repair. If there are any errors, repeat the repair until there are none.

6. Repeat this procedure for every 4.0*x* server on the network, whether or not you are upgrading it to NetWare 4.11.

You can now proceed to the following upgrade procedure.

Upgrading a NetWare 4.x Server to NetWare 4.11

First, make sure you have completed the procedure just above for all NetWare 4.0*x* servers. You should also have installed updated drivers as discussed in "Getting Patches and Drivers" in this chapter.

To avoid NDS base schema conflicts, always upgrade the server holding the master replica of the [Root] partition first. Use NetWare Administrator to determine which server holds the master replica. Choose Tools | Partition Manager. Select [Root], and then Replicas. The server holding the master replica is displayed.

1. Bring down the server.

2. Load the DOS drivers to use the CD-ROM from DOS.

3. Change to the NetWare 4.11 installation CD-ROM.

4. Type **INSTALL**.

5. Choose NetWare Server Installation.

6. Choose NetWare 4.11.

7. Choose Upgrade NetWare 3.*x* or 4.*x*.

8. When prompted, enter boot directory and language settings. SERVER.EXE is then loaded and multiprocessors are auto-detected.

9. If more than one processor is detected, you are prompted to load SMP (symmetrical multiprocessor) support.

10. Next, you are prompted to load device drivers. Select Load Device Drivers Manually if you have updated disk drivers (DSK, CDM, or HAM files) for your hardware. Otherwise, let the installation program auto-detect the hardware and load the appropriate drivers.

11. Verify that the settings (for interrupts, port values, DMA, and the like) are correct.

12. If you have a separate controller for your CD-ROM drive, continue accessing the drive via DOS. If not, attempt to mount it as a NetWare volume.

13. Supply a copy of the license disk when prompted.

14. Select Load LAN Drivers Manually if you have updated LAN drivers (LAN files) for your hardware. Otherwise, let the installation program auto-detect the hardware and load the appropriate drivers.

15. Verify the settings for your LAN drivers.

16. Install NDS. If there is an existing NetWare 4 server, the tree is discovered and you are prompted to install into this tree. If this is the only NetWare 4 server on the network, you are prompted to verify the DS information contained in the current directory.

If prompted for a type of time server, accept the default type.

17. You are presented with a suggested AUTOEXEC.NCF file. Accept it if the Ethernet frame type is okay. It should match the frame type used by your workstations. If you need both 802.2 and 802.3 frame types, you can load both. However, standardizing your workstations and servers on a single frame type will reduce unnecessary network traffic.

18. When the main part of installation is complete, reboot your server and troubleshoot any problems.

19. Log in and make sure the login scripts work correctly.

Summary

Upgrading a network doesn't have to be difficult, but it does take some time and preparation. First of all, you need to help your own users and management understand what's going on. Unless you're just upgrading the version of NDS running on your server, there'll be some interruption. For network administrators, that means working nights or weekends to avoid a devastating hit on the company's most productive hours.

It helps to be proficient on the Internet or CompuServe; that's where you'll find the latest drivers and patches. Software companies have grown accustomed to, even complacent about releasing buggy software and fixing the bugs later. That means administrators need to become accustomed to getting the fixes.

Workstation client software can be upgraded independently of the NOS, since the clients are backward-compatible with earlier NetWare versions. Novell's Client 32 for Windows 3.1 and Windows 95 provide better performance and features than the VLMs released with earlier versions of NetWare.

Novell probably supplies too many NOS upgrade procedures and utilities. There's MIGRATE.EXE, DSMIGRATE, INSTALL, and PUPGRADE. There are tools for doing the in-place upgrade, the same-server upgrade, the printing upgrade, the over-the-wire upgrade, the over-the-river-and-through-the-woods upgrade, and so on forever and ever, amen.

This chapter contains the most useful upgrade procedures, but if you have a special circumstance that calls for one of the other methods, you'll want to refer to the duly printed Upgrade manual.

Installing the
Network

THIS CHAPTER TAKES A two-pronged approach to explaining the process of installing new server hardware and networking software. In addition to guidance on buying assembled hardware and hiring hardware specialists to do the job for you, included here are tips for people who like to install hardware themselves.

You'll learn the simple procedure for finding Novell-approved hardware. You also get some tips on buying uninterruptible power supplies (UPSs), drives, controllers, and network adapters.

Finally, this chapter gives you procedures for preparing to create a NetWare server, and guides you through the critical decision points in the installation process. Also included is an easy way to install the client software and log in for the first time.

Selecting and Assembling New Hardware

AS YOU ACCEPT THE CHALLENGE of creating a new NetWare network, you might have some uneasiness about selecting and installing the hardware. How do I get the cable installed right? What hardware works with NetWare? How do I select network adapters, controllers, and disk drives?

This section explains the terms and coaches you through the task of getting the right stuff. The hard decisions are still yours because you know your company's situation best. But at least, with the help of this section, you'll know some of the hardware options available to you.

Do It Yourself? Pros and Cons

You have some options when it comes to installing cable, assembling a server, and hooking everything together. If you're of the hacker ilk, you might enjoy doing it all yourself. You can even save your company some money that way, and you'll certainly learn a great deal in the process. But there are drawbacks. Let's look at both sides of these issues.

Installing Your Own Cable

- Advantages: You know the quality of the work. If you purchase tools, they will be available when you need to repair broken cabling.

- Disadvantages: You need to buy tools and test equipment. You'll work much slower than experienced cable installers. Drilling into walls is unsafe.

Assembling Your Own Server

- Advantages: If you're experienced with PCs, you can build exactly the server you want. Another option is to buy a computer on sale and modify it for use as a server. That way you save money. You can also salvage the extra nonserver items—mouse, software bundles, SVGA monitor, and graphics card—for use on your workstations.

- Disadvantages: You get no guarantees or support for hardware you put together yourself. Improperly configured server hardware will plague your network later (if you can get it working at all).

A server is going to be your most important piece of hardware (if you don't count the boss's PC). Don't skimp when you buy it. A lot of vendors will assemble a PC to your specifications. It used to be that any old PC was thought to be adequate for a server, and this may be true for very small networks. But consider: What is the cost of downtime in dollars? How much will you really save by purchasing equipment of lower quality from a less reputable manufacturer?

Having Cable Installed

Since cable is the hardest component of your network to change, it pays to have it done right the first time (or, if your cabling already exists, have it done right *this* time). Probably the surest way to get it done wrong is to call a cabling contractor from the phone book and ask them to come down and put in some new cable.

It is estimated that about 90% of networking problems are cable related. Cabling is usually labor intensive. Since most of your money will go for the labor to install the cable, it doesn't make sense to spend all that money pulling cheap, low-cost/quality cable.

Consider the following guideline:

Step 1. Before you call anyone, meet with your manager and other interested parties to determine your company's needs and limitations. Some of the people involved in this discussion may be the phone system contractor, the building manager, and the facilities manager.

Discuss the physical limitations of your building, the possibilities for routing cables, locations of wiring closets, and possible sites for the servers and hubs. The phone system contractor may want to consider an upgrade to the phone cabling at the same time you have the network cabling done.

Step 2. Determine the locations of nodes, not just for the current head count but for a maximum head count. You don't want to run out of wall jacks when you hire more personnel or add more printers. It's said that if your cabling system lasts five years, you have planned well.

Step 3. Set the bandwidth requirement. Currently there is no reason to accept less than 100Mbps Category 5 wiring, even if you only use 10Mbps Ethernet now. Eventually, and perhaps very soon, you will want more speed.

Step 4. Establish a plan for using contractors. You will probably want to avoid using only one firm; using two or more means you have some capability to check on everyone's work. One consultant can help you write the specification and test the completed system, and a second contractor actually lays the cable.

Step 5. Make sure the following are part of the plan:

- Conformance with Category 5, 100Mbps testing defined by TSB-67, a specification for unshielded twisted-pair (UTP) cable channels. The specification calls for testing of the wire map (proper connectivity of all the wires), link length, attenuation (loss of signal strength), and near-end crosstalk (NEXT).

- Labeling of all jacks.

- As-installed diagram.

- Guarantee.

It is wise to become familiar with TSB-67, the cable specification mentioned above from the Telecommunications Industry Association/Electronic Industry Association (TIA/EIA).

Remember to have an independent company test the cabling when it's done. Of course you trust the installer; but you also want to verify that trust.

Selecting Novell-Approved Hardware

It's easy to verify that the server hardware you want to buy is Novell-approved. Call 1-800-NETWARE to order the following:

- A list of fax-back documents available from Novell Produce Certification. This list gives you a corresponding number for each category.

- The document regarding the hardware you need. For instance, you might order the document for "File Servers with PCI Bus" or "File Servers with NetWare 4.11."

You can also get information on Novell-approved hardware from the following sources:

- Network Support Encyclopedia, Professional Version (NSEPro on CD-ROM), available from Novell

- Novell's NetWire forum on CompuServe (GO NETWIRE)

- Novell's web site (`http://www.novell.com/`)

The information you get on approved products is very specific: the such-and-such server configured with the such-and-such controller using the version x disk driver.

Certification may take months, so the newest, hottest server from any given company may be "in the approval process," rather than approved. Remember that "in the approval process" in no way means "approved."

Uninterruptible Power Supplies

Imagine a malevolent intruder getting access to your company, gaining the confidence of your management and employees, and then systematically destroying the employees' work and sabotaging the company's computer equipment. If this sounds overly dramatic, just remember that it's always a possibility when you rely on public power for computers. On the average, every power outage—from a tripped circuit breaker, to an overloaded transformer, to a severed line—destroys two hours of work for every employee affected. Low-voltage conditions, called brownouts, can ruin a computer's RAM or cause other components to operate inconsistently. Power surges can fry delicate components.

The following power back-up and conditioning equipment are recommended for any company that relies on computers for any of its operations:

- *Servers.* Get a UPS for each server/monitor combination. This allows you to bring down the server or perform other server operations without line power. Also get software and an interface kit for downing the server automatically if you're not there when the power goes out.

- *Workstations.* Get a UPS for each CPU case. Plugging in the monitor or getting an interface kit to shut down the workstation automatically are optional, depending on your budget and the importance of keeping the workstation running. (This can be an expensive procedure, but some workstations may warrant such protection.)

- *Printers and Copiers.* The power requirements of typical printers and copiers are much larger than other computer equipment and less susceptible to damage. A surge suppressor should suffice for this equipment.

- *Hubs.* Get a UPS for each hub. This protects the hub from power fluctuations and allows users to save files on the server in case of a power outage.

If workstations, but not monitors, are on UPSs you'll want to ensure the users know the correct key sequence for saving their work if the power goes out. For instance, you might put a little "Ctrl+S" sticker on the Windows computers as a reminder. That way, when the monitor goes blank, the users know what to do and can do it quickly.

Network Adapters for Your Server

When buying a server's network adapter, remember that the NIC is the channel to the workstations (via the hub, MAU, or switch). As such, the adapter's performance will determine whether you characterize it as a pipeline or a bottleneck.

The requirements for your server's adapter are much more critical than those of any workstation. A workstation only makes the data transfers for one user, using on average one or two applications at a time. The server, however, manages data flow to and from many workstations, perhaps hundreds at once.

A server typically encounters brief periods of high CPU utilization, which can slow operations considerably for all users. A NIC that relies on the CPU for data transfers compounds the CPU utilization problem. Thus, the number of server CPU cycles a network adapter uses becomes a critical inverse measurement of the adapter's performance. A NIC that uses direct memory access (DMA) transfers data from the network to memory without relying on the CPU.

Using multiple network adapters can add multiples of channel bandwidth, but this approach also increases the importance of low CPU utilization. Make those adapters 100Mbps adapters, and the importance of low CPU utilization becomes even greater.

Choosing Network Adapters

In selecting a network adapter, it pays to check the most recent performance testing of adapters in periodicals such as *Network Computing*. Look for the following features when you shop:

- Physical interfaces appropriate for your server and your hub, MAU, or switch. Normally this means a PCI bus interface and one RJ-45 connector.

- Appropriate speed. For Token Ring, this means 4 or 16Mbps or both. For Ethernet, this means 10 or 100Mbps or both. Some adapters autosense the speed from the MAU or hub.

- Low CPU utilization.

- High throughput.

Getting the Right LAN Drivers

As a rule of thumb, you'll have the best performance and reliability from the latest version of LAN driver software for your network adapter. The manufacturer of your network adapter probably has a Web site, CompuServe forum library, or BBS for downloading the latest driver.

If you're installing a new NetWare server, make sure you have downloaded the newest driver before installing the operating system. The LAN driver software you need includes both the LAN driver (.LAN) and loader (.LDI) files. Keep them on a floppy for your server installation.

Disk Drives, CD-ROM Drives, and Controllers

If you're building your own server, you'll want to do some careful planning of the drive system. This will help you avoid the mistake of buying more PCI controllers than you have slots for, or of buying SCSI drives for your IDE controllers.

You'll want to avoid more subtle mistakes, too. For instance, you wouldn't want to cripple your EIDE speed by buying a slow controller. And for best reliability and performance, you'll want to get a dedicated SCSI controller and CD-ROM drive.

Selecting Drives and Controllers

In days gone by, you had numerous options for drive architecture: ESDI, RLL, IDE, SCSI, and others. Thankfully, the market has thinned down to a few varieties of Enhanced IDE (EIDE) and SCSI.

EIDE EIDE drives are getting faster and larger. So if price is important and you don't need 4GB or more from a hard drive, EIDE can suffice. There are actually a number of modes for EIDE, some of them giving woefully poor performance for a NetWare server.

- *Programmed Input/Output (PIO) Mode 0.* PIO Mode 0 is the old basic IDE mode, with transfer rates of 3.33Mbps.

- *PIO Mode 3.* This mode is an EIDE mode with an 11.1Mbps transfer rate.

- *PIO Mode 4.* This EIDE mode supports transfer rates of up to 16.6Mbps.

- *Multiword Direct Memory Access (DMA) Mode 1.* This mode goes to 13.3Mbps, using DMA to move data directly to RAM rather than via the CPU.

- *Multiword Direct Memory Access (DMA) Mode 2.* This mode goes to 16.6Mbps, using DMA to move data directly to RAM rather than through the CPU.

EIDE controllers limit the number of drives to four per channel; SCSI allows seven.

When you look at controllers, find out which transfer modes they support. Also ask if the transfer mode applies to all attached drives. Some controllers support the faster transfer modes on only one or two of the drives. Other drives are relegated to the snail's pace of PIO Mode 0.

In a server, CPU cycles matter. Look for an EIDE controller that supports one of the DMA modes. Then make sure the drive you select works well with the controller. It might be a good idea to call the controller manufacturer and find out which drives work fastest in combination with a given EIDE controller.

AT ATTACHMENT (ATA) TERMINOLOGY The term ATA comes from the original idea of running a drive directly off the AT computer bus (now called the ISA bus). ATA first appeared in 1985, when Compaq was developing its Portable II computer and needed a way to integrate a hard drive without using up an expansion slot for the controller. One year later, Compaq worked with Western Digital and the Magnetic Peripherals division of CDC (now part of Seagate) to produce a drive/controller combination. They coined the now familiar term, Integrated Drive Electronics (IDE). ATA and IDE have been used interchangeably ever since.

Other manufacturers competed in the ATA drive market, using proprietary methods of integrating the hard drive and controller. In 1988, the Common Access Method (CAM) Committee was formed to standardize the ATA interface. Three years later, an ATA standard was finally approved by the American National Standards Institute (ANSI).

Generally, ATA drives plug into a special slot on the motherboard, or into a special host bus adapter. Technically, the adapters shouldn't be called controllers, since the controller electronics are integrated with the drives—but everybody calls them controllers anyway.

To accommodate the addition of CD-ROM drives, the ATA Packet Interface (ATAPI) was developed by the Small Form Factor Committee. This interface adds jacks for audio signals to the 40-pin ATA cable and special commands for controlling the CD-ROM drive.

The original ATA specification limits drive size to 528MB. The ATA-2 standard, also called enhanced ATA, provides for logical block address (LBA) mode, which expands the address space to 8.4GB. LBA mode uses 28-bit addresses instead of cylinders, heads, and sectors to identify blocks.

Seagate's improvements on ATA are called Fast ATA and Fast ATA-2. Western Digital's are called Enhanced IDE. Given the continued divergence in integrated drive technology, it is always wise to buy your drive with a matching host bus adapter.

SCSI As a rule, you should put your CD-ROM drive on its own SCSI controller. This gives you reliable performance without slowing down the hard drives. SCSI drives still dominate the market for large drives. The relatively mature nature of the SCSI technology gives you good reliability, too.

You can buy your SCSI drives in an external subsystem, with its own power supply and cooling fans. SCSI drives and controllers generally come in three flavors:

- *Fast SCSI-2.* This version has an 8-bit data path that delivers data at 10Mbps.

- *Fast Wide SCSI-2.* This 16-bit version of SCSI handles transfer rates of up to 20Mbps.

- *SCSI-3.* This new SCSI specification allows for a new mode called Ultra-SCSI or Fast 20. This architecture gives burst transfer rates of up to 40Mbps on a 16-bit bus.

As with EIDE, it is always wise to buy your SCSI drive with a controller, or at least to get the drive manufacturer's recommendation on the controller to buy.

Getting the Right Drivers

For EIDE controllers and drives, you can use Novell's drivers. These drivers are loaded in the STARTUP.NCF file, which runs from the DOS partition of your server's boot drive. The following command is typical for EIDE servers.

```
LOAD IDEATA.HAM PORT=1F0 INT=E
```

This command loads the host adapter module (HAM) for your controller. The HAM checks for attached hard drives and CD-ROM drives. If the CD-ROM drive is present, it automatically loads the IDECD.CDM driver. If hard drives are present, it automatically loads IDEHD.CDM.

For SCSI drives and adapters, you should use the drivers recommended by the controller manufacturer. For instance, if you're using Adaptec's 2940 controller, the documentation will recommend loading the AIC7870 disk driver in your STARTUP.NCF file:

```
load aic7870.dsk slot=xx
```

For SCSI controllers, make sure you get the updated disk driver from the drive manufacturer before starting the NetWare installation.

You'll load the driver once for each controller in your server. You can mix both SCSI and IDE controllers in a NetWare server.

Installing Server Software

NOVELL HAS TESTED AND REVISED the server installation process many times to take out most of the headache and worry. What remains is a fairly simple procedure. If you follow the preparatory steps, use the F1 help and the manual when necessary, and consult the decision points outlined in this chapter, you should have no trouble installing your first NetWare server.

Preparation

Before you start your software installation, make sure you have what you need:

- Dedicated power line to servers and hubs.

- Network cabling and hubs in place.

- UPS for servers and hubs.

- Updated NetWare disk drivers and LAN drivers.

- Setup software for disk controllers and network adapters.

- A plan for your Directory tree, particularly the Organizational Unit (company) name, the server name, and the volume names and sizes.

- Enough RAM (normally at least 16MB, preferably 32MB). See the NetWare Installation manual for a complete formula.

1. Set Up UPSs

Install the UPSs according to the manufacturer's instructions. When you first plug the UPS into the site wiring, watch the Site Wiring Fault indicator if one exists. This light warns you of bad source wiring that will need fixing before you proceed.

Double-check the capacity of each UPS against the equipment plugged into it. Multiply the amperage of each server by 120 to get volt-amps (VA). For instance, if the sticker on the back of the computer says 5A, then multiply 5 by 120 to get 600 VA. The UPS in this case should have a rating of 600VA, plus additional capacity for monitors, hubs, and disk subsystems plugged into it.

Turn on the UPS, and plug a radio or other AC-powered device into it. Test the UPS by unplugging it from the wall or pushing the test button. It should beep audibly and the radio should stay on. You may need to let the UPS battery charge for a while before powering up the server.

2. Set Up Drives and Controllers

You'll need to install your SCSI CD-ROM drive and hard drive, and then run a SCSI setup utility for your SCSI controllers. The setup utility should come on floppy disk with the controller, or you can download the utility from the controller manufacturer.

Set up the controllers as appropriate for NetWare (there are sometimes differences between NetWare and DOS settings). In other words, follow the controller manufacturer's suggestions.

Also make sure the termination is correct and the SCSI ID numbers are set properly for the controllers and drives. The following rules apply to SCSI device termination and SCSI IDs:

- If you have both internal and external drives on a controller, do not terminate the controller. Otherwise, terminate it.

- Terminate only the last drive on the internal and external channels. Do not terminate other drives.

- All drives and controllers on a SCSI channel must have a unique SCSI ID number.

Write down the configuration settings you make. This will help you avoid conflicts among DMA channels, interrupts, SCSI IDs, and port addresses. Also, get the model numbers, revision numbers, and part numbers from the hardware if you haven't already done so. Worksheets for documenting your drive system are provided in Chapter 6, "Documenting the Network."

3. Configure the Network Adapter

Normally, you will configure each network adapter by running a software utility from a floppy drive. The card itself, as well, may have jumpers to set. Make sure you use the latest configuration utility from the manufacturer. Write down your interrupt and port address settings, and if you use multiple cards, check to see that the settings don't conflict. You will need to know the settings later when you run the NetWare installation.

Copy the setup software to the DOS partition on the hard drive, not only for NICs but for all cards you have in the server. Whether you have one NIC or many, set up an NWCLIENT subdirectory for each physical NIC card you have in the server. This will allow you to check the network adapter and make connections to other servers.

4. Create a DOS Partition on the Boot Drive

You can perform this step during the NetWare installation or beforehand. If you are mirroring or duplexing the boot drive, create bootable DOS partitions of the same size on both the mirrored drives. When the installation is complete, bring down the server and copy the entire DOS partition from the boot drive to the mirrored drive. This gives you a working boot partition in case your first drive should fail.

A good size for a DOS partition is 50MB. This gives you enough room for drivers and patches, in addition to repair information in case you have to perform a VREPAIR (volume repair) operation.

If an existing DOS partition occupies the entire boot drive, you will need to delete it and create a new, smaller one. Make sure you copy the CONFIG.SYS, AUTOEXEC.BAT, and other files you need onto floppy disks before deleting the partition.

Use the DOS FDISK utility to create the DOS partition and make it bootable, and the FORMAT utility to format the DOS partition with the system files. These utilities are contained on the NetWare installation diskette. The NetWare installation process will later format the remaining portion of your hard disk for the NetWare partition.

Using the computer's setup program, set the time on your server to the local time.

5. Boot the Computer with the CD-ROM Driver

To boot the computer with the CD-ROM driver, you'll need the driver in your CONFIG.SYS file, and the MSCDEX or equivalent software loaded in the AUTOEXEC.BAT file. Make sure there is no HIMEM.SYS loaded. After making any changes to CONFIG.SYS and AUTOEXEC.BAT, reboot the computer.

6. Make a Copy of the License Disk

Use the DISKCOPY command to make a copy of the license disk from the NetWare box. Now is a good time to lock away the copy to prevent piracy and to ensure you have a backup in case the original should fail.

Installation Decision Points

The following paragraphs cover the major events in the installation process that require your action or input. Not all steps are covered, so if you have questions consult online help (F1) or refer to the Installation manual.

1. Start the NetWare Installation from the CD-ROM

Change your current drive to the CD-ROM drive and type **INSTALL**. You will be presented with these three options:

- *NetWare Server Installation.* This option runs the NetWare Installation or Upgrade process. This is the option you will normally select.

- *DOS/Windows Client Installation.* Not for server installation. This option sets your computer up as a DOS/Windows client. You can use this option later from a workstation with a CD-ROM if you don't have NetWare client software. If you're running the installation program from another server, you can use this option to make it a client.

- *Create Disk.* This option allows you to create disks for booting the server, installing DOS/Windows clients, migrating a server, installing an OS/2 client, creating server upgrade diskettes, or OS/2 VLMBOOT.

2. Choose the Product You Want to Install

After choosing NetWare Server Installation, you are presented with the following choices:

- *NetWare 4.1.*   This is the normal installation for NetWare version 4.1. It also includes the upgrade from NetWare 3.1*x*.

- *NetWare 4.1 SFT III.*   Not for normal NetWare installation. This installs System Fault Tolerance level 3, which requires dual servers with a mirrored-server link between them.

- *Display Information (README) File.*   You should at least skim this file and then select the NetWare 4.1 option when finished.

3. Select the Type of Installation You Are Performing

After selecting NetWare 4.1 installation, you are given the following options:

- *Simple Installation of NetWare 4.1.*   This method makes the following assumptions, not allowing you to select other options:

   Booting from a DOS partition of at least 15MB

   No drive mirroring or duplexing

   One NetWare partition per drive

   One volume per NetWare partition

   Default volume names: SYS, VOL1, etc.

   No editing of NCF files during installation

   A Directory tree with one Organization, which contains all objects

- *Custom Installation of NetWare 4.1.*   Lets you customize the disk partitions, mirror or duplex drives, edit NCF files during installation, and create Organizational Units under the Organization in the Directory tree.

- *Upgrade NetWare 3.1x or 4.*   Only for existing NetWare 3.1*x* or 4.0*x* servers.

After selecting the type of installation, you type in a server name. If prompted, accept the randomly generated IPX internal network number. Then a preliminary copying of files to the DOS partition takes place. Accept the default language and file name format. Next, you select a disk driver.

4. Load Disk Drivers

If you have an updated disk driver on a floppy disk, insert the disk into the floppy drive. When prompted to select a disk driver from the list, press the Ins key and F3 to specify drive A. You will then be prompted to select the updated driver.

When prompted, confirm the parameters such as interrupt number and port address for your controller.

If you have more than one controller, load a corresponding disk driver for each controller.

5. Load LAN Drivers

If you have an updated LAN driver on floppy disk, insert the disk into the floppy drive. When prompted to select a LAN driver from the list, press the Ins key and F3 to specify drive A. You will then be prompted to select the updated driver.

When prompted, confirm the parameters such as port address for your network adapter. If a parameter is blank and you don't know the proper value, just leave it blank. Use the defaults unless the vendor documentation tells you otherwise.

If you have more than one network adapter, load a corresponding LAN driver for each adapter.

You may now get a disturbing message similar to the following:

```
ETHER.LAN did not load. Control will be switched to the
system console screen, where you may see the error.
(INSTALL-4.1-248)
Press <Enter> to continue.
```

Don't worry about this. Just press Enter as instructed and wait. After a few seconds, you will see the console prompt. Try to load the LAN driver manually by typing **LOAD** *driver,* where *driver* is the name of your LAN driver, such as ETHER. You will be prompted with the required values for the driver. You may need to try other parameters, such as different port addresses, to get the driver to load.

When the LAN driver loads, press Alt+Esc to return to the installation program. You will then supply the license disk and tell the installation program whether this is the first NetWare 4 server in the network.

---

6. Create NetWare Disk Partitions (Custom Configuration)

If prompted, you can have NetWare create other disk partitions automatically. However, if you want to mirror or duplex disks, select Manually.

Create NetWare partitions on the remaining space of the boot drive and on all other drives by the following procedure:

1. From the Disk Partition and Mirroring Options menu, choose Create | Delete | Modify Disk Partitions. If you have more than one disk drive, you will be prompted for the drive letter.

2. Choose Create NetWare Disk Partition.

3. Accept the default size and Hot Fix information by pressing Esc.

4. Repeat Steps 1 through 3 for each drive on your server.

---

7. Choose Disk Partition and Mirroring Options (Custom Configuration)

For mirroring or duplexing drives, choose Mirror and Unmirror Disk Partition Sets. To the NetWare server, mirroring is the same as duplexing. (With duplexing, the two disk drives just happen to be on different controllers.) A list of devices appears, each showing the Not Mirrored status. To mirror (duplex) drives, perform the following steps:

1. Select the primary drive (to which you want to mirror another drive).

2. Press Ins.

3. Select the drive you want to mirror to the primary drive.

4. Repeat Steps 1 through 3 to mirror additional drives.

8. Manage NetWare Volumes (Custom Configuration)

NetWare gives you a default volume setup, which has the required SYS volume occupying the boot disk, and additional volumes for each additional disk or mirrored disk pair.

Press Ins or F3 to modify any of the suggested volume sizes, names, or parameters. Among these parameters are block size (NetWare calculates a default size for you); file compression (default on); block suballocation (default on); and data migration (default off). Data migration is for servers equipped with a writable CD-ROM jukebox. This feature "migrates" seldom-used files to the slower media.

Make sure you are satisfied with your volume settings. Once you press F10 to save and mount volumes, the volume settings cannot be changed without deleting and re-creating the volumes.

When you are certain of the volume settings, press F10 and specify Yes to accept the changes to volume settings. The installation program then mounts the volumes. More files will be copied from the CD-ROM to the server. You will select your time zone.

9. Supply NDS Information

Next you are prompted to enter your company name. This name will become the Organization object.

You are also prompted for the ADMIN password. The User object ADMIN is the default administrative login account, with all authority over the network, so don't take this password lightly. A summary screen with information similar to the following appears. Write this information down as listed and give a copy to your manager.

```
For your information (note these for future reference
along with the administrator password)
Directory tree name: COMPANY
Directory Context:   O=COMPANY
Administrator name:  CN=Admin.O=COMPANY
Press <Enter> to continue
```

The main copying of files now occurs from the CD-ROM to your server.

10. Create **STARTUP.NCF** and **AUTOEXEC.NCF** Files

You will be prompted to create the STARTUP.NCF and AUTOEXEC.NCF files. You can accept the suggested commands for both files and continue, or you can edit the files as necessary.

Other Installation Options

These options include the NetWare for Macintosh product, NetWare MHS Services, protocols other than IPX, and online documentation. I recommend that you install at least the online documentation because Novell has seen fit to print only about 10% of it. The most important of this unprinted documentation is the Supervising the Network manual, which describes most of the day-to-day management procedures.

To install the manual set on the server, select Install Online Documentation and Viewers from the Product Options menu. This procedure creates DOC and DOC-VIEW directories at the root of the SYS volume. It also copies a SYSDOCS.CFG file to the PUBLIC directory.

The Windows application you will use to view the documentation is SYS:\ DOCVIEW\DTAPPWIN\DTEXTRW.EXE.

Logging In for the First Time

Once you have the server and hub running, you can start installing the NetWare client software on the workstations. There are a number of options for installing the client software. Probably the easiest way is to use the NetWare 4.1 Operating System CD-ROM.

Installing the DOS/Windows Client Software from CD-ROM

You can install either the Client 32 software (from Windows or DOS), or the VLM client. To install the VLM client, perform the following steps:

1. Put the NetWare 4.1 Operating System CD-ROM in your DOS/Windows workstation.

2. Change to the CD-ROM drive.

3. Type **INSTALL** and press Enter.

4. Select DOS/Windows Client Installation. Follow the prompts on the screen.

5. If the LAN driver for your workstation is not listed, you'll need to get the driver from the NIC manufacturer and specify the directory where you have it stored.

6. When the installation is complete, edit the NET.CFG file. Add the following line at the end of the file, replacing *organization* with the company name you specified during server installation. Do not omit the double quotes.

   ```
   NAME CONTEXT = "organization"
   ```

This is the context of the ADMIN user object, which you will use for logging in the first time.

Logging In

Restart your computer. The AUTOEXEC.BAT file will run the client software before other programs.

1. Change to the first network drive, usually F.

2. Type **LOGIN ADMIN** and press Enter.

3. When prompted, give the password you specified during server installation.

4. NetWare now automatically maps your drives to the server file system. To see the mappings, type **MAP** and press Enter.

Now you can update the DOS/Windows client software installation files on the server by following the procedure in Chapter 3.

Providing Access to the Network

THIS CHAPTER COVERS THE BASICS of getting your users connected to and enjoying the benefits of the network. First it describes NetWare Administrator, your Windows tool for managing the network. Then it gives instructions for creating new user accounts and getting the workstation software loaded and running.

A major portion of this chapter is devoted to rights. Users must have sufficient rights to do their work, but you need to restrict their rights to sensitive data. Some of the features of NetWare 4 that allow you to manage user access are container objects, drive mappings, Groups, and Organizational Roles.

Finally, this chapter gives instructions for running a remote console session from your workstation or over the phone lines from home.

Using NetWare Administrator

NETWARE ADMINISTRATOR IS the NetWare management utility for Windows. The program item runs NWADMIN.EXE (NWADMN95.EXE for Windows 95), found in the SYS:PUBLIC directory. Figure 5.1 shows the creation of the Nwadmin program item. Once you have created the program item, you can use NetWare Administrator to perform your day-to-day management tasks (see Table 5.1). Here's the icon for NetWare Administrator in the NetWare Tools group:

NetWare
Administrator

The main screen is illustrated in Figure 5.2.

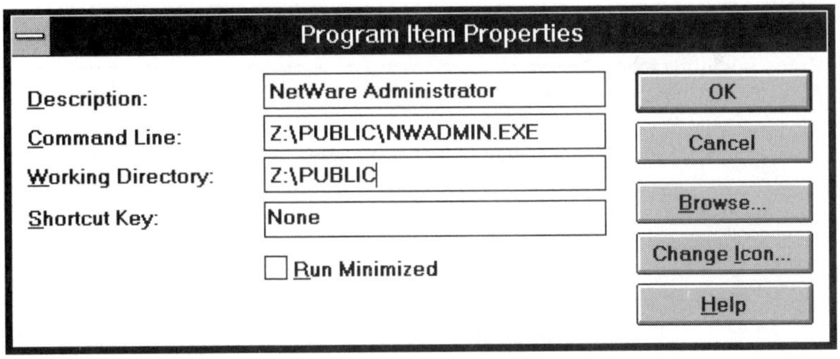

FIGURE 5.1

Creating the Nwadmin
program item from
NWADMIN.EXE in the
SYS:PUBLIC directory

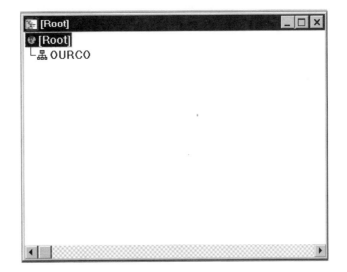

FIGURE 5.2

The main screen of
NetWare Administrator

	TASK	MENU	ITEM
TABLE 5.1 NetWare Administrator Tasks	Add a trustee of an object	Object	Trustees of This Object
	Change object properties	Object	Details
	Collapse a container	View	Collapse
	Combine partitions	Tools	Partition Manager
	Connect to the server console	Tools	Remote Console
	Connect remotely to the console	Tools	Remote Console
	Container object, move	Tools	Partition Manager
	Copy a file or group of files	Object	Copy
	Create a new object	Object	Create
	Create a new window	Tools	Browse
	Create a partition	Tools	Partition Manager
	Create a trustee of an object	Object	Trustees of This Object
	Create a User Template	Object	User Template
	Delete a partition	Tools	Partition Manager
	Delete a server	Tools	Partition Manager
	Delete an object	Object	Delete
	Exit NetWare Administrator	Object	Exit
	Expand the container object	View	Expand
	File, copy	Object	Copy
	File, delete	Object	Delete
	File, move	Object	Move
	File, purge	Tools	Salvage

TASK	MENU	ITEM
File, salvage	Tools	Salvage
Find objects or properties	Object	Search
Hide objects under this container	View	Collapse
Leaf object, move	Object	Move
Limit the classes of objects viewed	View	Include
Merge partitions	Tools	Partition Manager
Modify a User Template	Object	User Template
Move a container object	Tools	Partition Manager
Move a leaf object or file	Object	Move
Move a partition	Tools	Partition Manager
New object	Object	Create
New window	Tools	Browse
Object properties	Object	Details
Object search	Object	Search
Object, create a new	Object	Create
Partition, create	Tools	Partition Manager
Partition, delete	Tools	Partition Manager
Partition, join	Tools	Partition Manager
Partition, move	Tools	Partition Manager
Partition, split	Tools	Partition Manager
Partition, view	Tools	Partition Manager
Print a view of the Directory tree	Object	Print

TABLE 5.1 (continued)
NetWare Administrator
Tasks

TABLE 5.1 (continued)
NetWare Administrator
Tasks

TASK	MENU	ITEM
Properties, view or modify	Object	Details
Property search	Object	Search
Purge previously deleted files	Tools	Salvage
Recover deleted files	Tools	Salvage
Remote console	Tools	Remote Console
Rename an object	Object	Rename
Rights to other objects, search	Object	Rights to Other Objects
Salvage previously deleted file	Tools	Salvage
Search for a property value	Object	Search
Search for an object	Object	Search
Search for rights to other objects	Object	Rights to Other Objects
Set up printing	Object	Print Setup
Show server partitions	Tools	Partition Manager
Sort object classes	View	Sort by Object Class
Split a partition	Tools	Partition Manager
Template, User object	Object	User Template
Trustee, add or view	Object	Trustees of This Object
View a different part of the tree	View	Set Context
View object properties	Object	Details
View objects under this container	Object	Expand
View trustees of this object	Object	Trustees of This Object
Window, new	Tools	Browse

Creating a New User Template

K EEPING A TEMPLATE for new users will simplify the task of creating users in the future. The template for new users is actually a User object named USER_TEMPLATE. When you create USER_TEMPLATE, you set up property values that you want to apply to the User objects you will later create. The values you give to the template properties only apply to subsequent User objects, not those that already exist. In addition, they only apply to User objects created in the same container, not in other containers. Figure 5.3 shows the form displayed by NetWare Administrator when a User Template exists.

The most useful properties that you will supply for the User Template are the password restrictions, login script, and path to the home directory. The password restrictions most commonly applied are shown in Figure 5.4.

Most administrators do not want users to run a user login script or the default login script; they would rather manage only the container login script. To arrange this, you put a single character in the user login script. This keeps any user or default login script from executing. Typing a semicolon into the User Template login script has this effect (Figure 5.5). All subsequent User objects will have the semicolon in their login scripts by default.

FIGURE 5.3

When you create a new User object and a User Template exists, the Use User Template box is checked.

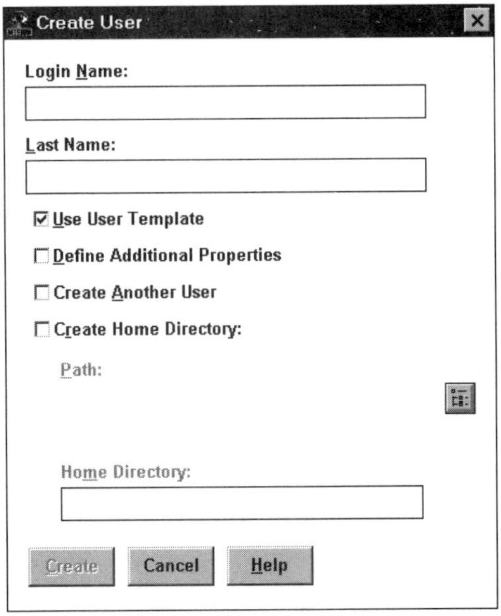

Create User

Login **N**ame:

Last Name:

☑ **U**se User Template

☐ **D**efine Additional Properties

☐ Create **A**nother User

☐ C**r**eate Home Directory:

Path:

Ho**m**e Directory:

Create   Cancel   **H**elp

FIGURE 5.4
Common password
restrictions for the
User Template

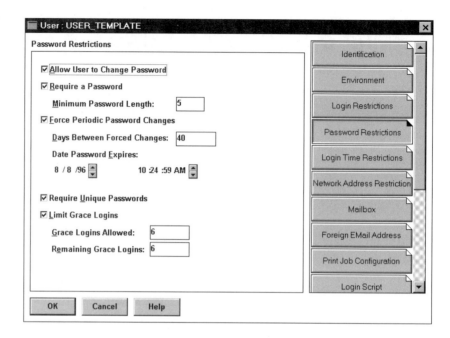

FIGURE 5.5
The semicolon prevents
both User and default
login scripts
from executing.

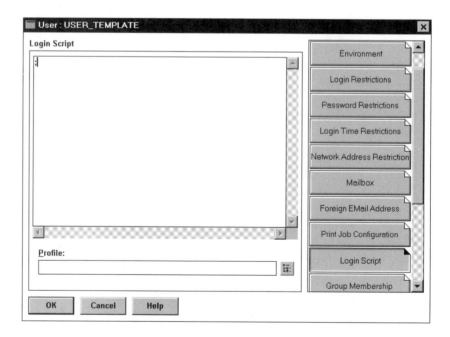

If you will have personal home directories for your users, be sure to specify a path in the User Template. This saves you considerable time when creating User objects later.

In NetWare 4.11, the User Template object is an object class, or a specific type of object, rather than a User object with a specific name and attributes. When defining the User Template in NetWare 4.11, you can specify rights to the file system and Directory objects, which you cannot do in 4.10.

To create a new User Template, follow these steps:

1. Using NetWare Administrator, highlight the container in which you will create more users.

2. From the Object menu, select User Template.

3. If you have created a User Template in the parent container, you are prompted to copy the parent container's User Template into the one you are creating. Answer Yes to copy the parent container's User Template, or No to create a new one.

4. Fill in the properties you want to apply to subsequent User objects in this container, and click OK when you're done.

In NetWare 4.10, you cannot give a User Template default rights to the file system or to Directory objects. If you want to give rights that apply to all users in a container, give those rights to the container itself, rather than to the User Template.

Creating New User Objects

YOU MUST CREATE NEW USER OBJECTS for each login account. This can be done in a number of ways. The first and simplest way for small networks is to use NetWare Administrator, as follows:

1. From NetWare Administrator, highlight the container object in which you want to create a new User object.

2. From the Object menu, select Create.

3. Highlight User and select OK.

4. Fill in the required Login Name and Last Name fields. The Login Name field is the name you will see next to the User object in NetWare Administrator. It is also the name the user will employ to log in.

5. Check the following options as desired:

   - *Use User Template* if you want the property values of the User Template to apply to this new User object. In NetWare 4.11, you will also need to select the template you want to apply, using the Browse button.

   - *Define Additional Properties* if you want to edit other optional User properties now.

   - *Create Another User* if you want to immediately add another User object without returning to the NetWare Administrator browser screen.

   - *Create Home Directory* if you want to create a personal directory for this user.

6. If you have checked the Create Home Directory box, verify the home directory name and the path to the home directory. Edit as necessary.

7. Select Create.

It usually takes a few seconds to create a new User object. The new object may not show up in the NetWare Administrator browser if the container is "collapsed." Double-click the container object to expand it and make sure the new object is there.

Installing Client Software on New Workstations

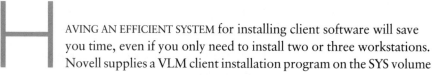

AVING AN EFFICIENT SYSTEM for installing client software will save you time, even if you only need to install two or three workstations. Novell supplies a VLM client installation program on the SYS volume of a NetWare 4.10 server. Both VLM and Client 32 installation programs are included with NetWare 4.11.

Your job as administrator is as follows:

1. Update the client installation areas on the server with the latest files. Chapter 3 contains procedures that tell you how to apply the latest client installation files, both for VLM and the Client 32 software.

2. Get the latest LAN drivers for your workstation network adapters. Chapter 3 tells you how to do this, as well.

3. Create disks for logging in from a workstation the first time. You'll need to do this to access the client installation programs on the SYS volume. The instructions for creating disks are in the upcoming section.

4. Log in using the disks created in Step 3, and run the updated client installation routine from each new workstation.

Creating VLM Client Installation Disks

As mentioned above, creating client installation disks is the third step in the process of installing client software on new workstations. The purpose of this step is to get yourself logged in for the first time from each new workstation, so you can run the complete installation routine with updated files over the network.

1. Obtain five formatted 3½" floppy disks.

2. On a workstation with a CD-ROM drive, insert the NetWare 4.1*x* operating system CD in the drive.

3. Change your current drive to the CD-ROM drive.

4. Type **INSTALL** and press Enter.

5. Select Create Disks.

6. Select the option for 3½" DOS and MS Windows Client (5 disks).

7. Type **A:** and press Enter. (The colon is required.)

8. Insert a blank formatted disk in drive A.

9. Follow the instructions on the screen to create all five client disks.

10. At each workstation, put the first client installation disk in the floppy drive, change to that drive, and enter the **INSTALL** command.

11. Follow the instructions on the screen.

Running the Client Installation

Once your users are able to log in to the network from the workstations, you can run the updated client installation routine over the network. This can be done manually or automatically.

- You can log in from each workstation and run the installation program for the client of your choice.

- Or you can set up the Automatic Client Upgrade (ACU) to run from the container login script. Then, when the user logs in, the client upgrade runs automatically.

From the Workstation

To upgrade the clients manually, complete the following steps from each workstation. If you're using NetWare 4.10, you will need to download the latest client software from NetWire.

1. Log in to the network.

2. Run one of the following client installation routines:

- *Client 32 for DOS:* Change to the SYS:\PUBLIC\CLIENT\CLIENT32 directory and run INSTALL.EXE.

- *Client 32 for Windows 3.1:* From Program Manager, choose File | Run. Click on the Browse button and change to the SYS:\PUBLIC\CLIENT\ CLIENT32 directory. Choose SETUP.EXE and follow the prompts.

- *Client 32 for Windows 95:* Run SYS:\PUBLIC\CLIENT\WIN95\ SETUP.EXE.

- *VLMs for DOS or Windows:* From DOS, switch to the SYS:PUBLIC\ CLIENT\DOSWIN directory and type **INSTALL**.

Using the Automatic Client Update (ACU)

With the Automatic Client Upgrade (ACU), you can automatically upgrade client software when a user logs in. If there is no need to upgrade, the client login just runs as usual.

If the client version on the workstation is older than the version on the server, the user can choose to upgrade the client software or not. After the files are updated, the user is prompted to reboot the workstation.

Here are the steps to use ACU:

1. Create a directory for the installation files, for example, SYS:PUBLIC\ CLIENT\WIN95\. This directory inherits the needed Read and File Scan rights.

2. Copy the installation files to the directory you created. For Windows 95, copy the downloaded Client 32 for Windows 95 installation files (including subdirectories) and the Windows 95 CAB files.

3. Access the container login script as follows (see Chapter 7 for more on login scripts):

   A. From Windows, start NetWare Administrator.

   B. Click on the container that contains your User objects.

   C. Choose Object | Details.

   D. Select the Login Script page (as shown in Figure 5.6).

4. Add the following lines to the container login script. Modify the file path as needed to agree with the path you copied the files to in Step 1.

   ```
   MAP ROOT J:=SYS:\PUBLIC\CLIENT\WIN95
   #J:\ENGLISH\SETUP.EXE /ACU
   ```

If you have several containers holding User objects, you will need to repeat this procedure for each container.

CONSIDERATIONS FOR USING ACU WITH WINDOWS 95 Before using the ACU with Windows 95, you should set up Windows 95 users with the NetWare Client 32 for Windows 95 software from disk. Otherwise, when Windows 95 workstations run the MS Client for NetWare Networks that ships with Windows 95, you will have to modify the users bindery login script to contain the SETUP command, rather than the container login script.

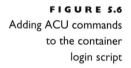

FIGURE 5.6
Adding ACU commands
to the container
login script

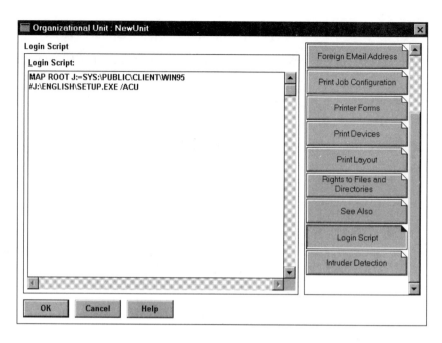

If the Windows 95 workstation is running MS Client for NetWare Networks Service for NetWare Directory Services, you must put the SETUP command in the login script that corresponds to the type of login (bindery or NDS).

FORCING AN UPDATE WITH ACU The SETUP.EXE file used in ACU checks the version of the client software installed, but it does not check the associated files used by the workstations. Should you decide to continue the upgrade regardless of whether the actual client software on the workstation is newer than the version on the network, you can force the ACU.

To force an ACU, you need to alter a "level" number in the NWSETUP.INI file (it's in the same directory as the other client installation files). You can locate the version number in the [Client Version] section. Look for four numbers separated by dots (for instance, 0.0.3.0), and increment the final number, which is the level number. So if the number is 0, make it a 1. The ACU compares the level numbers when the user logs in, finds the change, and upgrades the client software to the newer files.

Creating Bindery Users

When working in a small company, you'll likely find that funds for network hardware are often limited. Sometimes you are upgrading an old peer network, with old network adapters and printing arrangements. In some cases, the manufacturer of the network adapter is out of business, or perhaps you have no idea how to contact the company to get the newer ODI-style LAN drivers.

In such instances, you may be forced to use *bindery-only clients,* rather than VLM or newer clients that work with NDS. This is really no problem with NetWare 4.1*x,* as long as you make the following accommodations:

- Use bindery names.

- Use the 802.3 Ethernet frame type.

- Set a bindery context on the servers.

- Use a bindery login.

- Create bindery login scripts.

- Create bindery print queues.

Bindery User objects and the resources they need must be created in the container where the bindery services context is set.

Let's take a look at the process for all these tasks.

Using Bindery Names

If you have bindery clients on the network, you need to employ object names that can be used by such clients. Follow these special rules in object naming:

- Avoid spaces in object names. Replace spaces with underscores.

- Avoid object names longer than 47 characters. (We *know* you have at least a few of these.)

- Avoid using the following characters: / (slash); \ (backslash); : (colon); , (comma); * (asterisk); and ? (question mark).

Using the 802.3 Ethernet Frame Type

Packets for earlier versions of the Ethernet clients were formatted with the IEEE 802.3 frame type, rather than 802.2. This means that earlier clients can't communicate with a default NetWare 4.1*x* server. To resolve the issue of frame types, you can either standardize all stations and servers on the 802.3, or load both 802.2 and 802.3 on the server.

If you load both types on the server, some packets will be sent out twice, creating more traffic on the wire.

802.3 ONLY To standardize your network on the 802.3 frame type, make the following changes from the default setup:

1. In each server's AUTOEXEC.NCF file, change the

   ```
   LOAD lan driver
   ```

   commands to use the 802.3 frame type. Here's an example of the updated statement:

   ```
   LOAD PCNTNW.LAN PORT=FF40 INT=A FRAME=ETHERNET_802.3
   NAME=BASEMENT
   ```

2. If you have multiple servers, make sure you modify *all* the LAN driver load statements in the AUTOEXEC.NCF files of *all* servers.

3. Restart *all* servers by typing the commands

   ```
   DOWN
   EXIT
   SERVER
   ```

   at each server console during non-production hours.

4. Include the following line in the NET.CFG files on all DOS and Windows workstations. Put the line under the LINK DRIVER statement.

   ```
   FRAME ETHERNET_802.3
   ```

LOADING BOTH 802.2 AND 802.3 To use both frame types on the network, you need to duplicate the LOAD and BIND statements in the servers'

AUTOEXEC.NCF files. These statements in each server typically are similar to the following after a default installation:

```
LOAD PCNTNW.LAN PORT=FF40 INT=A FRAME=ETHERNET_802.2
  NAME=BASEMENT
BIND IPX TO BASEMENT NET=10
```

To add the new frame type, you need to duplicate the lines, changing the frame type and adding a unique net number. For example:

```
LOAD PCNTNW.LAN PORT=FF40 INT=A FRAME=ETHERNET_802.2
  NAME=BASEMENT
BIND IPX TO BASEMENT NET=10
LOAD PCNTNW.LAN PORT=FF40 INT=A FRAME=ETHERNET_802.3
  NAME=B2
BIND IPX TO B2 NET=12
```

This creates a separate "virtual" cable segment for the additional frame type.

1. Following the previous example, alter the LOAD and BIND statements for each LAN driver loaded on your server. Make sure you modify *all* LAN driver LOAD and BIND statements in the AUTOEXEC.NCF files of *all* servers.

2. Restart *all* servers by typing the commands

```
DOWN
EXIT
SERVER
```

at each server console during nonproduction hours.

Setting a Bindery Context on the Servers

You'll need to set a server's bindery context to the containers that hold the bindery User objects. Set the bindery context using a typeful name for the containers, with multiple contexts separated by semicolons.

You can set the bindery context from the server console's command line, in the AUTOEXEC.NCF file, or in the STARTUP.NCF file. Use syntax similar to the following:

```
set Bindery Context = OU=ACCT-DEPT.O=COMPANY; OU=PROD-DEPT.O=COMPANY;
```

Once this line has executed, the server looks for all bindery users and other bindery objects in the containers listed.

Creating Bindery Login Scripts

A login script in NetWare 4.1*x* is a property of an NDS object, such as a container or user, but this is not the case with bindery users. Login scripts for these users are files in the SYS:MAIL directory. The files are in ASCII text form, and are called LOGIN.

Each bindery user gets a unique directory under SYS:MAIL for the LOGIN file. This directory and the LOGIN file are created and left empty the first time a user logs in with the /B parameter (example: LOGIN DOUG /B) or uses dedicated IPX rather than IPXODI. After you log in with a bindery login, you will see a file and directory similar to the following:

```
Volume in drive G is SYS

Directory of G:\MAIL\DB000001

LOGIN                   0  06-26-96  5:31p
           1 file(s)              0 bytes
```

The easiest way to create bindery login scripts is to log in as the bindery user, and then use the NETUSER utility in bindery mode. Follow these steps:

1. Log in as a bindery user. (The user must be created in a container listed as a server's bindery context.) For example, type

   ```
   LOGIN SERVER1/DOUG /B
   ```

2. Type NETUSER to start the NETUSER utility.

3. Select Attachments.

4. Choose the server you want the user to log in to.

5. Select Login Script.

You can now edit the login script, putting in the commands that would normally run in the container login script. Avoid the commands that apply only to NDS and not to the bindery.

Creating Bindery Print Queues

For bindery users to be able to print on network printers, you must create bindery-style print queues. Bindery users can then capture local printer ports to the queue, which will be serviced by a print server. Follow these steps:

1. Make sure the bindery context is set to a container that has a Print Server object.

2. Log in to a server as SUPERVISOR. This User object is similar to Admin in bindery mode. Type the following, replacing SERVER1 with the server name:

   ```
   LOGIN SERVER1/SUPERVISOR /B
   ```

3. Type **PCONSOLE** to start the PCONSOLE utility.

4. Select Print Queues.

5. Press the Insert key. Then type in the name of the bindery queue you want to create, and press Enter.

6. Press Enter again to access Print Queue Information.

7. Select Users to specify who can use the queue.

8. Press Insert to add users. Then highlight each user you want to add, and press F5 to mark the user name.

9. Press F10. The users you marked appear on the Print Queue Users list on the right.

10. Press Esc twice to return to the Print Queue Information screen.

11. To specify which print server will service this queue, select Print Servers.

12. Choose a print server from the list and press F10.

13. Press Esc four times, and then choose Yes to confirm that you want to exit.

14. Log in to the network as Admin. For instance, type the following command (you may need to type it twice, depending on the version of NetWare):

    ```
    LOGIN .Admin.OURCO
    ```

15. Start Windows, and then start NetWare Administrator.

16. Choose the Printer object you want to assign to the print queue you created.

17. Select Object Details, choose the Assignments button, and click Add.

18. Browse on the Directory Context list until you see the Print Queue object you created on the left. Then double-click on the Print Queue.

19. Select OK.

20. If the bindery User objects are in a different container than the print server, do the following to add them as queue users:

   A. Select the Print Server object you want to service the queue.

   B. Access the object details, and select the Users button.

   C. Select Add.

   D. Browse until you see the container of the bindery user objects on the left, then double-click it.

   E. Click on OK.

21. Restart the print server.

22. Access the Details of the Print Server object, and click on Unload.

23. Click on OK. The Status will show Going Down.

24. Go to the server console and reload the Print Server. For instance, type

```
LOAD PSERVER .ACCT-PS.ACCT-DEPT.OURCO
```

At this point, bindery users should be able to capture printer ports to the bindery queue.

To automate this process every time a bindery user logs in, add the #CAPTURE command to the bindery login script. The process of creating bindery login scripts is described in the preceding section, "Creating Bindery Login Scripts."

Managing Rights

DEPENDING ON YOUR SITUATION, your daily network management tasks may or may not include managing rights for network users. NetWare's default rights make these duties fairly minimal, even when setting up the network.

Sooner or later, though, you'll get involved in rights management. You may need to set up special rights for a group of users to access an application, or give a user rights to administer part of the Directory tree.

In order for your users to utilize any resource on the network, they need the appropriate rights. When you give a user rights, you are making that user a *trustee*. Thus, in NetWare, rights are often called *trustee rights*.

Making Trustee Assignments

The object to whom rights apply is called the *target object*. For instance, when User object Amy is made a trustee of the Directory Map object WP, WP is the target.

Targets that are Directory objects are different from targets that are in the file system. (This distinction will be explained shortly.) Rights that apply to Directory objects fall into two categories: object rights and property rights.

Let's return to user Amy. When she is made a trustee of a container object, you can give her any of the following rights to *the container object itself:*

- Supervisor

- Browse

- Create

- Delete

- Rename

You can also give Amy any of the following rights to *all the properties* of that container object:

- Supervisor

- Compare

- Read

- Write

- Add Self

Finally, you may also give Amy any of the rights above to any *selected property* of the container object. For instance, if you wanted Amy to manage the container login script alone, you could give her the Supervisor right to the Login Script property.

The NetWare Administrator utility shows you lists of object and property rights, as shown in Figure 5.7.

Rights to Objects and Properties

In NetWare Administrator, making trustee assignments is a fairly easy task. All you need to do is drag the User object onto the target object, and then fill in the dialog that pops up. For instance, if I wanted the User object Me to be a trustee of the container object OURCO, I would drag Me on top of the container. In the Trustees of NewUnit dialog (Figure 5.7), I would check the options for Me's rights and click on OK. User Me thus becomes a trustee of the target container OURCO with the rights I specified.

FIGURE 5.7
NetWare Administrator illustrates the distinction between object rights and property rights.

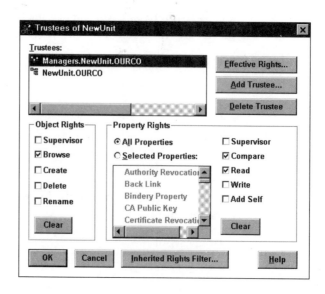

You might expect that dragging one object to another place in the Directory tree moves the object. This is not the case. Dragging one object onto another confers trustee rights.

If you need help with which rights to assign, click on the Help button in the Trustees dialog. It gives detailed definitions of each object and property right.

CONTROLLING INHERITANCE Rights flow from the target down through the Directory tree. So if you make user Amy a trustee of [Root], then Amy will have the same rights to all objects below [Root] in the tree. Since that includes the whole tree, Amy will have a significant trustee assignment with far-reaching effects. This phenomenon is called inheritance. All "children" of a target container object, without gaining a trustee, are subject to the trustee assignments of the parents, grandparents, great grandparents, and so on.

There are two ways to control inheritance. One way is to create a new trustee assignment. For instance, suppose you have made Amy a trustee of the [Root]. If you want that assignment to change or stop at a certain container below [Root], you make Amy a new trustee assignment at that container. The rights she was granted at [Root] will cease with the new target and below. Of course, the *new* assignment will flow down to (and be inherited by) the target's children.

Another way to control inheritance is to create an inherited rights filter (IRF), as described next.

INHERITED RIGHTS FILTERS (IRFS) An IRF stops the inheritance flow from a target object. Let's suppose you want Amy to have Supervisor right to the [Root] object, but you only want her to have Browse right in a child container. You can set an IRF at that container to "filter" out all rights except Browse.

IRFs apply to all trustees, so beware of cutting off a branch of the tree from your administration! Before setting an IRF, grant at least yourself (Admin) a specific trustee assignment with Supervisor rights at the same container.

Use the following procedure to filter object or property rights:

1. Select a target object.

2. Give Admin all rights.

   A. From the Object menu, choose Add Trustee to make Admin a trustee.

    B. Browse using the right-hand Directory Context box until the Admin object appears on the left-hand Object box.

    C. Double-click on Admin.

    D. Check all the rights boxes to give all rights to Admin.

3. Choose the Inherited Rights Filter button.

4. Check the boxes next to the trustee rights that you want to be inherited. That is, uncheck the boxes to turn off every right you want filtered out. To change the Inherited Rights Filter for specific property rights, you must also choose Specific Property and select a property from the Properties list.

5. Click OK twice to close first the IRF dialog and then the Object Details box.

The Supervisor right includes the other rights. Therefore, if you have granted someone the Supervisor right at a higher target in the Directory tree and want to block (filter) a right to child targets, make sure you also filter the Supervisor right. See the Warning earlier in this section.

Making Multiple-User Trustees

Sometimes you want to make a single trustee assignment for multiple User trustees. For example, you might want to grant several User objects the right to access a Profile (login script) object in another container. You have a number of options for granting trustee rights to a number of trustees.

- You can make the container a trustee. When you do this, all objects below the container receive the same rights as the container.

- You can create a Group object and make it a trustee. Then you add Users from anywhere in the Directory tree to the Group's membership.

- You can create an Organizational Role object and make it a trustee. Similar to a Group object, you would then add individual User objects to the Organizational Role's membership.

Use the questions in Table 5.2 to help you decide which of the above methods will work best for you.

TABLE 5.2 How to Grant Multiple Users a Trustee Assignment	WHAT YOU WANT TO ACCOMPLISH	RECOMMENDED METHOD
	You want all Users in a container to be trustees.	Make the container object a trustee.
	You want selected User objects (possibly from multiple containers) to be trustees, and these selected Users will not change very often.	Create a Group object and add selected User objects to the Group.
	You want selected User objects (possibly from multiple containers) to be trustees, and these selected Users will change frequently.	Create an Organizational Role object and add selected User objects to its occupants list.

Rights to the File System

Probably the most common rights assignment you will make is to file system targets. Users, Groups, Organizational Roles, and container objects can be trustees of the file system. In fact, you can make any object except [Root] a trustee of the file system, though the objects just mentioned make the most sense.

Remember that rights to the file system are different from rights to Directory objects. To give object rights, you can drag a User object on another object; however, the procedure is different for granting file system rights. Use the following procedure.

1. Using NetWare Administrator, highlight the prospective trustee. This may be a User, Group, Organizational Role, or container object.

2. Select Object | Details.

3. Click on the Rights to Files and Directories button on the right.

4. Click on Add.

5. In the Directory Context box, browse until the target directory or file appears in the left-hand Files and Directories box. You can select multiple files and directories by Shift-clicking or Ctrl-clicking.

6. Choose the rights you want to grant from the Rights checkboxes, and click OK when you're done.

INHERITANCE Just as trustee assignments are inherited down through targets in the Directory tree, they also are inherited down through targets in the file system. Therefore, if you make Amy a trustee of SYS:\APPS, she will also have the same rights to SYS:\APPS\WORDPROC\WORD.

If User objects are trustees of a Volume object, you might expect the object rights to flow down to the files and directories on that Volume. This is not the case. You must make a specific trustee assignment to files or directories on that Volume.

DIRECTORY RIGHTS The following rights apply to directory targets in the file system.

DIRECTORY RIGHT	DEFINITION
Supervisor	Includes all rights to the directory, to its files, and to its subdirectories and their files. The Supervisor right can only be revoked from the target directory in which it was originally granted, because filters below that point are ignored. In this way, the Supervisor right in the file system is different from the Supervisor right for objects.
Read	The right to open and read all files in the directory (unless you make a trustee assignment at the file level that does not include Read). Includes the right to execute programs in the directory.
Write	The right to open and modify files in the directory (unless you make a trustee assignment at the file level that does not include Write).
Create	The right to create files and subdirectories below this directory. If Create is the only right to this directory and below it, it is a "drop box" directory. Users can create a new file in the directory or copy a file to the directory, but after the file has been closed, the user can't see or read from it.
Erase	The right to delete the directory. This also applies to subdirectories and their files, unless other rights are assigned below it.

DIRECTORY RIGHT	DEFINITION
Modify	The right to rename or change the attributes of the directory. As with other rights, this applies to all subdirectories and files below it. It does *not* include the right to see or modify any directory or file's contents.
File Scan	The right to see files in the directory, unless that right is blocked by other rights below the directory level.
Access Control	The right to alter the trustee assignments and IRF of the directory. Applies to any files or subdirectories below it unless blocked. *Caution:* Be careful with this right, because users can grant all rights (except Supervisor) to other trustees, *including rights that they themselves have not been granted.*

FILE RIGHTS The following rights apply to files:

FILE RIGHT	DEFINITION
Supervisor	Includes all rights to the file. A user with this right can grant any right to another trustee and modify the file's IRF. The Supervisor right cannot be blocked by an IRF.
Read	The right to open and read the file.
Write	The right to open and write to the file.
Create	The right to salvage the file after it has been deleted.
Erase	The right to delete the file.
Modify	The right to rename the file or change its attributes. Does not include the right to see or modify the file's contents.
File Scan	The right to see the file when viewing the directory. This includes the right to see the directory structure above the file, including the directory structure back to the root of the volume.
Access Control	The right to change the file's trustee assignments or IRF. Be careful with this right, since a user with this right can grant to other trustees all rights except Supervisor, *including rights that they themselves have not been granted.*

CONTROLLING INHERITANCE WITH IRFS Just as with Directory objects, an IRF in the file system stops inheritance from targets above. Let's suppose you want users to have Read, Write, and Create rights to the SYS:\APPS directory, but you only want them to have Read in the SYS:\APPS\DLLS directory. You can set an IRF at the SYS:\APPS\DLLS directory to filter out all rights except Read.

Unlike the Supervisor object right, you can't filter out Supervisor right in the file system. Therefore, if you want to grant all rights and reserve the possibility of filtering in subdirectories, grant all rights except the Supervisor right.

Here's how to make an IRF in the file system:

1. In NetWare Administrator, double-click on the volume object that contains the target file or directory.

2. Continue double-clicking on directories that lead to the target file or to the directory where you want to create the IRF.

3. Highlight the file or directory target that will have the IRF.

4. Choose Object | Details.

5. Click on the Trustees of this Directory button on the right. You will see the Inheritance Filter rights list. If you don't have rights to create an IRF, the list is grayed out.

6. Uncheck the boxes for the rights you want filtered. That is, check the boxes for the rights you want to be inherited. Notice that the Supervisor right is grayed out. You cannot filter the Supervisor right in the file system.

7. Click on OK when you're done.

Security Equivalence

Another way to grant rights is to make a *security equivalent*. For instance, if you want to have the object rights of Admin while logging in as Doug, you can make Doug a security equivalent to Admin.

Security equivalence is not transitive, so if Charlie is security equivalent to Betty, and Betty is security equivalent to Andrew, Charlie is NOT security equivalent to Andrew.

To make a security equivalent, perform these steps:

1. Select the object to which you want to give security equivalence. For instance, in the scenario mentioned above, you would select the object Doug to make it equivalent to Admin.

2. Choose Object | Details.

3. Scroll down to the next page of buttons. Click on the Security Equal To button on the right.

4. Click on Add.

5. Browse in the Directory Context area on the right until the object you want appears on the left (Admin, for this example), and double-click it.

6. Click on OK.

Figuring Effective Rights

Rights can get complicated. In order to anticipate the rights that a trustee has and can actually use, you need to consider a number of factors.

Among these factors are the rights granted automatically when the server, Directory tree, and User object were created. Another factor is the rights that are inherited by a trustee. Then, of course, you need to consider the rights obtained by membership in a Group or Organizational Role. From these rights you must subtract rights filtered by IRFs, and add the ones gained by security equivalence.

The rights that a User object can actually *employ* to see or change a particular directory, file, or object are called *effective rights*. NetWare calculates these rights every time a user or service initiates an action. Following are some rules you can use to figure what the effective rights will be for a trustee:

- When the trustee is a container, all objects below that container inherit the rights. When the target object is a container, the trustee gets rights to all objects below the target in the tree.

- When you make a trustee assignment, and an assignment already exists for the same trustee up the tree from the target, the new assignment overrides the existing one. This occurs even if the new assignment has fewer rights than the higher one.

- Rights obtained by security equivalence or membership in a Group or Organizational Role are added to those of the trustee in question.

- IRFs filter all specified rights, whether those rights were obtained by direct assignment, by membership, or by security equivalence. The one exception to this rule is Supervisor right in the file system, which cannot be filtered.

Though it's important that you are able to predict a user's effective rights to Directory and file system objects, you can also use NetWare Administrator to calculate and display them for you, as described next.

Viewing File System Targets

The following procedures get NetWare Administrator to calculate effective rights for you and display them in an Effective Rights window.

1. From NetWare Administrator, double-click on the Volume object that has the target file or directory.

2. Double-click on the directories in the path of the target file or directory until you see the target.

3. From the Object menu, select Details.

4. Click on the Trustees of This Directory button.

5. Click on the Effective Rights button.

6. Click on the Browse button.

7. Browse with the Directory Context area on the right until you see the object whose rights you want to check on the left.

8. In the left-hand Objects box, double-click on the object whose rights you want to check.

NetWare Administrator now displays the Effective Rights window (Figure 5.8). The effective rights of the object appear in bold display; others are grayed out. In Figure 5.8, the User object Deone has no rights.

FIGURE 5.8
Effective rights are
displayed bold in the
Effective Rights window.

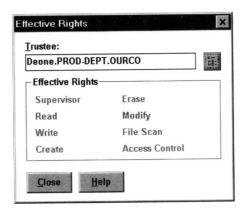

FIGURE 5.8
Effective rights are
displayed bold in the
Effective Rights window.

Calculating Directory Object Targets

1. From NetWare Administrator, highlight the Directory object target you want to check to examine a trustee's rights.

2. From the Object menu, select Trustees of This Object.

3. Click on the Effective Rights button.

4. Click on the Browse button.

5. Browse the Directory Context area on the right until you see the trustee object on the left whose rights you want to check.

6. In the left-hand Objects box, double-click on the object whose rights you want to check.

NetWare Administrator displays the same Effective Rights window shown in Figure 5.8. As described just above, the trustee object's rights are shown in bold, and others are grayed out.

Restricting the PUBLIC Trustee

NetWare Administrator shows PUBLIC in the trustee list of a target object to indicate the rights given any object that requests access and for which no other rights are effective. Before logging in, a user has all of the trustee rights of PUBLIC. For this reason, it's important to restrict the use of PUBLIC as a trustee to secure areas.

PUBLIC has the Browse object right to the [Root] object when NetWare 4.1x is installed. This allows all objects to see all other objects until you create other trustee assignments or IRFs.

To restrict the rights of PUBLIC, add PUBLIC as a trustee whenever you are defining trustees of a target object. You can also delete PUBLIC as a trustee of any object or file.

Creating New Containers

N CHAPTER 2, FIGURE 2.17 GIVES a decision tree for determining whether to create multiple OUs in your Directory tree. You may decide to create them if your network meets either or both of the following criteria:

- There are more than 200 User objects.

- There are more than 20 User objects and your organization does little resource sharing among departments.

When you create an OU, you see a Create Organizational Unit dialog. There you enter a name for the OU and choose one of the following options: to define additional properties, or create another OU, or define user defaults.

The most useful of the properties you can set up for the new object are the rights to files and directories, and the login script property.

Defining Rights and the Login Script

By assigning the rights to files and directories for the OU object, you can make trustee assignments to file system targets. Since the assignment "flows down," all objects you create in the OU (including User objects) will inherit the rights. To make the trustee assignment, complete the following steps:

1. Click on the Rights to Files and Directories button.

2. Click on the Add button.

3. Browse on the right-hand list to select the volume and then the directory and subdirectory, until the directory or file you want appears on the left.

4. Double-click on the directory or file target on the left.

5. Select check boxes for the rights you want to give.

6. Repeat Steps 2 through 5 to make additional trustee assignments.

To create the login script, click on the Login Script button and edit the login script box. All User objects in the OU will run the login script contained in the OU's login script property.

You can cut, copy, and paste text from one login script to another, using standard Windows editing tools: Cut=Ctrl+X, Copy=Ctrl+C, and Paste=Ctrl+V.

Login scripts are discussed in Chapter 7, "Automating Access to Network Resources."

Creating Drive Mappings

D RIVE MAPPINGS GIVE YOUR USERS access to the files they need in their work. As network administrator, you will create drive mappings quite often, most commonly in login scripts.
You can create drive mappings from the DOS command line or from NetWare User Tools in Windows. It's important to know how to create drive mappings in DOS with the MAP command, since you will use the same syntax in login scripts.

Mapping Drives with User Tools

When you install client software on a Windows 3.1 workstation, a program item is created called NetWare User Tools. This item points to the NWUSER.EXE program. You can use this program to map drives in Windows by performing the following steps:

1. From Windows, start the NetWare User Tools program.

2. Click on the Drive Mapping button.

3. Browse on the right-hand side of the window to select the directory you want.

4. Drag the directory you want to the drive letter on the left.

5. (Optional) If desired, make the drive mapping a root mapping by clicking on the Map Root check box.

6. (Optional) If desired, make the drive mapping permanent by clicking on the Permanent button at the bottom of the window.

Mapping Drives with Network Neighborhood

Perform the following steps to map a drive using the Network Neighborhood in Windows 95:

1. Start the Network Neighborhood program (see Figure 5.9).

2. Click on the Map Network Drive button.

3. The next available drive letter appears. You can accept the drive or select a different one with the drop-down box.

4. Select the desired volume from the Path drop-down box.

5. (Optional) If you want the drive mapping to occur every time Windows 95 is started, click on the Reconnect at Login check box.

FIGURE 5.9
Network Neighborhood gives you usable client options for Windows 95.

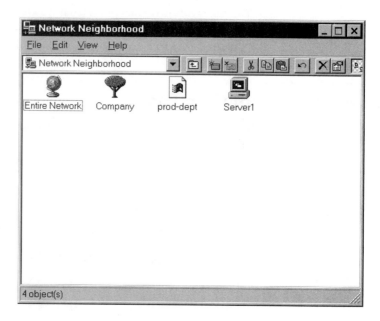

Mapping Drives Using the MAP Command

Use the MAP command when mapping drives from the DOS command line, from DOS batch files, or from NetWare login scripts. The basic syntax of the MAP command is as follows:

```
MAP x:=volume:path
```

where *x* is the drive letter you want to assign; *volume* is the NetWare volume on which the desired directory resides; and *path* is the full path to the directory.

Here is an example of the basic MAP command:

```
MAP F:=SYS:\APPS\CODE
```

After typing the above command, the user could change to the F: drive, and the current directory would be SYS:\APPS\CODE.

If you wanted the directory to appear as the root directory, you would insert the ROOT parameter, as in

```
MAP ROOT F:=SYS:\APPS\CODE
```

Now when the user changes the current drive to F:, the SYS:\APPS\CODE directory becomes the current directory, but it appears as the root (F:\).

If you don't know or care what your next available drive letter is, you can use the N (Next) parameter with the MAP command, as shown in the next example:

```
MAP N SYS:\APPS\CODE
```

If the next available drive letter is G:, then G: gets mapped to SYS:\APPS\CODE.

If you have more than one server on your network, you will need to supply the server name before the volume name. For example:

```
MAP H:=SERVER1/SYS:\DATA\EXCEL
```

To delete a drive mapping, use the DEL parameter, as in this example:

```
MAP DEL G:
```

G: is now an invalid drive letter. If your current drive is G:, you are informed of this face when you type the command to delete the mapping. Your next move should be to change to a valid drive letter.

Search Drives

Use *search drives* to point to executable files, just as you would use a path statement in DOS. The basic syntax of a search drive mapping is as follows:

```
MAP Sn:=volume:path
```

where *n* is an integer representing a position in the search order; *volume* is the NetWare volume on which the desired directory resides; and *path* is the full path to the directory.

For instance, if you wanted to create a path (a search drive mapping) to a batch file directory, you might type the following command:

```
MAP S3:=SYS:\PUBLIC\BATCH
```

After you type in this search drive command, the workstation looks for executable files in the BATCH directory whenever you type a command. More specifically, the workstation software looks in the current directory, then in search drive S1, search drive S2, search drive S3, and so on until the command is found. To indicate that the workstation should look in the search drive as a last resort, specify S16 in the MAP command.

If you've assigned S3 a search drive and S3 is already in use, you overwrite the existing assignment. To insert a search drive and bump the other assignments without overwriting them, use the INS option. For example:

```
MAP INS S1:=SYS:\PUBLIC
```

In this case, if there were an existing assignment for S1, it would get bumped to S2, and S2 to S3, and so on.

MAP Command Summary

The full formal syntax of the MAP command is as follows:

MAP [*option* | /VER] [*search*:=[*drive*:=]] | [*drive*:=] [*path*] [/W]

OPTIONS

INS	Inserts a search drive.
DEL	Deletes a drive mapping.
N	Maps the next available drive.
R	Makes the drive a root directory.
P	Maps a drive to a physical volume on a server.
C	Changes a regular drive to a search drive or a search drive to a regular drive.

SWITCHES

/VER	Displays MAP command version information.
/W	Does not change the master environment.
/?	Displays the help screen.

Creating and Using Group Objects

USING A GROUP OBJECT is a convenient way to manage User objects. You can add specific User objects from a single container or from multiple containers as members of a Group object. Here are the steps to create a Group object and add members to it:

1. Using NetWare Administrator, highlight the container object where you want to create the new Group.

2. From the Object menu, select Create.

3. Choose the Group object class and click on OK.

*Type **G** to move down the selection list directly to the Group object class.*

4. Type in a name for the new Group object, such as **Managers.**

5. Click on the Define Additional Properties check box.

6. Click on the Create button.

7. Click on the Members button.

8. Click on the Add... button.

9. Browse on the Directory Context side of the screen until the User object you want to add appears.

10. Highlight the User object(s) on the left that you want to add to the group. To add multiple User objects from the same container, use the Ctrl button while clicking on each User.

11. Click on OK.

12. Repeat Steps 8 through 11 to add more User objects from other containers.

You can now grant rights to the Group that will apply to all Users you have added. Beware of granting rights to Server objects or container object targets. If you make a Group a trustee and grant it the Supervisor object right to a Server target, then all members of the Group will inherit all rights to all files and directories on all volumes on that server. The same thing occurs if you assign the Supervisor right to a container that contains a Server object anywhere in its branches. Check effective rights carefully to avoid unintended consequences of trustee assignments.

The IF MEMBER OF Statement

Once you have created a Group, assigned its members, and granted rights to the file system, you'll probably want to map a drive to the directory in a container login script. To map the drive only for the Group, use an IF MEMBER OF statement in the container login script, similar to the following:

```
IF MEMBER OF Managers THEN MAP R:=SYS:\REPORTS\WEEKLY
```

Remember to add the IF MEMBER OF statement to all container login scripts that hold Group members.

When the Group is in a different container, use a relative object name in the statement, as in

```
IF MEMBER OF ACCT-DEPT.Managers. THEN MAP R:=SYS:\REPORTS\WEEKLY
```

If you have more than one server on the network, add the server name to the volume, as in

```
IF MEMBER OF Managers THEN MAP R:=SERVER2/SYS:REPORTS\WEEKLY
```

If you want the login script to execute more than one command for the Group, use multiple lines and an END statement (indenting improves readability).

```
IF MEMBER OF "Managers" THEN
    MAP R:=SYS:REPORTS\WEEKLY
    #CAPTURE LPT2 Q=QXEROX NB NFF TI=1
END
```

Creating and Using Organizational Role Objects

YOU CAN USE AN ORGANIZATIONAL ROLE (often called Org Role) object in much the same way that you would use a Group object. The difference is that the Org Role object is intended for one or two *occupants* (rather than members), and the occupants may change more often than a Group's members do.

You can add selected User objects from a single container or from multiple containers as occupants of an Org Role object. Here are the steps to create an Org Role object and add occupants to it:

1. Using NetWare Administrator, highlight the container object where you want to create the new Org Role.

2. From the Object menu, select Create.

3. Select the Organizational Role object class and click on OK.

Type **O** *to move down the selection list directly to the Organizational Role object class.*

4. Type in a name for the new Org Role object, such as Salvage.

5. Click on the Define Additional Properties check box.

6. Click on the Create button.

7. Click on the browse button next to the Occupant field.

8. Click on the Add button.

9. Browse on the Directory Context side of the screen until the User object you want to add appears.

10. On the left, highlight the User object(s) that you want to add to the Org Role's occupants list.

11. Click on OK.

12. Repeat Steps 8 through 11 to add more User objects to the occupants list.

You can now grant rights to the Org Role as you would for any other object. Beware of granting rights to Server objects or container object targets. If you make an Organizational Role a trustee and grant it the Supervisor object right to a Server target, then all occupants of the OR will inherit all rights to all files and directories on all volumes on that server. The same thing occurs if you assign the Supervisor right to a container target that contains a Server object anywhere in its branches. Check effective rights carefully to avoid unintended consequences of trustee assignments.

Accessing the Server Console

ADMINISTRATORS OFTEN NEED access to the console when they are not physically near the server. Most of the time this will occur when you need to change a SET parameter or load an NLM. Sometimes you will need to restart the server or edit an NCF file.

NetWare includes *remote console* utilities to make these remote tasks easier to take care of. Remote console works from the NetWare Administrator utility in Windows or from DOS. You can use the utilities from a workstation over the network or from a remote location over phone lines.

Enabling Remote Console

If you need to access the server console from your workstation, you just need to run the proper software at the server and workstation. It's not much harder to do over the phone lines; all you need are a modem and the proper software, both at the server and at the remote workstation.

For LAN Access

To enable remote console for access over the LAN, you need to load REMOTE .NLM and RSPX.NLM. The REMOTE file requires a password. If you load RSPX, it will load REMOTE automatically and prompt you for a password. Here are the commands to load these files:

```
LOAD REMOTE
//you are prompted for a password//
LOAD RSPX
```

You can load REMOTE and RSPX from the console using the same syntax shown above, supplying the password as a parameter of REMOTE (for example, LOAD REMOTE MYPASS). You can also put the two commands in the AUTOEXEC.NCF file.

For Modem Access

To enable remote console for use over a modem, you need to load REMOTE .NLM, RS232.NLM, AIO.NLM, AIOCOMX.NLM. Of course, you will also need to connect a modem to a serial port on the server. Here are the commands you'll need to enter:

```
LOAD REMOTE
//you are prompted for a password//
LOAD AIO
LOAD AIOCOMX
LOAD RS232 1 9600
```

The parameters supplied with RS232 in the foregoing example are for the communications port and the modem speed. If you don't give these parameters, you will be prompted for them. RS232 supports speeds of 2400, 4800, 9600, 19200, and 38400. Add the C parameter to enable Callback or an N to communicate over a Null modem cable. If you use the C option to enable Callback, create a text file entitled CALLBACK.LST in the SYS:SYSTEM directory listing the acceptable callback numbers.

You can run these commands from the console, supplying the password as a parameter of REMOTE (for example, LOAD REMOTE MYPASS). You can also put the two commands in the AUTOEXEC.NCF file.

Using Remote Console from NetWare Administrator

To access remote console from a workstation running NetWare Administrator, you must first enable remote console for LAN access at the server as instructed just above. Then perform these steps:

1. Select Tools | Remote Console.

2. The remote console session will start as a DOS menu program. You'll see a warning message and then a prompt for the type of session. The mouse will not work, so move the selection bar with the arrow keys and press Enter to make a selection.

3. Select SPX.

4. In the Available Servers menu, choose the server whose console you want to access.

5. You will see the console screen, where you can enter commands just as you would at the console.

   ■ To get a menu of commands specifically for this remote console session, press Alt+F1. Among other tasks, you can view files on or transfer files to the server's DOS partition.

   ■ To switch console screens, press Alt+F4.

6. To quit the remote console session, press Alt+F2 and then Esc.

Using Remote Console by Modem

To access remote console from a computer via modem, you must first enable remote console for modem access at the server as instructed earlier. You will also need a modem on the remote computer connected to a phone line.

I. Copy the following files from the network to a directory on the remote computer:

_RUN.OVL	SYS:PUBLIC
_AIO.OVL	SYS:PUBLIC
IBM_RUN.OVL	SYS:PUBLIC
IBM_AIO.OVL	SYS:PUBLIC
RCONSOLE.EXE	SYS:PUBLIC
TEXTUTIL.IDX	SYS:PUBLIC
RCONSOLE.HEP	SYS:PUBLIC\NLS\ENGLISH
RCONSOLE.MSG	SYS:PUBLIC\NLS\ENGLISH
TEXTUTIL.HEP	SYS:PUBLIC\NLS\ENGLISH
TEXTUTIL.MSG	SYS:PUBLIC\NLS\ENGLISH

2. Make sure the modem is turned on and connected to the computer.

3. Change to the directory where you copied the remote console files.

4. Type **RCONSOLE**.

5. In the Connection Type menu, choose Asynchronous.

6. **If this is your first connection,** perform the following steps; otherwise, go on to Step 7.

   A. Select Configuration and enter the data for your modem. You can get this information from the modem manual, or just accept the default if you're not sure.

B. Fill in the User Connection ID and Call Back Number fields. The User Connection ID is the identifier that will show on the server console when the session starts and ends. The Call Back Number will only be used if you enabled RSPX at the server using the C parameter and created a Callback list.

C. Press Esc and confirm Yes to save changes.

7. Select Connect to Remote Location.

8. Press the Insert key to enter a location and phone number to dial. Press Esc to return to the menu of phone numbers.

9. Highlight the number and press Enter to dial.

- If you have enabled the Callback option at the server, the callback will take place. Otherwise, proceed to Step 10.

10. You will see the console screen, where you can enter commands just as you would at the console.

- To get a menu of commands specifically for this remote console session, press Alt+F1. Among other tasks, you can view files on or transfer files to the server's DOS partition.

- To switch console screens, press Alt+F4.

11. To quit the remote console session, press Alt+F2 then Esc.

Summary

THIS CHAPTER COVERED THE BASICS of getting you and your users connected and enjoying the benefits of the network. NetWare Administrator is your "Swiss Army knife," containing all the tools of your network trade. You use it to create and manage all the Directory objects and to control many aspects of the file system.

Despite NetWare's careful work in creating a useful set of default rights, you'll need to manage rights to some extent. You need to grant users sufficient rights to access the file system for their work, and restrict their rights to sensitive files and directories.

The inheritance of rights through the Directory tree and the file system gives you a nice shortcut for new users, files, and directories. But be cautious of inheritance—you don't want to be surprised by unintended consequences of your trustee assignments. Make sure you check effective rights whenever you change an assignment.

Used correctly, NetWare's administration features can save you time. You can create container objects for departments that don't share many resources with the rest of the network. You can create Groups to simplify rights and login script administration. Organizational Role objects are like Group objects in many ways.

Finally, you can work at the console from your workstation or over the phone lines from home. Just enable REMOTE and its supporting NLMs at the server console, and run RCONSOLE from your workstation or a remote computer.

Documenting
the Network

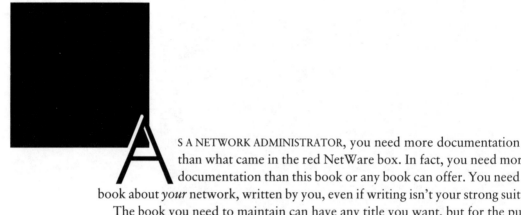

A S A NETWORK ADMINISTRATOR, you need more documentation than what came in the red NetWare box. In fact, you need more documentation than this book or any book can offer. You need a book about *your* network, written by you, even if writing isn't your strong suit.

The book you need to maintain can have any title you want, but for the purposes of this chapter, let's call it your Network Documents binder.

Why Do You Need a Network Documents Binder?

C ONSIDER THE FOLLOWING SCENARIOS, which illustrate only some of the problems you'll see if you don't document your network. Let's hope they don't already sound familiar.

Scenario #1: The LAN Gets Too Long

After adding a length of coaxial cable to connect a new workstation, the network slows to a crawl and errors start multiplying on the console statistics screen. Does the workstation have a bad network adapter? Is there a bad cable, T-connector, or terminator? Have you exceeded the recommended cable segment length?

Solution: If your network documentation includes a current diagram of your cabling system, you'll be able to look up that cable length in less than a minute. You can also see where your cabling contractor laid the previous cable and installed the repeater. Getting your network back on track becomes a much easier job if you don't have to trace cables through the ceiling with a measuring tape in your teeth.

Scenario #2: You Take a Vacation

Some administrators can't even imagine taking a vacation, for fear of what may go wrong while they're gone. What if you get the flu? Or take a three-day seminar in Atlanta? Do you really *enjoy* wearing a pager?

Solution: If you have written down what kinds of backups to do, how to do them, and how to recover from the most common network disasters, you can leave that pager with someone else.

Scenario #3: The Server Runs Out of Disk Space

You're sitting in your manager's office asking for a new disk subsystem. The manager says, "I'll see if I can get it approved for next year's budget."

You say, "No, you don't get it. We need it *now*! We're out of disk space!"

Your manager taps her pencil on the desk a few times and turns to stare out the window at the parking lot. She asks, "And why didn't you warn us that this was going to happen?"

You have no answer.

Solution: If you faithfully track disk space and other statistics such as processor utilization, in writing, on a weekly basis, you can forecast future hardware needs. Then you submit a proposal in writing, with your line graph pointing the way to disaster, two months *before* you need that disk subsystem.

Scenario #4: You Call Customer Support

One of your users is getting errors running an application. The Customer Support person starts asking questions over the phone. "What version of VLM is the workstation running?" You tell the customer support person to hold on while you run over to the workstation and type VLM /VER. You run back.

"How many users are on the network?" asks Customer Support. You run to the workstation again.

"Does the user's workstation have a VGA monitor?"

Solution: By the time you have gathered all the information Customer Support needs to isolate the problem, your sneakers are worn out and your telephone bill is up around the size of the national debt. On the other hand, if you're keeping a Network Documents binder, the answers will be right on the pages in front of you.

Scenario #5: You Get Promoted

If you do a good job of documenting your excellent work, you may get promoted sooner than you think. Wouldn't it be nice to move your books and plants into the office with the window overlooking the parking lot, and never have to worry about the network again?

If you keep your Network Documents binder up to date, you're more likely to get recognized for your work. (After all, it'll be documented!) Then, when you get the promotion, you can train your successor quickly, and your successor won't always be calling you to unearth long-forgotten details.

What Goes into a Network Documents Binder?

START WITH A THREE-RING BINDER. Then add seven tabbed section dividers, labeled as follows:

Log

Procedures

Server

Workstations

Cabling

File System

Directory Tree

You now have the seven sections that you need in your Network Documents binder. In those sections you'll put samples and blank worksheets. You can make copies of the blank worksheets or create worksheets of your own. Buy some lined three-hole paper for taking notes and writing addenda to the worksheets. Get a three-hole punch for documents without holes that you need to include in the binder.

Now here are the details of what will go into each section of the binder.

Log

The first thing you'll ask yourself when something goes wrong is, "What was the last thing I did to the network?" The next question will be, "Have we ever had this problem before, and if so, how did we solve it?"

It only makes sense that the most current problem will be related to the last thing you changed. That's why you should keep all changes in a log. For instance, suppose user Jim comes back from vacation to find he can't run his favorite word processor. The last time he used it was ten days ago and it worked fine.

Your log will tell you what happened over the last ten days that might be affecting Jim's situation. Did you change the login script? Did you update the word processor application on the network? Did you alter the trustee assignments? Has anyone modified Jim's workstation while he was gone? Keeping track of all such activities will give you an immediate source of troubleshooting data.

The log contains two types of entries: Maintenance and Errors. Maintenance entries give you the "what I changed" information that helps you in Jim's case. A Maintenance entry lists the following:

- Date

- Time

- Description of the action taken

An Error entry helps you analyze recurring problems. For instance, suppose user Kristen gets the message "An internal system error occurred during CX's attempt to canonicalize the context: ACCT-DEPT.OURCO."

You vaguely remember seeing that word *canonicalize* before…. If you look back in your log, you will find the last time it happened and what you did to fix it. When you enter an error into the log, you should include the following:

- Date

- Time

- Error number

- Error text

- Suspected cause

- Actions taken

Table 6.1 illustrates a sample Maintenance entry in the log. Notice that information for other worksheets is included in the entry, for recording at the end of the day. It's like recording accounting events in a general ledger for posting to other ledgers later.

TABLE 6.1 Sample Maintenance Entry in the Log	**DATE**	**TIME**	**ERROR REPORT (INCLUDE ERROR NUMBER) OR MAINTENANCE INFORMATION**
	9/19/97	6:30am	Installed a new 10/100 (EtherExpress Pro/100) network card in Al's workstation. Serial number 8634E. MONITOR shows the node ID as 0040052A56C6. Driver version 1.03.

Table 6.2 shows a sample Error log entry. Notice that it includes the error number and text, along with the cause and action taken. Register all errors that occur, whether users see them on workstations or you get them from the server's error log.

TABLE 6.2 Sample Error Report in the Log	**DATE**	**TIME**	**ERROR REPORT (INCLUDE ERROR NUMBER) OR MAINTENANCE INFORMATION**
	9/20/97	8:04am	Al got error when logging in: "MAP-4.10-115: Drive K: is mapped to a bad directory handle. Try remapping it." I had deleted the directory last night, but forgot to take the drive mapping out of the container login script. Edited the container login script to remove K drive mapping.

Procedures

This is the section of the Network Records binder that will maintain your good reputation with management. It's what helps others do your job when you go on vacation or to that seminar in Atlanta. The Procedures section should contain the following sheets:

- Daily Routine

- Master Schedule

- Backups

- Statistics Gathering

- Contingency

When you have your next performance review with your manager, take your Network Documents binder in with you. Show her the Procedures section. You can tell her, "This is what I do every day. This is what I did last month. This is my schedule for backing up data, so we don't lose important stuff. These are the statistics I keep, so I can predict future needs and avoid downtime. These are the procedures for disaster recovery, which anyone can perform when something goes wrong, like a power outage."

Even if you've copied some of the procedures out of this book or out of the NetWare Supervising the Network manual, your manager will be impressed. She'll think, "This is an administrator who knows the job, who has the self-discipline to write things down, and who can organize the work."

Daily Routine

Once you have performed the daily routine a few times, you don't really need it written down. The person who *does* need it in writing is the administrator who takes your place when you're sick or on vacation. You may want to keep the Daily Routine sheet posted by your desk, ready for anyone who replaces you while you're away.

Table 6.3 shows a sample Daily Routine sheet.

Master Schedule

The Master Schedule lists the tasks that are not performed every day. It will contain the things you do weekly, monthly, or on another routine. Table 6.4 gives a sample Master Schedule.

	TIME	JOB	PROCEDURE
TABLE 6.3 The Daily Routine Sheet	8:00am	Check the server error log for new messages. Record errors in the Log section of the binder and resolve.	1. Start NetWare Administrator. 2. Highlight SERVER1. 3. From the Object menu, select Details. 4. Select Error Log. 5. Scroll to the end for most recent errors.
	8:45	Check Backup log from last night's scheduled backup.	Use text editor to view log in SYS:SYSTEM\BACKUP.
	9:30-10:00	Resolve user support calls and tasks from Master Schedule.	As required.
	10:30	Record processor utilization, disk space information, and long term cache hits.	See the Statistics Gathering worksheets and procedures.
	11:30	Lunch	
	1:00-5:00pm	Resolve user support calls and tasks from Master Schedule.	As required.
	5:00	Back up accounting database.	Run DBACKUP.BAT in the C:\DOS directory while logged into the network.

Backups

Backup strategy and tactics are covered in Chapter 10. Make sure you document both the strategy and the day-to-day procedures of network data backup and restoration. Then include the backup documents in the Backups section of the Network Documents binder.

TABLE 6.4 The Master Schedule	FREQUENCY	JOB	PROCEDURE
	Weekly (Wednesdays)	Test backups	Restore part of the backed-up data.
	Biweekly (first and third Tuesday)	Full backup	Full backup of servers and Directory; store tapes off site.
	Biweekly (second and fourth Tuesday)	Differential backup	Back up files changed since last full backup. Do not reset Modify bit.
	Monthly (first Monday)	Report to management	Line graphs of processor utilization and disk usage to management. Predictions of future hardware, software, and personnel needs.
	Monthly during off hours (first Sunday)	Test server UPS	1. Unplug UPS from wall to test automatic shutdown. 2. Down the server and unplug it from UPS, plug in radio to UPS, unplug UPS from wall.
	Quarterly	Review contingency plans	1. Schedule this meeting w/manager two weeks in advance. 2. Provide written plans and agenda two days in advance. 3. Review contingency plans with upper management.

Statistics Gathering

Use this section of the Network Documents binder to record the statistics you gather. You'll use the statistics to project future hardware needs and thus prevent downtime from server crashes or lack of disk space.

This section should also contain written procedures for obtaining the statistics you use (and how you intend to use them). Table 6.5 gives such an explanation of the statistics.

TABLE 6.5 Written Procedures for Obtaining and Using Statistics	STATISTIC	PROCEDURE	USE
	10:30 Utilization	Between 10:15 and 11:00 AM, watch utilization on the main MONITOR console for about 2 minutes. Write down the average.	If processor utilization approaches 100% for long periods of time, server will be slow. To alleviate, change to network adapters and disk controllers that use DMA. Balance print services, files, and applications among all NetWare servers. Add servers after other options have been exhausted.
	Long-term cache hits	From the main MONITOR console screen, select "Cache utilization." Then select "Long term cache hits." Write down the percentage.	Server uses RAM as cache. If short on RAM, cache utilization will drop below 90% and server response will slow. When this happens, unload unnecessary NLMs to free up RAM for cache. If long-term cache hits still languish under 90%, add RAM.
	SYS: % disk space / dir entries	Record this statistic for each volume on each server. Using NetWare Administrator, highlight the volume. Select Object | Details | Statistics. Record % of disk space and % of directory entries.	Tracking disk space over time helps estimate when it will run out. Should add disk space before that time arrives. The directory entries statistic should stay about even with the disk space %. If it advances well ahead of disk space, make sure application temp files are properly deleted and purged.

Contingency

Good contingency planning distinguishes a great network administrator from an average one. This kind of planning uses the negative side of your imagination, with which you suppose the destructive consequences of events.

Take an hour sometime to just imagine what could go wrong. Get somebody who knows something about your company's business to help you. Put Pollyanna on leave. Brainstorm the big and little things that might go wrong. At this point, you can include the absurd and save sensible evaluation for later. Here's a sampling of what you might come up with:

- Both you and your replacement administrator take ill on the same day. That same day, the server goes down with an abend.

- Your backup software fails during the nightly backup session.

- A workstation's network adapter goes bad.

- A server's network adapter generates bad packets until the hub partitions it from the network.

- The server's hard drive begins to sound like a garbage disposal.

- The accounting database application corrupts all existing data.

- A disgruntled employee deletes all the personnel files on the server.

- The boss's monitor goes blank.

- You change your password and immediately forget it before you get it written down.

- A construction crew severs power to the building. It will take 24 hours to restore it.

- A tornado destroys your building.

- A coffee spill ruins your backup tapes.

- An earthquake levels your part of town.

Now it's time for a more level-headed evaluation. What possibilities are absurd? Eliminate those. Rate the remaining possibilities according to how devastating each would be to your business. Rate them by probability, too.

Now devise and document contingency plans for the most devastating and most probable of these events. Your plans are likely to include some of the following preparations.

SPARES Keeping spare parts of your server hardware allows you to respond quickly to failure. Sure, it costs money; and part of your job is to evaluate those costs against the cost of down time. Whatever your decisions, document them. Show them to your manager.

Write down the procedure for replacing bad parts, so that someone else will do the right thing if something goes bad when you're not there.

You can install an extra network adapter in your server without loading its driver. Then, if an adapter goes bad, just unload its driver and unbind it from IPX. Then load the spare adapter driver, bind it to IPX, and reconnect the cable from the old card to the spare one. You're back in business without downing the server.

MIRRORING Mirroring and duplexing are discussed in Chapter 2. If these techniques are part of your contingency plan, you should document the procedure for replacing one of the mirrored drives.

STORING BACKUP TAPES OFF SITE Sure, it's most convenient to store your backup tapes in a pile next to the tape drive. But if catastrophe strikes, you'll save the day (or month) by coming up with a complete backup from your off-site hiding place.

Consider storing your weekly complete backup at a location known to you and your manager. Keep a record of the storage locations for tapes in the Procedures section of your Network Documentation binder.

PASSWORD PROCEDURES Write down the Admin password and the passwords of all other administrative user accounts. Give the list to your manager, to be kept under lock and key. Then write down what should happen when a user or another administrator needs a password.

MAINTENANCE CONTRACTS A maintenance contract with your hardware maintenance provider or cabling contractor can provide security in case of failures. Make sure the procedures and telephone numbers for accessing this maintenance service are written in the Procedures section of your Network Documentation binder.

PROCEDURES FOR REROUTING NETWORK TRAFFIC Take some time to consider the likely events if a hub or patch cable to the server were to go out. Then compose a procedure for routing around the problem. You may need to cascade two hubs off one network adapter on the server. Or you may need to prioritize the ports so that the mission-critical workstations and printers stay on line.

Server

Document your server hardware and software thoroughly. This will make the replacement or reconfiguration of critical parts go much faster. When the server is down and a few dozen employees are out of work, you and they (and management) will appreciate the minutes and hours your documentation can save.

Also, if you decide to order RAM for the server, you can just look up the brand, size, and speed of the existing SIMMs in your binder—no need to open up the server's case.

Documentation for the server also helps with preventive maintenance. For instance, suppose you learn that certain problems are related to some revisions of BIOS. If you have the BIOS version written in the binder, you don't need to figure out how to check it while the server is running.

Start with an overview of the server configurations. A worksheet like the one in Table 6.6 can save you hours of explanation to someone unfamiliar with your network.

TABLE 6.6
Server Overview Worksheet

SERVER	DRIVES	VOLUMES	APPLICA-TIONS	ADAPTERS
Server1	2 @ 1 GB duplexed 2 @ 2 GB duplexed 1 tape drive	Spanned SYS: (0.5GB) USR: (1.5GB) SBT: (1GB)	USR: • Office • Market Msgr SBT: • SBT Print queues on SYS: • Qsales • Qexec	NICs: • NDC Coax • NDC TP I/O Combo card UPS card Video SCSI Adapters: • 2940 • 2940
Server2	2 @ 1 GB duplexed 2 @ 1 GB duplexed 1 CDROM drive	Spanned SYS: (0.5GB) USR: (1.5GB)	USR • Installation • Drivers • Concierge • NSE Pro Print queues on SYS • QTek	I/O Combo card UPS card Video NICs: • NDC Coax • NDC TP SCSI Adapters: • 2940 • 2940

Motherboard, CMOS, BIOS, and RAM

You'll need to shut down the server during off hours to get this information for adding to the Server section of the binder. If you have a manual for your motherboard, you can make copies of the important pages and insert them into the binder. (You'll get to use your three-hole punch!) Table 6.7 illustrates a sample worksheet for recording motherboard-related details.

TABLE 6.7 Worksheet for the Motherboard	COMPONENT	PARAMETER	VALUE
	Motherboard	Serial #	B1262-NO2-00400
		Slots	1: ISA - empty 2: PCI - NE5500+ (net=10) 3: PCI - NE5500+ (net=20) 4: ISA - empty 5: ISA -empty
		RAM	1: LGS GM71618160AJ7 (1X32) 2: LGS GM71618160AJ7 (1X32) 3: PNY 4MB upgrade 1X32 32178 4: PNY 4MB upgrade 1X32 32178
	BIOS settings	Version	AMI 10/10/94
		Serial ports	3F8, 3E8
		Parallel port	378
		Base memory	640KB
		Extended memory	40320KB
		Controller 1	Master: user defined 1653 cylinders, 16 heads, 65535 WP, 1654 LZ, 63 sectors, 814MB, LBA 32-bit block transfer enabled Slave: none
		Controller 2	CD-ROM only
		Disabled features	Advanced power management, mouse, floppy drive swapping, external cache, VGA "palette snooping"
		PnP IRQs	Bh (decimal 11), Ah (decimal 10)

Hard Drives

You can probably read the hard drive information directly from the sticker on the outside of the drive. Tables 6.8 and 6.9 illustrate worksheets for IDE and SCSI drives.

TABLE 6.8 Worksheet for the IDE Drives	**IDE DRIVE**	**PARAMETER**	**VALUE**
	Controller 1 master	Manufacturer	Western Digital
		Model	Caviar 2850 (WDAC 2850-00F)
		Description	AT Compatible Intelligent Drive
		Drive parameters	1654 cylinders, 16 heads, 63 sectors per track, 853.6MB
		Part number	99-004178-003
		CCC	C2 22 Mar 96
		DCM	CNBC SEG
		Serial number	WT303 136 4627

TABLE 6.9 Worksheet for the SCSI Drives	**ADAPTER**	**LUN**	**PARAMETER**	**VALUE**
	Adapter 1	2	Manufacturer	Seagate
			Model	ST-34371W
			Size	4.32GB
			Serial number	34371W9430872 Mar 95
			Sectors/track	163 average
			Tracks	51,670
			Cylinders	5,167 user
			Heads	10
			Disks	5
			Termination	Active external
			Interface	Ultra SCSI

Controllers

More and more motherboards come with built-in controllers, both EIDE and SCSI. For the built-in controllers, you can get the information you need from your computer manual and the BIOS setup. For controller boards that you add to the system, you can get information from the manual or directly from the manufacturer. Since SCSI adapters use a separate BIOS setup program (such as SCSISelect for Adaptec), you need to record the important settings from it.

Tables 6.10 and 6.11 show sample documentation for EIDE and SCSI controllers.

	CONTROLLER	PARAMETER	VALUE
TABLE 6.10 Built-in EIDE Controller Information	Controller 1	Model	Built-in Intel PCI/IDE
		Type	EIDE
		PIO mode	4
		Max drives	2
		IRQ	14
		DMA	no
		Bus	PCI
	Controller 2	Type	EIDE
		PIO mode	4
		Max drives	2
		IRQ	15
		DMA	No
		Bus	PCI

TABLE 6.11	ADAPTER	PARAMETER	VALUE
SCSI Controller Setup Information	Slot 1	Model	Adaptec 2940
		Serial number	AHA2940-0324890B
		DMA	1
		Slot	2
		SCAM support	Yes
		Termination	Automatic
		Host adapter SCSI ID	7
		SCSI parity checking	Enabled
		Initiate sync negotiation	Yes (Enabled)
		Maximum sync transfer rate	10 MB/sec
		Enable disconnection	Yes (Enabled)
		Send start unit SCSI command	No (Disabled)
		Host adapter BIOS	Enabled
		Extended BIOS translation for DOS drives > 1GB	No (Disabled)
		Display Ctrl+A message during BIOS initialization	Enabled
		Multiple LUN support	Disabled
		BIOS support for more than 2 drives	Enabled
		BIOS support for bootable CD-ROM	No (disabled)
		BIOS support for IRQ 13 extensions	Enabled
		Disk driver	AIC7870.DSK
		Configuration utility	SCSISelect
		Load parameters	Tag disable=ffff max_nontags=1

Network Adapters

Table 6.12 shows a sample worksheet for network adapters.

TABLE 6.12 Sample Worksheet for Network Adapters	ADAPTER	PARAMETER	VALUE
	Slot 1	Model	Microdyne NE5500
		Driver	PCNTNW.LAN
		Name	Marketing
		Frame type(s)	Ethernet_802.2
		Protocols(s)	IPX
		Network number(s)	10
		Serial number	AHA2940-0324890B
		DMA	1
		IRQ	Ah
		Memory port	FF80h
		Configuration utility	JMPSTART.EXE
		Load parameters	INT=B PORT=FF80 TP CDCOFF

Workstations

Experience will tell you which information you need to maintain for workstations. Obviously, hundreds of workstations will be harder to keep up with than a dozen or so. Either way, your documentation will make things easier. Table 6.13 shows a sample summary worksheet for ten workstations.

	USER	NODE	PRIMARY APPLICA-TIONS	OPERATING SYSTEM	NETWORK ADAPTER
TABLE 6.13 A Workstation Summary Worksheet	ALASSEN	0040052A56C0	Word CServe	Win95	NE5500+
	BHOLT	008A789BC9B2	WP Office 3 Net. Nav. 1.2	Win 3.1	3C509B
	CDAVIS	00DB6DB76423	AutoCAD Designer	Win 3.1	NE2000+
	DJONES	0DB6898D6798	Office 95 IExplorer	Win95	Ether16
	ESHANNON	00DB9DB67DDA	WebServer WP6.1	WfW 3.11	Maxtech Combo
	FBURNS	0016578DB765	SBT Goldmine	Win 3.1	3C579
	GPATTON	9337004576D6	SBT	DOS	NE1000
	HROBBINS	0021DB432A0	Quattro Pro WP 6.1	Win 3.1	Ether Express 16C
	ICRANE	00D79B876876	Word 6 CServe	Win 3.1	TC5048T
	JMITCHEL	00567C7DB6A0	Persuasion Pagemaker	Win95	LiteLink 10
	KCLINE	0079CBA87456	Ami Pro 3.1 1-2-3 5.0	Win95	Creditcard II
	LBJOHNSO	00CBDDD97678	Project Word	Unixware	3C595TX

Table 6.14 is a more detailed worksheet that will help you diagnose problems over the phone, if that's your principle means of communication.

If you have more than a dozen or so workstations, a database application can help you sort and access records quickly.

TABLE 6.14 Workstation Worksheet with More Details	USER	COMPUTER MODEL	NODE
	DJONES	Gateway P5-166	00DB6DB76423
	Bus type	**Drive controller**	**Network adapter**
	PCI/ISA	(2) EIDE Mode 4	LinkSys Ether16
	Disk Drive	**CDROM Drive**	**Floppy Drive**
	WD 2.5GB IDE	Toshiba 8X	3[one-half]"
	RAM	**Modem**	**Processor**
	16 MB EDO 70ns	US R 14.4 Fax	Pentium 166MHz
	Video Adapter	**Monitor**	**Operating System**
	Trio 2MB 128+ PCI	Gateway Vivitron 17	Win 95
	Video Driver	**Network Driver**	**Hub and Port**
	STB Lightspeed 128	ETHER.LAN	A-6
	Client Software	**Client Revision**	**Email Address**
	Novell C32 / Win95	2.02	dwjones@axxis.com
	Other Hardware		
	Plustek Scanner		
	Primary Applications		
	Office 95	Internet Explorer	Visio
	Image-In		

Cabling

The as-installed cabling diagram you keep in the Network Documents binder should come from the contractor you hired to put in the cabling. If you inherited the network without a diagram, you can do a rudimentary drawing yourself.

It may help to have a cable list similar to the one in Table 6.15. That way, if you suddenly get calls from about half of your users, you can quickly see whether a single cable segment is at fault.

	PORT NUMBER	HUB 1 (NETWORK NUMBER 10)	HUB 2 (NETWORK NUMBER 20)
TABLE 6.15 A Cable Segment List	1	UFISCHER	ALASSEN
	2	BHOLT	VBORGA
	3	CDAVIS	WABBOTT
	4	XHOLLAND	DJONES
	5	ESHANNON	YMARTINEZ
	6	ZBEATTY	FBURNS
	7	GPATTON	AROMEO
	8	HROBBINS	BHART
	9	CHANSEN	ICRANE
	10	JMITCHEL	DKILMER
	11	KCLINE	ESEALAND
	12	FGEORGE	LBJOHNSO
	13	MJORDAN	GSTODDARD
	14	HHUNTER	NREAGAN

TABLE 6.15 (continued) A Cable Segment List	PORT NUMBER	HUB 1 (NETWORK NUMBER 10)	HUB 2 (NETWORK NUMBER 20)
	15	OSTONE	IKURIAKI
	16	PDUKE	JLEWIS
	17	KFRANZ	QBUCKNER
	18	RWEAVER	LLOUIE
	19	SSIMMS	MANTOINE
	20	TDUNCAN	NKIDMAN

File System

You probably don't want a listing of every file on the network, but a diagram of the major directories can help you remember where things are. To print a file system diagram like the one in Figure 6.1, you can use Network Administrator as described in the following steps:

1. Select View | Set Context.

2. Using the Browse button, choose the context where your volume exists on the right-hand side of the screen.

3. Double-click on the Volume object on the left-hand side of the screen. A new browser appears with the volume object alone at the top.

4. Double-click on the Volume object to expand the view, showing all the directories and files at the root of the volume.

5. Double-click on the directories you want to expand.

6. Select Object | Print.

7. In the Print dialog, choose two-column printing if desired.

8. Click on OK.

9. Repeat this process for each volume, or for different views of the current volume.

FIGURE 6.1
NetWare Administrator
creates a useful file
system diagram.

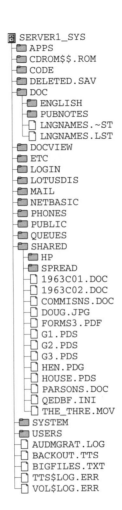

```
SERVER1_SYS
  APPS
  CDROM$$.ROM
  CODE
  DELETED.SAV
  DOC
    ENGLISH
    PUBNOTES
    LNGNAMES.~ST
    LNGNAMES.LST
  DOCVIEW
  ETC
  LOGIN
  LOTUSDIS
  MAIL
  NETBASIC
  PHONES
  PUBLIC
  QUEUES
  SHARED
    HP
    SPREAD
    1963C01.DOC
    1963C02.DOC
    COMMISNS.DOC
    DOUG.JPG
    FORMS3.PDF
    G1.PDS
    G2.PDS
    G3.PDS
    HEN.PDG
    HOUSE.PDS
    PARSONS.DOC
    QEDBF.INI
    THE_THRE.MOV
  SYSTEM
  USERS
  AUDMGRAT.LOG
  BACKOUT.TTS
  BIGFILES.TXT
  TTS$LOG.ERR
  VOL$LOG.ERR
```

Directory Tree

If your Directory tree is at all complex, a diagram (see Figure 6.2) will help you remember the names and locations of Directory objects. Network Administrator will print a diagram of the tree; follow these steps:

1. Select View | Set Context.

2. Using the Browse button, set the context where you want the diagram to start (usually [Root]).

3. Double-click on the container objects to expand the view, showing all the Directory objects.

FIGURE 6.2

A Directory tree diagram printed by NetWare Administrator

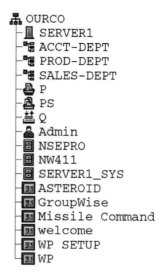

4. Select Object | Print.

5. In the Print dialog, choose two-column printing if desired.

6. Click on OK.

7. Repeat this process for various views of the Directory tree.

Blank Worksheets

THE PAGES FOLLOWING THE SUMMARY are blank worksheets. You can copy them up to 8.5" X 11" to fit in your Network Documents binder. Enlarge the worksheets by copying them at 129%. These worksheets are also available in the Downloads area of the Sybex Web site.

Summary

N THE BUSINESS OF NETWORK ADMINISTRATION, there are two types of professionals. One type enjoys knowing what other people don't. Type 1 views the world of knowledge as a zero-sum game; that is, his knowledge has less value if someone else knows it also. He imagines that his job security and self-esteem depend on his knowing all the secrets. He memorizes what he must and improvises the rest. If something goes wrong, he spouts enough buzzwords to imply that it's not his fault (and he resents any insinuation that it is).

Administrator Type 2 documents the network, knowing that the information can be used to train others and make his job more satisfying and easier to perform. His value to the company lies in his ability to forecast needs, prepare for contingencies, and thus keep the network as reliable and invisible as possible.

If you're the first type of administrator, you probably skipped this chapter and aren't even reading this. If you're Type 2, you will document your network. You might use the binder with the sections described in this chapter, or you will devise your own (better) method. Either way, I know which administrator I'd hire to run *my* network.

LOG SHEET

DATE	TIME	MAINTENANCE INFORMATION OR ERROR REPORT (INCLUDE ERROR NUMBER)

DAILY ROUTINE SHEET

TIME	JOB	PROCEDURE

THE MASTER SCHEDULE

FREQUENCY	JOB	PROCEDURE

LOG SHEET FOR SERVER STATISTICS

DATE	SERVER 1			SERVER 2		
	10:30 UTILIZATION	LONG TERM CACHE HITS	SYS: % DISK SPACE/ DIR ENTRIES	10:30 UTILIZATION	LONG TERM CACHE HITS	SYS: % DISK SPACE/ DIR ENTRIES

PROCEDURES FOR OBTAINING STATISTICS AND AN EXPLANATION FOR THEIR USE

STATISTIC	PROCEDURE	USE

SERVER OVERVIEW WORKSHEET

SERVER	DRIVES	VOLUMES	APPLICATIONS	ADAPTERS

MOTHERBOARD WORKSHEET

COMPONENT	PARAMETER	VALUE

WORKSHEET FOR IDE DRIVES

IDE DRIVE	PARAMETER	VALUE
Controller 1 Master	Manufacturer	
	Model	
	Description	
	Drive Parameters	
	Part Number	
	CCC	
	DCM	
	Serial Number	
Controller 1 Slave	Manufacturer	
	Model	
	Description	
	Drive Parameters	
	Part Number	
	CCC	
	DCM	
	Serial Number	

WORKSHEET FOR SCSI DRIVES

ADAPTER	UNIT #	PARAMETER	VALUE
Adapter 1		Manufacturer	
		Model	
		Size	
		Serial Number	
		Sector/Track	
		Tracks	
		Cylinders	
		Heads	
		Disks	
		Termination	
		Interface	
Adapter 2		Manufacturer	
		Model	
		Size	
		Serial Number	
		Sector/Track	
		Tracks	
		Cylinders	
		Heads	
		Disks	
		Termination	
		Interface	
Adapter 3	2	Manufacturer	
		Model	
		Size	
		Serial Number	
		Sector/Track	
		Tracks	
		Cylinders	
		Heads	
		Disks	
		Termination	
		Interface	

BUILT-IN EIDE CONTROLLER INFORMATION

CONTROLLER	PARAMETER	VALUE
Controller 1	Model	
	Type	
	PIO Mode	
	Max Drives	
	IRQ	
	DMA	
	Bus	
Controller 2	Model	
	Type	
	PIO Mode	
	Max Drives	
	IRQ	
	DMA	
	Bus	

SCSI CONTROLLER SETUP INFORMATION

ADAPTER	PARAMETER	VALUE
Slot 1	Model	
	Serial Number	
	DMA	
	IRQ	
	SCAM support	
	Termination	
	Host Adapter SCSI ID	
	SCSI Parity Checking	
	Initiate Sync Negotiation	
	Maximum Sync Transfer Rate	
	Enable Disconnection	
	Send Start Unit SCSI Command	
	Host Adapter BIOS	
	Extended BIOS Translation for DOS Drives > 1GB	
	Display Ctrl+A Message During BIOS Initialization	
	Multiple LUN Support	
	BIOS Support for More Than 2 Drives	
	BIOS Support for Bootable CD-ROM	
	BIOS Support for IRQ 13 Extensions	
	Disk Driver	
	Configuration Utility	
	Load Parameters	

WORKSHEET FOR NETWORK ADAPTERS

ADAPTER	PARAMETER	VALUE
Slot __	Model	
	Driver	
	Name	
	Frame Type(s)	
	Protocol(s)	
	Network Number(s)	
	Serial Number	
	DMA	
	IRQ	
	Memory Port	
	Configuration Utility	
	Load Parameters	
Slot __	Model	
	Driver	
	Name	
	Frame Type(s)	
	Protocol(s)	
	Network Number(s)	
	Serial Number	
	DMA	
	IRQ	
	Memory Port	
	Configuration Utility	
	Load Parameters	

WORKSTATION SUMMARY WORKSHEET

USER	NODE	PRIMARY APPLICATIONS	OPERATING SYSTEM	NETWORK ADAPTER

WORKSTATION WORKSHEET

USER	COMPUTER MODEL	NODE
BUS TYPE	**DRIVE CONTROLLER**	**NETWORK ADAPTER**
DISK DRIVE	**CDROM DRIVE**	**FLOPPY DRIVE**
RAM	**MODEM**	**PROCESSOR**
VIDEO ADAPTER	**MONITOR**	**OPERATING SYSTEM**
VIDEO DRIVER	**NETWORK DRIVER**	**HUB AND PORT**
CLIENT SOFTWARE	**CLIENT REVISION**	**EMAIL ADDRESS**
OTHER HARDWARE		
PRIMARY APPLICATIONS		

CABLE SEGMENT LIST

PORT NUMBER	HUB 1: (NETWORK NUMBER___)	HUB 2: (NETWORK NUMBER___)	HUB 3: (NETWORK NUMBER___)
1			
2			
3			
4			
5			
6			
7			
8			
9			
10			
11			
12			
13			
14			
15			
16			
17			
18			
19			
20			
21			
22			
23			
24			
25			
26			
27			
28			
29			
30			
31			
32			
33			
34			
35			
36			

Automating Access to Network Resources

UTOMATION, IN NETWARE 4.10 TERMS, means providing the file system and printing resources your users need when they log in. NetWare 4.10 automates with *login scripts*. NetWare 4.11 provides the same login script automation, with the added option of presenting network applications at login. You replace or augment login scripts with NetWare Application Launcher (NAL).

The first part of this chapter deals with login scripts. The second part explains the NetWare Application Launcher.

If you have a NetWare 4.10 network, you can add NAL automation by getting the Client 32 kit from Novell.

Using Login Scripts

OUR FIRST TASK IS to evaluate how users log in—do they log in with their AUTOEXEC.BAT file, or do they use the OS/2, Windows, or Windows 95 login process?

For DOS and Windows users, the default login process consists of STARTNET.BAT, called from AUTOEXEC.BAT. You may prefer to have Windows users run the Client 32 login in their Windows startup group. Windows 95 users should run the default login utility included in the Client 32 for Windows 95 bundle.

This chapter covers the events that occur after the login utility has started. You will automate these events by using a combination of login scripts, Directory Map objects, Alias objects, Profile objects, and NetWare Application Launcher (NAL). Here are some brief definitions of these items.

A *login script* is a list of commands that run when a user logs in. There are four kinds of login scripts: container, profile, user, and default. Novell has created the default login script for you. You'll have to create the rest.

A *container login script* runs for each User object in a container.

A *Profile object* is a special Directory object whose prominent feature is its login script. When you add a user to a Profile's membership, the Profile login script runs when that User logs in. It runs after the container login script if there is one.

A *User login script* is a property of the User object. If a User login script exists, it runs after any container or Profile login scripts run. A *default login script* runs if the User login script is blank.

Actually, the default login script will *not* run if any of the following are true:

- There is a User login script.

- The container or profile login script contains the NO_DEFAULT command.

- The container or profile login script contains the EXIT command.

The default login script has the following commands:

```
MAP DISPLAY OFF
MAP ERRORS OFF
MAP 1:=SYS:
MAP 1:=SYS:%LOGIN_NAME
IF "%1"="ADMIN" THEN MAP 1:=SYS:SYSTEM
MAP P:=SYS:PUBLIC (only if the user logs in from an OS/2
   workstation)
MAP INS S1:=SYS:PUBLIC
MAP INS S2:=SYS:PUBLIC\%MACHINE\%OS\%OS_VERSION (only if
   the user logs in from a DOS workstation)
MAP DISPLAY ON
```

Run Order of Login Scripts

Login scripts run in the following order:

1. Container

2. Profile

3. User (or default)

Managing Login Scripts

NetWare 4 gives you numerous ways to manage login scripts. Here is a summary:

- You can manage one container login script for each container with Users. This is the recommended and easiest method. For users with specific needs, you can create groups and use the IF MEMBER OF construction to run specific commands for them.

- You can use Profile login scripts. With this method, you maintain multiple login scripts that are usually interrelated.

- You can create User login scripts. With this method, you have to maintain numerous scripts: one for each user. Troubleshooting is an ordeal, because you have to update all of the scripts whenever you change the network.

- You can use a combination of Profile, User, default, and container login scripts. If you like frustration, this is the highest level of torture.

- You can avoid login scripts altogether, allowing the default login script or NAL (discussed later in this chapter) to make the basic drive mappings. On one hand, this sounds simple for you, the administrator—no login script maintenance! On the other hand, setting up applications and data directories using the limited drive mappings in the default script or NAL may cause more trouble than you want. Still, if your company only has a narrow range of network needs, this option has its advantages.

Creating a Profile Login Script

If you have users with similar needs, you can create a Profile object and add them as members. Figure 7.1 shows a Profile object named MGRSCRIPT.

If you use a Profile object, each User object must have Read right to the Profile's Login Script property.

After you have created the Profile object and created its login script, you can add it to each of the User objects. Here's the procedure:

1. Using NetWare Administrator, select a User object.

2. From the Object menu, select Details.

FIGURE 7.1
You can create a Profile
object for users with
similar needs.

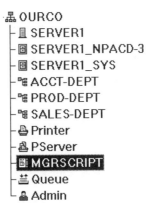

FIGURE 7.1
You can create a Profile
object for users with
similar needs.

3. Choose the Login Script page. A screen similar to the one shown in Figure 7.2 appears.

4. Use the Browse button beside the Profile box to select the Profile object.

5. Click on OK.

FIGURE 7.2
To use a Profile object,
you add it in the Profile
box at the bottom of the
User's login script page

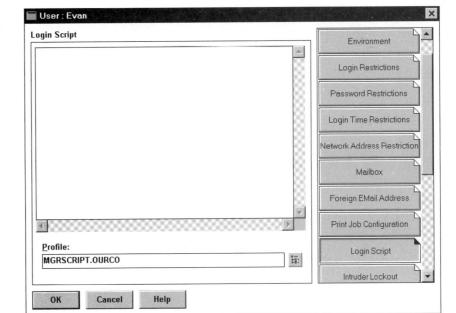

Be aware of context. The User objects who run the Profile login script may have different contexts. If you MAP drives or CAPTURE to queues in the Profile, use relative naming or use Directory Map and Alias objects that will work for all Users who run it.

Another way to assign users to a Profile is with the PROFILE command in a container login script. Example:

```
IF MEMBER OF "MANAGERS" THEN PROFILE MGRSCRIPT.
```

The Rule of No Distinguished Names

Novell's login utilities have a weakness when it comes to distinguished names. (You remember that a *distinguished name* is one that starts with a period and includes all the containers to the [Root].) This weakness is due to the fact that login script commands often refer to Directory objects. Specifically,

- MAP commands refer to Volume objects.

- CAPTURE commands refer to Queue or Printer objects.

- IF MEMBER OF constructions refer to Group objects.

When the objects in a login script command are in the current context, then there's no problem. Sometimes, though, you need to refer to objects outside the workstation's current context. For these objects you would probably opt to supply a fully distinguished object name from the command line.

But the login utility (LOGIN) has trouble interpreting distinguished names in login scripts—it's likely to choke on anything that begins with a period. You have to use relative naming or create Alias or Directory Map objects in the current context that point to objects in other containers. The following paragraphs will help you devise ways of doing that.

Using Relative Names

Consider the situation depicted in Figure 7.3. You have a Server and a Volume at the Organization level, with User objects in three OUs. Your login scripts will need to map drives to the Volume object and capture printing ports to the Queues. In this case, you could create your printing objects at the Organization level, as shown in Figure 7.4.

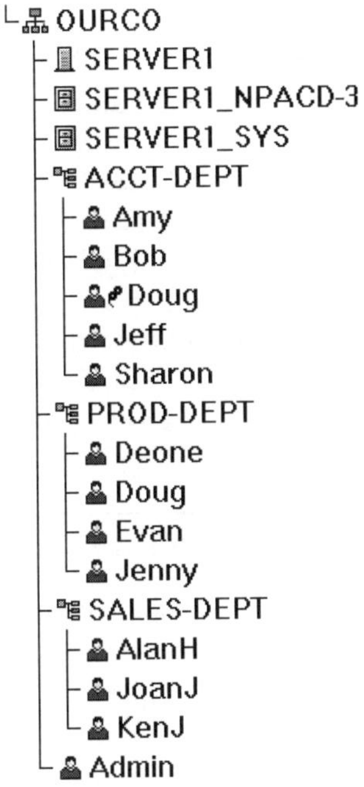

FIGURE 7.3

In this organization,
you'll need to address
objects outside the
Users' context.

```
└ 品 OURCO
    ├ ▤ SERVER1
    ├ 回 SERVER1_NPACD-3
    ├ 回 SERVER1_SYS
    ├ ▣ ACCT-DEPT
    │   ├ & Amy
    │   ├ & Bob
    │   ├ &✐ Doug
    │   ├ & Jeff
    │   └ & Sharon
    ├ ▣ PROD-DEPT
    │   ├ & Deone
    │   ├ & Doug
    │   ├ & Evan
    │   └ & Jenny
    ├ ▣ SALES-DEPT
    │   ├ & AlanH
    │   ├ & JoanJ
    │   └ & KenJ
    └ & Admin
```

FIGURE 7.3

In this organization, you'll need to address objects outside the Users' context.

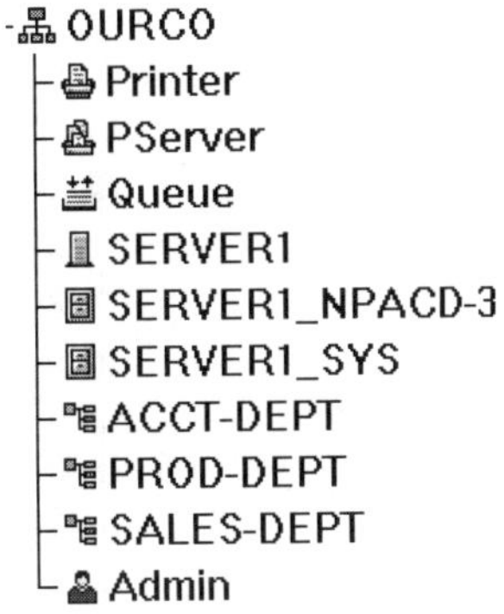

FIGURE 7.4

Here we've created print
objects under the
Organization object.

```
- 品 OURCO
    ├ 🖨 Printer
    ├ & PServer
    ├ ≛ Queue
    ├ ▤ SERVER1
    ├ 回 SERVER1_NPACD-3
    ├ 回 SERVER1_SYS
    ├ ▣ ACCT-DEPT
    ├ ▣ PROD-DEPT
    ├ ▣ SALES-DEPT
    └ & Admin
```

FIGURE 7.4

Here we've created print objects under the Organization object.

Now, in your login scripts, you simply employ relative naming by adding a period at the end of each object name. In the following examples, the object names are shown in boldface.

```
MAP INS S1:=SERVER1_SYS.:\PUBLIC
MAP ROOT H:=SERVER1_SYS.:USERS\%LOGIN_NAME
#CAPTURE Q=QUEUE.
```

Notice the period after each object name. The period causes the MAP and CAPTURE utilities to search the context directly above the current one, which happens to be the correct location of the objects.

Using Alias and Directory Map Objects

If the whole idea of relative object names gives you hives, then consider using Alias objects and Directory Map objects. Figure 7.5 shows a Directory Map object called APPS. When this object is created, it points to the APPS directory in the SERVER1_SYS volume.

With this setup, when you create a drive mapping in a login script for Doug, Deone, Evan, or Jenny, you only need to use the Directory Map object. For example:

```
MAP INS S2:=APPS
```

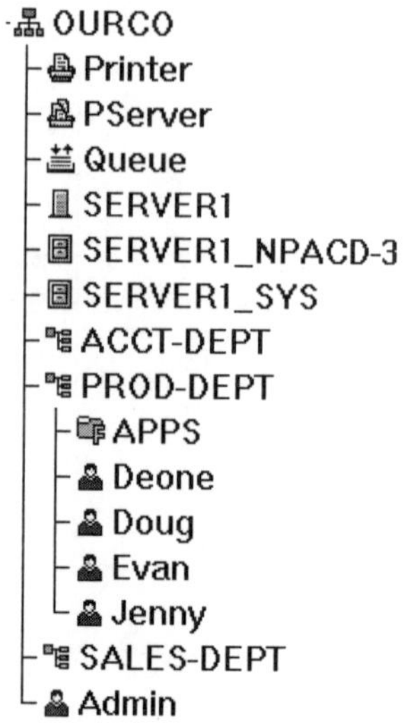

FIGURE 7.5
The APPS Directory Map object points to a directory on the SYS volume.

```
OURCO
├─ Printer
├─ PServer
├─ Queue
├─ SERVER1
├─ SERVER1_NPACD-3
├─ SERVER1_SYS
├─ ACCT-DEPT
├─ PROD-DEPT
│  ├─ APPS
│  ├─ Deone
│  ├─ Doug
│  ├─ Evan
│  └─ Jenny
├─ SALES-DEPT
└─ Admin
```

For printing, you'll need an Alias for the Print Queue object, as shown in Figure 7.6. Now your CAPTURE statement for Doug, Deone, Evan, or Jenny only needs to refer to the local queue alias:

```
#CAPTURE Q=QUEUE NB NFF TI=2
```

If you have users in other containers who need the queue and directory, you'll need to create the Alias and Directory Map objects in each container. Since NDS allows you to have duplicate names in different contexts, you can use the names QUEUE and APPS repeatedly.

FIGURE 7.6
Create an Alias for the Print Queue object so your CAPTURE statements can refer to a local name.

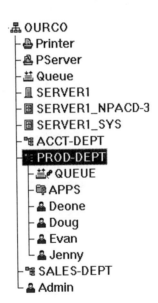

Login Script Commands

Novell's Supervising the Network manual contains an exhaustive reference on login script commands. This section lists and describes the most useful ones, giving you plenty of fodder for effective script programming. Here's a summary of what is covered in this chapter:

#	FDisplay	PCCompatible
Attach	If...Then	Profile
CLS	Include	Remark
Context	Map	Set
Display	No_Default	Set_Time
Drive	NoSwap	Swap
Exit	Pause	Write

(Execute External Program)

The # command runs a program that is external to the login script. In the following example, CAPTURE.EXE is the external command:

```
#CAPTURE Q=Qaccounting NB NFF TI=2
```

Make sure you have already established a search drive mapping to the external command. If the command fails, consider the following possible causes.

- You have not established a search drive to the external command. In the example above, you would need a search drive to SYS:PUBLIC.

- The User does not have the proper trustee rights to the external command. In the example above, the User would need Read and File Scan rights to the SYS:PUBLIC directory.

MAP is both an internal login script command and an external program, so you don't need to precede it with #.

ATTACH (Make a Bindery-Style Connection)

Use ATTACH to make a bindery-style connection to a pre-NetWare 4 server or a NetWare 4 server running bindery services. No additional login script will run when the user attaches, but the user will be authenticated to use the server's file system.

In this example:

```
ATTACH Server1/Guest
```

Server1 is the server and Guest is the bindery user account. If you don't include the user name, LOGIN interrupts the login script to prompt the user for the login name.

CLS (Clear Screen)

The CLS command clears the workstation screen, just as the DOS CLS command does.

CONTEXT (Change the Workstation's Context)

The CONTEXT command sets the workstation context. For example:

```
CONTEXT .PROD-DEPT.OURCO
```

You can use a complete context or a relative context. For instance, to move up two containers from the workstation's current context, use two periods:

```
CONTEXT ..
```

DISPLAY (Display a Text File)

Use the DISPLAY command to show the contents of a text file on the user's screen when the user logs in. Example:

```
DISPLAY SYS:SYSTEM\WELCOME.MSG
```

DRIVE (Set the Default Drive)

Use the DRIVE command to set the default drive while the login script is executing. Example:

```
DRIVE G:
```

When logging in from OS/2, Windows, Windows 95, or Windows NT, DRIVE is only effective during the login process. When the login script completes, the workstation returns to the drive in effect before the login script ran.

Make sure the drive letter exists as a local drive or is already assigned with the MAP command. Unless this command is in your login script, the default drive is set to the first network drive, which is assigned in your NET.CFG file.

EXIT (Terminate Script and Run an External Program)

The EXIT command ends the login script and transfers control to an external program. Example:

```
EXIT "VIRUSCAN"
```

The length of information between quotes may not exceed the workstation's keyboard buffer length minus 1 (typically 15 − 1 = 14 characters). This command does not apply to users logging in via OS/2, Windows, Windows 95, or Windows NT. EXIT prevents other login scripts from running.

Make sure you have mapped a search drive to the command specified in quotes. You should also add the PCCOMPATIBLE command to the login script before the EXIT command.

FDISPLAY (Display a Formatted File)

The FDISPLAY command shows the text of a word processing file on a workstation's screen when the user logs in. It works just like the DISPLAY command, except that FDISPLAY interprets and strips out the formatting codes in most word processor files. Example:

```
FDISPLAY SYS:SYSTEM\WELCOME.WPD
```

IF...THEN (Conditional Structure)

The IF...THEN construction allows you to run commands only under certain conditions. Example:

```
IF LOGIN_NAME="Admin" THEN MAP ROOT
  G:=SYS:\SYSTEM\PATCHES
IF MEMBER OF "Managers" THEN DISPLAY MGRMSG.TXT
```

Here LOGIN tests the variables and values with current workstation and user settings.

The conditional part of the construction often uses identifier variables. As shown in the preceding example, some identifier variables require the equal sign (=) and some don't. Identifier variables are explained later in this chapter.

You can use AND or OR to include two or more conditional statements in an IF...THEN structure. If you put multiple commands on separate lines, use an END statement. Example:

```
IF LOGIN_NAME="JMARBLE" AND DAY_OF_WEEK="MONDAY"
THEN
    MAP ROOT Q:=SYS:BACKUPS
    CLS
    FDISPLAY Q:\BACKUP.WPD
    DRIVE Q:
    PAUSE
    #PBACK.BAT
END
```

If you include a WRITE command as part of an IF...THEN structure, the WRITE command must be on a separate line.

You can nest IF...THEN structures. Notice in the following example that two END statements are required and that indenting is used to make the structure clear:

```
IF DAY_OF_WEEK="MONDAY" THEN
    MAP 6:=VOL1:APPL\WP
    IF MEMBER OF CLERKS THEN
        WRITE "Your report is due immediately!"
    END
END
```

Your IF commands can contain any of the symbols in the following list. Here's an example usage of the >= symbol:

```
IF HOUR24>="12" THEN DISPLAY Z:PM.MSG
```

SYMBOL	DEFINITION
=	Equal
<>	Not equal
>	Greater than

SYMBOL	DEFINITION
>=	Greater than or equal to
<	Less than
<=	Less than or equal to

You can use ELSE commands in an IF...THEN structure. Example:

```
IF LOGIN_NAME="Amy" AND DAY_OF_WEEK="TUESDAY" THEN
    WRITE "Remember your status report."
    ELSE
    WRITE "A brain is only as strong as its weakest
    think."
END
```

INCLUDE (Run Other Scripts)

The INCLUDE command runs external files as scripts, or it runs another object's login script.

- You can include any *file* containing valid login script commands, providing the user has Read and File scan rights to the directory.

- You can include any *login script*, providing the user has Read right to the Login Script property and Browse right to the Directory object. Here are a couple of examples:

```
INCLUDE SYS:\PUBLIC\LOGIN2.TXT
INCLUDE PROFILE2
```

The nesting of INCLUDE scripts is limited only by available memory. This means that one subscript file can call another subscript file, which can call yet another subscript file, and so on.

MAP (Manage Drive Pointers)

The MAP command works in login scripts much as it works from the command line. Chapter 4 gives an overview of the MAP command as used from the command line. MAP is both an internal and an external command and therefore requires no #. Example:

```
MAP ROOT K:=SERVER1_SYS:\APPS
MAP INS S1:=SERVER2/SYS:PUBLIC
```

The map parameters C (change), DEL (delete), INS (insert), N (next), P (physical), and ROOT work as they would from the command line. For login scripts, the MAP command has some additional options:

MAP OPTION	DESCRIPTION	EXAMPLE
DISPLAY (ON or OFF)	(Valid only in login scripts.) Controls whether the drive mappings are displayed when the user logs in. The default setting is ON.	MAP DISPLAY OFF
ERRORS (ON or OFF)	(Valid only in login scripts.) Controls whether error messages are displayed when the user logs in. You'll probably want errors ON while you are debugging your login script and OFF thereafter. The default setting is ON. You must place a MAP ERRORS OFF command before the MAP commands in the login script.	MAP ERRORS OFF

OS/2 workstations are always mapped to the root of a drive. Also, OS/2 workstations do not use search drives. Instead, they use the PATH, DPATH, and LIBPATH commands in their CONFIG.SYS files.

Use the MAP DISPLAY OFF command at the beginning of the login script. Then add the lines MAP DISPLAY ON and MAP to the end of the login script. This sequence of commands displays a clearer set of drive mappings for the users as they log in.

If you have installed a network application that requires a certain drive letter, use the following command syntax to map a search drive to that drive letter:

```
MAP S16:=K:=SYS:\APPS\SPREADSH
```

NetWare uses search drives in reverse order (Z, Y, X…). That is, S1 is assigned to drive Z: and searched first. For instance, if the INSTALL.EXE command existed in S1 (normally Z:) and S4 (W:), the command in Z: would run when the user typed **INSTALL** at the command line. To map the next available search drive without disturbing existing search drives, use the MAP S16: command. Example:

```
MAP S16:=SYS:APPL\DATABASE
```

If you have created a Directory Map object, you can use it in a MAP command. Example:

```
MAP S16:=WP
```

NO_DEFAULT (Prevent Default Login Script from Running)

The NO_DEFAULT command in a container login script prevents the default login script from running.

Without the NO_DEFAULT command, the default login script runs if there is no user login script. The user default login script overwrites drive mappings made in the container login script, so using NO_DEFAULT is advised when you don't have user login scripts. Example:

```
NO_DEFAULT
```

NOSWAP (Prevent LOGIN from Swapping Out of Conventional Memory)

The NOSWAP command prevents the LOGIN utility from moving out of conventional memory into higher memory when an external (#) command runs. Example:

```
NOSWAP
```

PAUSE (Temporarily Halt Execution)

Use PAUSE to create a pause in the execution of the login script. This is similar to the PAUSE command used in DOS batch files to stop execution until the user has time to read a message. The message "Strike any key when ready..." appears on the workstation screen. Example:

```
CLS
DISPLAY SYS:PUBLIC\LOGINMSG.TXT
PAUSE
```

PCCOMPATIBLE (Enable Exit Command)

The PCCOMPATIBLE command tells LOGIN that the workstation is a DOS machine that can run an external command. LOGIN first checks the LONG MACHINE NAME variable for the IBM_PC value. If the test is False, the EXIT command won't run unless PCCOMPATIBLE is set before the EXIT command. Example:

```
PCCOMPATIBLE
EXIT "NMENU MAIN.MNU"
```

The PCCOMPATIBLE command does not work in login scripts executed from OS/2, Windows, or Windows 95.

PROFILE (Set User's Profile Login Script Assignment)

The PROFILE command in a container script specifies a Profile script, which will run when the container login script is complete. PROFILE is useful when defining a group profile using the IF MEMBER OF construct. Example:

```
IF MEMBER OF "MANAGERS" THEN PROFILE MGRPROF
```

REMARK (Add Explanatory Text)

The REMARK command and its equivalents (REM) and (;) allow you to insert explanatory text into your login script. The use of explanatory text is highly recommended, so that you or your replacement can easily understand and maintain the script. The text does not show on the users' screens. Example:

```
REMARK This line will not print or be executed.
REM This one won't either.
; Neither will this one.
```

Set (Set Environmental Variable)

The SET command establishes the value of a DOS or OS/2 environment variable. For OS/2 workstations, SET only affects the environment while the login script is running. Example:

```
SET PROMPT="LOGGED IN $P$G"
```

This command does not work in a login script if the DOS workstation's environment space is limited. In that case you should increase the environment size in the CONFIG.SYS file using the SHELL command.

After you set an environment variable, you can use that variable in other login script commands. To include an environment variable as an identifier variable in a command, enclose the name of the variable in angle brackets—for example, <EMAILUSER>. To include an environment variable in a MAP command, precede the variable with a percent sign (%). Examples:

```
IF MEMBER OF MANAGERS THEN SET STATUS="SUPERIOR"
    ELSE SET STATUS="MORTAL"
END
MAP ROOT SYS:REPORTS\%STATUS
WRITE "DO YOU FEEL "; <STATUS>; " TODAY?"
```

SET_TIME (Synchronize Workstation Time to Server)

The SET_TIME ON command synchronizes workstation time with server time. This command is especially useful for network applications that use time stamps, such as e-mail and scheduling applications. Example:

```
SET_TIME ON
```

The synchronization only occurs when the login script runs. There is no automatic synchronization of workstation time unless the user logs in again.

(The better-known time synchronization feature of NetWare refers to server-to-server synchronization.)

SWAP (Move LOGIN Out of Conventional Memory)

The SWAP command transfers LOGIN out of conventional memory into higher memory, if available, or onto the hard drive. This allows execution of a # command and LOGIN at the same time. Example:

```
SWAP G:
```

Write (Display Text)

The WRITE command displays messages on the workstation as a user logs in. Example:

```
WRITE "Good day, %FULL_NAME"
```

Text strings can include the following special characters:

CHARACTERS	EFFECT AT WORKSTATION
\r	Carriage return
\n	New line
\"	Quotation mark
\7	Beep sound

Identifier Variables

As described earlier for the IF...THEN and SET login script commands, identifier variables can help you make the login script more personalized for the user and more flexible for you. When you put an identifier variable in a login script, the LOGIN utility replaces the variable with its current value when the user logs in.

For example, consider the following line:

```
IF MONTH_NAME="JANUARY" THEN WRITE "Cold, ain't it!"
```

Here LOGIN looks up the value of MONTH_NAME and compares it to JANUARY. When the test is True, LOGIN proceeds with the WRITE command.

Tables 7.1 through 7.6 list and describe login script identifier variables.

IDENTIFIER VARIABLES FOR THE DOS ENVIRONMENT You can return any DOS environment variable in angle brackets (for instance, <PATH>). To use a DOS environment variable in a MAP command, add a percent sign (%) in front of the variable. For example:

```
MAP S16:=%<PATH>
```

OBJECT PROPERTIES You can use property values of NDS objects as variables. Use the property values just as you do any other identifier variable. If the property value includes a space, enclose the name in quotation marks.

TABLE 7.1 Login Script Identifier Variables for Dates	IDENTIFIER VARIABLE	FUNCTION
	DAY	Day number (01–31)
	DAY_OF_WEEK	Day of week (example: Monday)
	MONTH	Month number (01–12)
	MONTH_NAME	Month name (example: January)
	NDAY_OF_WEEK	Number (1–7; 1=Sunday)
	SHORT_YEAR	Last two digits of year (example: 97)
	YEAR	All four digits of year (example: 1997)

TABLE 7.2 Login Script Identifier Variables for Time	IDENTIFIER VARIABLE	FUNCTION
	AM_PM	Day or night (A.M. or P.M.)
	GREETING_TIME	Time of day (morning, afternoon, or evening)
	HOUR	Hour (12-hour scale; 1–12)
	HOUR24	Hour (24-hour scale; 00–23; 00=midnight)
	MINUTE	Minute (00–59)
	SECOND	Second (00–59)

TABLE 7.3 Login Script Identifier Variables for Users	**IDENTIFIER VARIABLE**	**FUNCTION**
	CN	User's login name as it exists in the Directory.
	ALIAS_CONTEXT	Y if REQUESTER_CONTEXT is an Alias.
	FULL_NAME	User's FULL_NAME property; spaces are replaced with underscores.
	LAST_NAME	User's last name property (full login name in bindery-based NetWare).
	LOGIN_CONTEXT	User object's context.
	LOGIN_NAME	Login name truncated to 8 characters.
	MEMBER OF *Group*	True if the User is a member.
	NOT MEMBER OF *Group*	False if the User is a member.
	PASSWORD_EXPIRES	Number of days until password expires.
	REQUESTER_CONTEXT	Workstation's context when login started.
	USER_ID	Unique number assigned for UNIX clients.

TABLE 7.4 Login Script Identifier Variables for the Network	**IDENTIFIER VARIABLE**	**FUNCTION**
	FILE_SERVER	NetWare server name.
	NETWORK_ADDRESS	IPX external network number of the cabling segment (8-digit hexadecimal number).

TABLE 7.5 Login Script Identifier Variables for the Workstation	IDENTIFIER VARIABLE	FUNCTION
	MACHINE	Type of computer (e.g. IBM_PC).
	NETWARE_REQUESTER	Version of the VLM or NetWare Requester for OS/2.
	OS	Type of operating system on the workstation (example: MSDOS).
	OS_VERSION	Operating system version on the workstation (example: 6.22).
	P_STATION	Workstation's node number (12-digit hexadecimal).
	SHELL_TYPE	Version of the workstation's DOS shell (example: 1.01); supports NetWare 2 and 3 shells and NetWare 4 Requester for DOS.
	SMACHINE	Short machine name (example: IBM).
	STATION	Workstation's connection number.

TABLE 7.6 Miscellaneous Login Script Identifier Variables	IDENTIFIER VARIABLE	FUNCTION
	ACCESS_SERVER	Whether the access server is functional (True=functional, False=not functional).
	ERROR_LEVEL	Value of DOS ERROR LEVEL variable (0=no errors). Many external commands set a return code or "error level" when they finish. The value returned by such commands can be tested with the ERROR_LEVEL identifier variable.

To use a property name with a space in a WRITE statement, you must place it at the end of the quoted string:

```
WRITE "Howdy, %GIVEN_NAME"
IF "%MESSAGE SERVER"="MS1" THEN MAP INS
  S16:=MS1\SYS:EMAIL
```

Many properties of the User object can be used as identifier variables in login scripts. The most useful are as follows:

ACCOUNT BALANCE	INCORRECT LOGIN ATTEMPTS
CITY	LAST NAME
DATE PASSWORD EXPIRES	LOCATION
DEFAULT SERVER	LOCKED BY INTRUDER
OU	LOGIN TIME
DESCRIPTION	NETWORK ADDRESS
FULL NAME	TITLE

USING IDENTIFIER VARIABLES Identifier variables are most useful with IF...THEN constructs and MAP or WRITE commands. Remember to enclose DOS environment variables in angle brackets. If you use an identifier variable in a WRITE statement, remember to use all uppercase letters and precede it with a percent sign.

In the following example, if User ALassen logs in during the afternoon, the first line will display, "Good morning, Lassen." The next line will display "My workstation's language is ENGLISH."

```
WRITE "Good %GREETING_TIME, %LAST_NAME"
WRITE "My workstation's language is %NWLANGUAGE."
```

Managing Applications with NAL

NETWARE 4.11 GIVES YOU the power to present Windows applications to users automatically, employing a program called NetWare Application Launcher (NAL). As of this writing, NAL works on Windows, Windows 95, and Windows NT. It can present DOS, Windows, and Windows 95 applications.

To a user, NAL works like this:

1. The user logs in and starts Windows.

2. NAL opens up its own window and presents the applications you have made available, as shown in Figure 7.7.

FIGURE 7.7
When you put NAL in the Startup group, it presents the applications to the user when Windows starts.

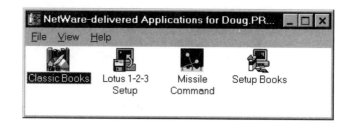

3. The user can double-click on a NAL application to run it.

Before we cover the advantages and disadvantages of NAL, you should have an idea of how to make it work.

1. You do a one-time setup of NAL.

2. You set up the applications you want to run from the server. For instance, to set up the Lotus 1-2-3 installation, you run the installation program from your workstation, which copies disk images to a directory on the server.

3. You create an Application object. This is a new Directory object that represents your application, such as the 1-2-3 installation program.

4. You select the User, Group, or container objects you want to offer the application.

Now, whenever the user runs NAL, the applications you have made available are presented in the NAL window. You can always add, delete, or change the applications from your workstation.

Benefits and Drawbacks of NAL

NAL gives you the following benefits:

- *Control.* You decide which applications to present and specify the users they are presented to. Only you—and not the users—can add, change, or delete the applications presented.

- *Automation.* Suppose you wanted to distribute the 1-2-3 application. You could set it up on the network *without* NAL, but it would never get presented to the users. You would have to train the users on running the setup application. NAL, however, presents the application conveniently right there in front of the user, displaying the name and icon you select. Or you can make it even simpler and have the application run automatically, without any intervention from the user.

- *Maintenance.* Suppose you want to move the application to a different volume. All you do is copy it over to the new volume and change the pointer on the Application object. The change causes no disruption to the users whatsoever. An added benefit is that you can use NetWare Administrator, your familiar standby, to manage applications.

- *Portability.* If a user logs in from another workstation, NAL provides the network applications that are set up for that user. Without NAL, each workstation has its own unique environment, independent of the user.

In addition, NAL can obviate the need for login scripts. You can arrange the system so that whenever a user runs an NAL application, any drive mappings or printer captures are made either temporarily (for that application only) or permanently.

Using NAL does have its drawbacks:

- *Limited to NDS Only.* Since NAL uses Directory objects, support for bindery attachments doesn't exist. All users must use an NDS client (VLM or Client 32).

- *Complexity.* Getting applications to work over the network is hard enough. Figuring out which drive mappings and environment variables are required by NAL may cause you premature graying.

- *Setup.* It takes some time to set up NAL. You need to use a "snap-in" application with NetWare Administrator, add NAL to the Startup groups at each workstation, delete the local versions of the applications at each workstation, and then create and maintain the Application objects. It's probably not worth the trouble for only one application.

If you're accustomed to login scripts, you may be inclined to avoid NAL altogether. Looking ahead, however, I think NAL will be the application management tool of choice for administrators. Its integration with both NDS and Windows makes it a significant automation tool.

Setting Up NAL

There are two phases to using NAL. First, you need to accomplish the one-time setup tasks. These include arranging the NAL files and updating NetWare Administrator and the Directory schema.

In the second phase, you set up each application, including getting it to run on the network, deciding who gets to run it, and creating the Application icon.

Setting Up NAL the First Time

Use the following procedure to set up NAL the first time. NetWare 4.11 administrators can skip the first five steps and begin with Step 6.

1. If you have NetWare 4.10, pick a directory to hold the NAL application and the NetWare Administrator snap-in application. (NetWare 4.11 already has the NAL application files set up for you.)

   Since this directory must be available to all users, a good choice is SYS:PUBLIC or a subdirectory thereof; for example, you might set up the subdirectory SYS:\PUBLIC\NETAPPS.

2. Copy the NAL files and NetWare Administrator snap-ins to the directory you created in Step 1. (These files can be downloaded from Novell's Web site.)

   Following are the NAL files required at the time of this writing:

APPSNAP.DLL	CLNWIN16.DLL	NAL.EXE
APPRES16.DLL	CLNWIN32.DLL	NALW95.EXE
NALBMP.DLL	CLXWIN16.DLL	NALW31.EXE
NALBMP32.DLL	CLXWIN32.DLL	ADDICON.EXE
NALRES.DLL	LOCWIN16.DLL	APPSNAP.GID
NALRES32.DLL	LOCWIN32.DLL	APPSNAP.HLP
NETWIN32.DLL	NCPWIN16.DLL	NAL.HLP
AUDWIN32.DLL	NCPWIN32.DLL	ADDICON.MSG
CALWIN16.DLL	NETWIN16.DLL	
CALWIN32.DLL	AUDWIN16.DLL	

3. Flag application and message files as Read Only (RO) and Shareable (SH), so that all users can access them at the same time.

It's a good idea to flag all network applications Read Only and Shareable. For instance, from the SYS:\ directory, you could type the following lines:

```
FLAG *.EXE RO SH /S/C
FLAG *.DLL RO SH /S/C
FLAG *.MSG RO SH /S/C
```

4. On the workstations from which you run NetWare Administrator, edit NWADMIN.INI in the Windows directory. Add lines pointing to the APPSNAP.DLL file. The proper syntax, using the directory you created in Step 1, is as follows:

```
[Snapin Object DLLs]
SNAPIN1 = \\Server1\SYS\PUBLIC\APPSNAP.DLL
```

5. Run NetWare Administrator from the workstation you updated in Step 4. You are prompted to modify the schema. Click Yes to confirm. If successful, you'll see a window acknowledging the schema change.

If the schema change didn't work, make sure you have updated to the latest version of NDS and that you have Supervisor object right at the [Root] of the Directory tree.

6. For both NetWare 4.10 and 4.11, the next step is to test and troubleshoot the NAL.EXE application from a Windows and a Windows 95 workstation.

7. Go to each Windows (including Windows 95) workstation and place the NAL.EXE program in the Startup group.

With the one-time setup of NAL completed, you can proceed to setting up each application.

Application Setup for NAL

NAL assembles a set of application icons from objects and properties in the Directory. First NAL examines the logged-in User object for any Application objects associated with that User. Then NAL looks at every Group object in which the User is a member, and incorporates any Application objects associated with that Group. Finally, NAL examines the container objects for the User.

You can specify the number of generations of parent (and grandparent) containers to be checked. Applications assigned to those containers are added, as well, to the set of icons presented to the User.

Duplicate applications are eliminated. Also, Windows 95 applications are eliminated from Windows 3.x users.

Important Guidelines for Application Setup

As you work through the steps of setting up applications for users under NAL, keep the following in mind.

DRIVE MAPPINGS FOR APPLICATIONS You can map drives dynamically with each application provided to users. But you'll want to be careful with drive mappings. If you create one of these "dynamic" drive mappings and the drive letter is already taken, the user will get an error. (Actually, the dynamic mapping will succeed if it maps the drive to where it's already mapped.)

The user can also manually map the needed drive and launch the application.

You'll find application management works best when you keep a master list of drive mappings. If you have seven networked applications, make sure you always assign seven different drive letters, in case a user tries to use both at the same time.

MAKING INI FILES AND REGISTRY SETTINGS Most Windows applications use INI files and/or Registry settings. Using an NAL pre-launch script, you can make these settings each time the application runs. You can also tear down these settings with a post-termination script.

DESIGNATING UNC PATHS NetWare supports the use of Universal Naming Convention (UNC) names in dialog boxes. In UNC names, a network resource such as a print queue or file is identified using backslashes (\\). Here are a couple of examples of valid UNC paths:

\\SERVER2\SYS\APPS\SOLITAIRE\SOL.EXE\.

\\SERVER1\PQUEUE\

TIMED REFRESH SETTING The Timed Refresh setting determines whether additions or deletions of applications available to a user will or will not be made while the application launcher is open.

The default setting for Timed Refresh is Off, because frequent refreshes of large numbers of users can adversely impact network traffic. If you have a small network with under 50 users, you can set Timed Refresh to On.

Network Application Setup Procedure

The process of adding an application to a user's application launcher consists of only two steps: Create an Application object and specify its properties, and then associate the Application object with a User, Group, or container object.

CREATING APPLICATION OBJECTS

Before beginning this process, make sure you have completed the one-time NAL setup procedure.

1. Start NetWare Administrator.

2. Select Object | Create.

3. From the object list, choose Application (DOS), Application (Windows 3.x), Application (Windows 95), or Application (Windows NT). Figure 7.8 shows the available Application object types. Click OK to confirm.

   Note that the Application object classes refer to the type of application, not to the type of workstation. For instance, choose Application (DOS) for a DOS application such as FILER, even if it will be run on Windows 3.*x* and Windows 95 workstations.

4. Give the Application object a name.

5. Specify the path of the application, using the Browse button to select the application file.

6. Click on the Define Additional Properties check box.

7. Select Create. The Identification page is displayed.

8. Use the properties pages as necessary for this application. You may want to edit some of the properties listed in Table 7.7.

FIGURE 7.8
Choose from four
object classes for the
Application object

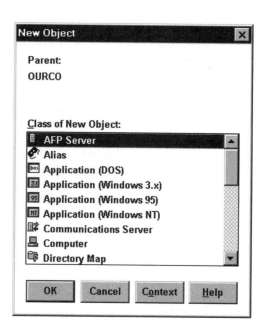

TABLE 7.7
Application Object
Properties

PROPERTY	DESCRIPTION
Application Icon Title	Title that will be displayed in the Application Launcher.
Command Line Parameters	Parameters specified at application startup. For instance, you can specify /d-C:\TEMP with WordPerfect 6.1 for Windows to direct temporary files.
Working Directory	Many Windows applications require a working directory. Use the Browse button to construct the proper UNC name.
Run Minimized	Check this to run the application minimized.
Clean Up Network Resources	Default setting is on, because Normally you'll want the command line parameters and other settings eliminated after the application closes. However, if the application is a "wrapper" and actually calls another application, turn this setting off so the resources are available to the next application.

	PROPERTY	DESCRIPTION
T A B L E 7.7 (continued) Application Object Properties	Drives to be Mapped	Maps specific drives for the application, if necessary. Make sure these don't conflict with other drive mappings in login scripts.
	Ports to be Captured	Captures specific printer ports for the application, if necessary. Make sure these don't conflict with other CAPTURE statements in login scripts.
	Description	This field does not affect the running of the application. However, a user can view this field for information about the application.
	Script to Run Before Launching	These are commands you want to run before the application starts.
	Script to Run After Termination	These are commands you want to run after the application ends.
	Contacts	These are contacts available to users of the application. The phone numbers and e-mail names are retrieved from the properties of the User you select.
	Associations	With this page, you can associate the Application object with Users, Groups, or Containers. If you do so, you can skip the procedure in the upcoming section.

ASSOCIATING THE APPLICATION

If you add objects to the Application's Associations page (see "Associations" in Table 7.7), you have already associated the Application. If not, you can associate the Application with User, Group, and/or container objects using the following procedure.

1. Start NetWare Administrator.

2. Select the container, Group, or User object with which you want to associate the Application object.

3. Choose the Applications page. You'll see two lists of applications: "Launched by user" and "Launched automatically."

To run "Launched by user" applications, the user must double-click the application icon. This list will already include any application you associated with the User via the application's Associations property. Applications in "Launched automatically" are launched when the NAL.EXE file is executed at the users' workstations.

4. Using the Add button, select Application objects to add to the appropriate list.

5. Select the Launcher Configuration page, and use Help to decide whether to accept the default option.

6. Click on OK to save changes to the object.

Some NAL Strategies and Examples

With a little imagination, you can think of a way for NAL to solve most of your workstation management issues. Here are a couple of examples.

Eliminating Login Scripts

Suppose you don't want to use login scripts, but you need to make sure each user can access e-mail and scheduling software (GroupWise). You can create an application for GroupWise that runs automatically when NAL starts. That first Application can also designate the drive mappings to shared directories and CAPTURE to the network printers.

You start by creating the Application (Windows 3.*x*) object. The Create Application dialog then appears, as shown in Figure 7.9.

Figure 7.10 shows the GroupWise Environment page. Notice that the /PO parameter is supplied here, as it would be if you created a Program Item for the application. (/PO points to the post office location.)

Also notice that the Clean Up Network Resources box is not checked, since you want the drive mappings and printer ports to remain after the application runs. This gives the Application similar capabilities to a login script.

Figure 7.11 shows the Drives/Ports page. Since this Application object will be used automatically, the drive mappings and printer ports are designated for the entire network session. Note that you can't capture to the home directories using the %LOGIN_NAME variable.

In Figure 7.12 you see the container object's Applications page. GroupWise runs automatically, while the network application WP is available to the users.

FIGURE 7.9
The Create Application
dialog gives the name
and path to the
GroupWise application.

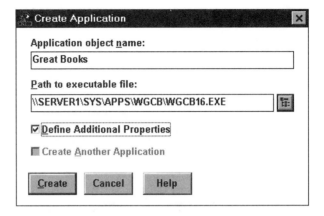

Create Application

Application object **name:**

Great Books

Path to executable file:

\\SERVER1\SYS\APPS\WGCB\WGCB16.EXE

☑ **Define Additional Properties**

☐ Create **Another** Application

Create   **Cancel**   **Help**

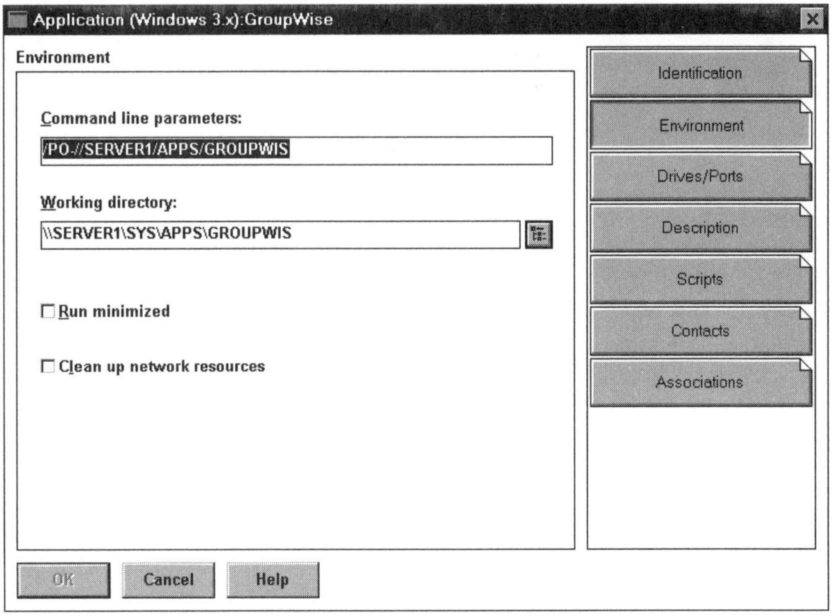

FIGURE 7.10
The Environment page
sets up the post office
location (/PO) and
working directory for
GroupWise.

Application (Windows 3.x):GroupWise

Environment

Command line parameters:

/PO-//SERVER1/APPS/GROUPWIS

Working directory:

\\SERVER1\SYS\APPS\GROUPWIS

☐ **Run minimized**

☐ **Clean up network resources**

Identification

Environment

Drives/Ports

Description

Scripts

Contacts

Associations

OK   Cancel   Help

FIGURE 7.11
The Drives/Ports page
establishes drive
mappings and printer
ports for the user's
entire network session.

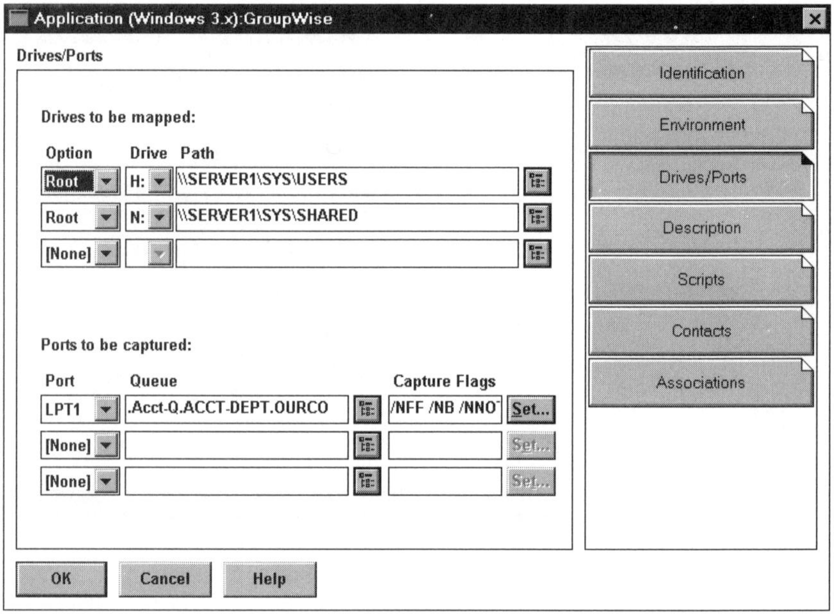

FIGURE 7.12
The Applications page
of a container object
shows which applications
are automatic and
which ones are available
to the users.

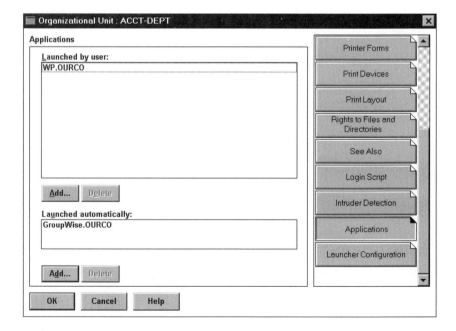

AUTOMATICALLY STARTING NETWARE CLIENT 32 FOR WINDOWS 95 INSTALLATION Suppose you want your users to install NetWare Client 32 when they log in. First, you create an image of Client 32 on a network server. Then follow these steps:

1. Using NetWare Administrator, create an Application (Windows 95) object.

2. Name the Application object and set the path to the executable file for Client 32's SETUP.EXE. For instance:

   \\SERVER1\PUBLIC\CLIENT32\WIN95\SETUP.EXE

3. (Optional) Enter other properties, such as contact information.

4. Select the container object whose users you want to upgrade.

5. Add the new Application object to the Applications page on the Launched Automatically list.

Summary

AUTOMATION MEANS USERS don't have to know much about the network; things just happen for them, thanks to your behind-the-scenes work. Your users can concentrate on their own jobs.

Novell has provided two impressive tools for automation: login scripts and NetWare Application Launcher (NAL). Login scripts give you diverse capabilities. You can set up User, Profile, and/or container login scripts, each altering the environment seen by the user at login.

Considering the interplay of these three levels of login scripts (along with the additional "default" login script), you'd do best to simplify. I recommend using only container and, if necessary, Profile login scripts.

Login script commands can accomplish the following and more:

- Run external commands, such as CAPTURE

- Display a text file or formatted word-processor file

- Control drive mappings (including search drive)

- Run commands conditionally, using a wide array of variables

- Include other login scripts

NAL opens a new world of automation for your Windows users. After a one-time setup, you can create Application objects and control their presentation to users. If you want, you can even eliminate login scripts for Windows users.

Setting Up Printing

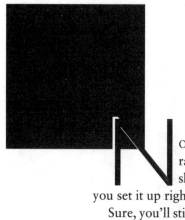

OTICE THAT THIS CHAPTER is entitled "Setting Up Printing" rather than "Managing Printing." There's a reason for that: You shouldn't have to do any managing of printing to speak of, if you set it up right. It pretty much manages itself.

Sure, you'll still have the jobs of clearing jammed printers, calling the printer repairperson, and managing the Print Queue. But these tasks can be handled by a print operator who's not so proficient in NetWare (and who probably isn't as busy) as you.

This chapter covers the "theory" of NetWare printing, a short discussion on planning your printing operations, procedures for setting them up, and maintenance.

How NetWare Printing Works

HE NETWARE PRINTING PROCESS INCLUDES the following steps:

1. Capturing a print stream

2. Queuing a print job

3. Servicing the print job

4. Driving the printer port

NDS uses Directory objects called a Print Queue for queuing, a Print Server for servicing, and a Printer for driving the printer port.

Figure 8.1 illustrates the printing process described in the following paragraphs.

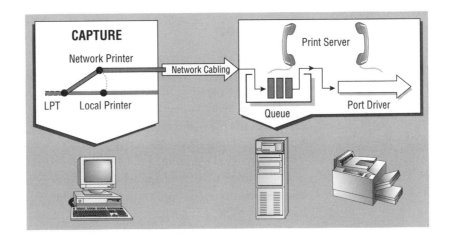

FIGURE 8.1
This simplified view of the network printing operation shows the capture, queue, and port driver functions.

Step 1: Capturing a Print Stream

The capturing of a print stream occurs at the workstation. Primarily, it involves converting a print stream into packets that can travel over the network and sending those packets to the network adapter.

Since the beginning of NetWare printing, applications have printed to the local printer port (LPT1 or LPT2). The workstation was then required to load CAPTURE.EXE to snatch print jobs directed to that port. The CAPTURE command still works today, and may be executed from the DOS command line, from a batch file, or from a login script. For workstations running Windows, you can capture printer ports using the User Tools. For Windows 95 and Macintosh workstations, the NetWare client uses a more "native" approach. That is, applications do not send data to an LPT port, which is then intercepted; instead, they send the print stream directly to a native (Windows 95 or Macintosh) printer device, which may be a network print queue.

Regardless of the workstation type, the capturing process works the same: Print streams are broken into packets and sent out the network adapter to the desired print queue.

Step 2: Queuing a Print Job

Print queues are special directories on a NetWare server's file system. Print Queue objects represent the actual queue directories for management purposes.

A NetWare server with a print queue receives packets comprising a print stream over its network adapter. The server reassembles the packets into a file and places the file in the print queue directory. The programmers who designed NetWare printing would not put it so simply, but really that's the essence of it. The print stream comes in, and—plunk—it drops into the queue.

Queue users are those users who have NDS rights to send jobs to the queue. You can make User, Group, and container objects queue users. A *queue operator* has special rights to manage the queue, including the power to rearrange jobs that haven't yet been printed.

Queues are associated with Printer objects and Print Server objects. The Printer object represents the port driver that will accept jobs from the queue. For example, if the NetWare server has a local printer attached and runs NPRINTER to drive its port, the queue may be associated with that port driver (and therefore the local printer).

A Print Queue may be associated with more than one Printer object, but the normal arrangement is one Printer per Print Queue. The Print Server object that is associated with a queue is the program that monitors both the Printer and the Print Queue. The Print Server feeds the print jobs to the Printer.

Step 3: Servicing the Print Job

The Print Server represents a service, not a physical object. The service may be provided by a NetWare server, a PC board in a network-ready printer, or a third-party network device. The service works like an expediter who is constantly on the phone with the Print Queue and the Printer. "Hello, Printer? You ready for a print stream yet? Coming right up! Hello, Print Queue? I'm sending Amy's print stream to the Printer. Hey Printer, you ready for another job yet?"

The Print Server may actually be PSERVER.NLM loaded on a NetWare server or a firmware program inside an HP JetDirect print server (or similar third-party device). One Print Server can handle all the print queues in a small network, with very little processing load on the NetWare server. Since you associate Print Queues with Printers, the Print Server knows what to do with each print job in each of its queues.

Step 4: Driving the Printer Port

A port driver is the interface software that resides on a printer's host device. It relays the printer's status to the Print Server and interrupts the host device to transfer the print stream to the printer port. The nature of this software depends on the host.

- If the network printer is attached to the NetWare server, the port driver is NPRINTER.NLM, which you load at the server console.

- If the network printer is attached to a DOS/Windows or OS/2 workstation, the port driver is NPRINTER.EXE, which you load from a batch file or at the DOS prompt.

- If the network printer is attached to a Windows 95 workstation, the workstation runs NPTWIN95.EXE as its port driver.

- If the printer is "network ready," it has a built-in port driver.

Printer objects represent port drivers in NDS. A printer can be local or remote, depending on its relationship with the print server. If the port driver and Print Server reside on the same computer, the port driver is local. If the port driver resides on a workstation or network device apart from the Print Server, it is a remote Printer.

Planning Your Printing Operation

N PLANNING A PRINTING SYSTEM, your first objective is to satisfy the customers—your fellow employees—by locating the printers where they'll be most convenient and least bothersome.

Consider the disadvantages of sitting next to a printer. The noise, the traffic—would you want everybody in the company tracking by *your* cubicle to get their printouts? When would you play Solitaire!? The worst neighborhood in the company will predictably be next to the printer.

Figure 8.2 shows some of the options for connecting printers to the network.

Network-ready printers offer you the most versatility because you can put them wherever you have an open connection to the network. If you have a printer

FIGURE 8.2
There are many ways
to share printers
on the network.

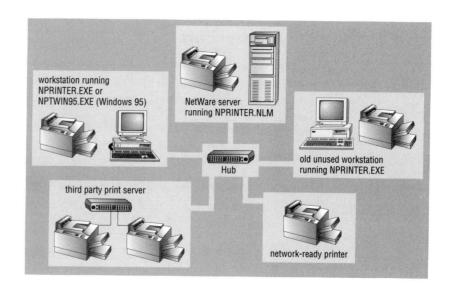

you are happy with but it's not network-ready, there may be an add-on network card you can buy for it. If not, you can always get a third-party print server.

If you buy a third-party print server or a network card for your printer, make sure it supports NDS. Older models don't.

Do you have an old 386SX-20 computer around that's just taking up space? You can easily load NPRINTER.EXE on it and use it as a port driver, connecting printers to the computer's parallel and serial ports.

You can add printers to the server's parallel and serial ports. The advantage of this arrangement is that the network traffic of print jobs from the queue to remote printers is eliminated. This solution is inexpensive, as well, because you don't need to occupy a workstation with a network printer or buy a third-party print server. The disadvantage of this arrangement is having your server out in the open, making it susceptible to both malicious and innocent harm.

Another option is to make a printer that is cabled to a workstation into a network printer. This option is inexpensive, since no third-party equipment is required. But consider the disadvantages:

- The workstation user will be bothered by the noise of a constantly running printer and the foot traffic of everyone who uses it.

- If an application on the workstation hangs or the user shuts off the workstation, the printer also stops.

- The workstation's performance may suffer from the memory or processing cycles needed to run NPRINTER.EXE, the port driver for the printer.

The best solution I've seen for a small company is to have a centrally located printer room, with a third-party print server or an old workstation driving the printers. You can keep all your printing supplies in that room, as well, and install a spring-loaded door to keep the noise inside. Large companies may be able to use several printing rooms.

Setting Up Network Printing

PRINTING SETUP CAN BE PRETTY EASY if you use Novell's automated Quick Setup option in PCONSOLE.EXE. Or it can be fairly easy even if you don't. Whether the setup process is automated or not, the following steps are involved:

1. Create Print Queue objects.

2. Create Print Server objects.

3. Load print server and port driver software.

4. Enable printing from workstations.

First, we'll cover the Quick Setup way of setting up a printing environment, and then we'll do it the manual way. Last, we'll walk through the process of setting up printing using Hewlett-Packard JetDirect print servers.

Quick Setup

NetWare has an easy way to create and associate the printing objects, called Quick Setup. After running Quick Setup, you only need to load the Print Server and port driver and then enable printing from the workstations.

Create and Associate the Objects

To run Novell's Quick Setup, follow these steps:

1. Log in as Admin (or the equivalent).

2. Change context to the Organization object. From the DOS prompt, type (for example) **CX .OURCO.**

3. Start PCONSOLE from the DOS prompt.

4. Select Quick Setup. You are presented with a complete setup on one screen, including the new print server, printer, and print queue names (Figure 8.3).

5. Edit the Quick Setup screen to customize it to your environment. For example:

- Change the names of the Print Server, Printer, and Print Queue objects, if desired. If you will have multiple print queues, you can choose appropriate names for the Print Queue and Printer instead of accepting "P1" and "Q1."

- If you have already created a Print Server, select it rather than creating a new one. Highlight the Print Server and press Enter to specify the existing Print Server.

FIGURE 8.3
The Quick Setup option of PCONSOLE presents the whole setup in one screen.

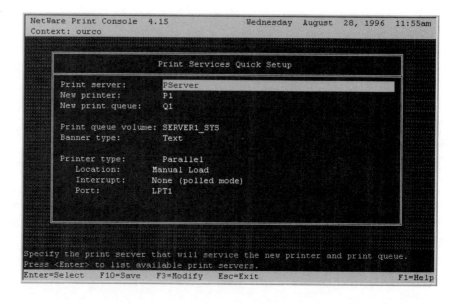

- Change the Print Queue volume if desired. You can use any read/write volume (no CD-ROM volumes) on any server. Highlight the volume, press Enter, and then press Ins to select from a list of volumes.

- Change the banner type if desired; text and PostScript are the options. If you want PostScript, make sure your printer supports the PostScript language.

- Change the printer type if desired. This is the type of port that the printer is attached to, generally parallel or serial. For third-party print servers, select Other/Unknown.

- Change the location, if desired. Auto Load means the printer is attached to the NetWare server. In this mode, the Print Server automatically loads the port driver (NPRINTER.NLM). Manual Load means the printer is not attached to the NetWare server and you'll need to manually load a port driver somewhere.

- Select polled mode or an interrupt. If you don't know which to select, try polled mode first. This avoids interrupt conflicts and normally provides good performance. If polled mode gives slow printing, try interrupt mode. The normal interrupts for printer ports are as follows:

LPT1 :	Interrupt 7
LPT2 :	Interrupt 5
COM1:	Interrupt 4
COM2:	Interrupt 3

- Select the printer port. If you specified a serial port, specify the settings supported by the COM port you select.

6. Press Esc and select Yes to save the customized configuration.

Load the Print Server and Port Driver

Here are the steps to load the Print Server and Port Driver:

1. To load the print server, go the server console and type the following command, replacing PS1 with the Print Server name you specified with Quick Setup: **LOAD PSERVER PS1** and press Enter.

2. Add the LOAD command to the AUTOEXEC.NCF file to load the printer server every time you boot the server. To edit the file, type **LOAD EDIT AUTOEXEC.NCF** and press Enter.

Now, for the port driver. If the printer is connected to the server and you specified Auto Load in the Location field during Quick Setup, the port driver (NPRINTER.NLM) loads automatically. If you specified Manual Load, you need to load a port driver at the computer that has the printer physically attached.

3. If you attached the printer to a DOS or Windows 3.1 workstation, go to that computer. In whatever batch file runs LOGIN, add **NPRINTER P1** after LOGIN. If your Printer is not named P1, specify the correct name you gave the printer in Quick Setup.

4. If you attached the printer to a Windows 95 workstation, put NPTW95.EXE in that workstation's Startup group.

5. Restart the Windows 95 workstation and, when prompted, select the Printer you created with Quick Setup (default: P1).

6. You may need to restart the Print Server after loading the remote port driver(s). If so:

   A. At the server console, type **UNLOAD PSERVER PS1** (where PS1 is the name you specified) and press Enter.

   B. Type **LOAD PSERVER PS1** (where PS1 is the name you specified) and press Enter to restart the Print Server.

Enable Printing from Workstations

You'll need to put a #CAPTURE command in the login script for each container that has Users. You can capture to a Print Queue or Printer object. Example:

```
#CAPTURE Q=Q1 NB NFF TI=2
```

Table 8.1 describes CAPTURE's most useful parameters. If you're not sure which to use, start with NB, NFF, and TI=2. Then try other parameters as necessary for your printing environment.

TABLE 8.1
CAPTURE's Most
Useful Parameters

PARAMETER	EXAMPLE	MEANING
LPT port	L=<1–10>	Declares which printer port is to be routed to the printer.
No Banner	NB	A banner is (usually) a wasted sheet of paper declaring who sent the print job.
Queue	Q=<queue name>	Name of the Print Queue or Alias. If the Print Queue is not in the workstation's current context, you should make an Alias in the current context and use it.
Printer	P=<printer name>	Name of the Printer or Alias. If the Printer is not in the workstation's current context, you should make an Alias in the current context and use it.
Tabs	T=<1–18>	Don't use tabs if you have a laser or ink-jet printer.
No Tabs	NT	Default; works best for most printers.
Timeout	TI=<0–1000>	Specifying a timeout is necessary for most laser printers.
Form Feed	FF	Adds a form feed at the end of a print job. Not necessary for most print jobs.
No Form Feed	NFF	Prevents the wasting of paper by letting the application specify form feeds at the end of print jobs.
Autoendcap	(AU)	Ends capturing when an application closes.
No Autoendcap	(NA)	Retains capturing when an application closes.
Notify	(NOTI)	Sends a message to the user when a print job is finished.
No Notify	(NNOTI)	Disables user notification of finished print jobs.

Windows 95 users need to configure network printing from the workstation. To do so from the Start menu, choose Settings and then Printers. Choose Add Printer, and follow the instructions to add a network printer.

Manual Setup

The difference between Quick Setup and manual setup is in how you create and associate the Printer, Print Queue, and Print Server objects. Loading the Print Server and port driver, as well as enabling printing from the workstations, are done in exactly the same way as for Quick Setup.

Following are the steps for manually setting up printing with NetWare Administrator:

1. Using NetWare Administrator, select the Organization object that represents your company.

2. Select Object | Create and choose Print Queue. Click on OK.

3. Save the Print Queue a name and select a volume using the Browse button.

4. Click on the Create button.

5. With the Organization object still highlighted, select Object | Create and choose Printer. Click on OK.

6. Give the Printer a name and select Assign Additional Properties.

7. Click on the Create button.

8. Select the Assignments page, click the Add button, and select the Print Queue you created.

9. Select the Configuration page, and specify the printer type (usually parallel or serial).

10. Click on the Communication button. Fill in the parameters appropriate for the port. Select Auto Load for printers attached to the NetWare server running PSERVER, and select Manual Load for other printers.

11. Click on OK twice to save the settings.

12. With the Organization object still highlighted, select Object | Create and choose Print Server.

13. Give the Print Server a name and select Define Additional Properties.

14. Click on the Create button.

15. Select the Assignments page, click the Add button, and select the Printer you created.

16. Click on OK.

Now you can start the Print Server and port driver as described in the "Quick Setup" section of this chapter.

HP JetDirect Setup

The following procedure applies to Hewlett-Packard JetDirect Print Server cards that support NDS. If you're not sure whether your JetDirect card supports NDS, check the card's firmware version. It must be at least A.03.14, B.03.14, C.03.14, or D.04.06 (D.04.20 EX+3).

1. Install the JetAdmin software (available from Hewlett-Packard). You should use the latest version of JetAdmin; only versions A.01.08 and later support NDS.

2. Using the Quick Setup procedure and PCONSOLE, create new Print Server, Printer, and Print Queue objects. Make sure the Printer type is "Other/Unknown."

3. Start JetAdmin.

4. Select the + next to the Printer object you created in Step 1.

5. Highlight the LAN Hardware Address and choose Configure.

6. In the Name field, type in the name of the Print Server object you created in step 1. Choose Next.

7. Verify that the Operating Mode is Queue Server. Choose Next.

8. Choose Next again to skip bindery queues, which are not used for printing in NDS.

9. Choose Next again, skipping the Default Printer Driver setup.

10. If desired, select objects to be notified if there is a printing problem. Choose Next.

11. Select your Directory tree.

12. In the Print Server NDS Context field, type in the context where you created the printing objects. Normally this means the Organization object. Choose Next.

13. If desired, set a password. Choose Finish.

14. When prompted, confirm Yes to save the configuration.

15. Test the setup by highlighting the JP JetDirect card, choosing Printer, and then Self-Test Page.

Print Queue Operator Tasks

YOU'LL PROBABLY WANT TO DESIGNATE someone besides yourself as queue operator. It makes sense that users consistently take their print queuing problems to the same person who clears jammed printers and fills the printers with paper and toner. Here are the steps to assign a queue operator:

1. In NetWare Administrator, select the Print Queue object.

2. Select Object | Details.

3. Select the Operator page and click on the Add button.

4. Select the User object for the new queue operator, and click on OK.

The operator now has the power to perform the task of managing the Print Queue, which includes the jobs listed in Table 8.2.

You'll need to make sure the queue operator knows how to start NetWare Administrator or PCONSOLE.

Table 8.3 gives the procedures for performing common tasks. If the queue operator uses NetWare Administrator, it is assumed that the operator has selected the Print Queue object and its Details dialog. In PCONSOLE, it is assumed that the operator has selected Print Queues and the specific queue being managed.

TABLE 8.2 Print Queue Operator Tasks	**TASK**	**EXPLANATION**
	When problems occur, stop users from repeatedly submitting print jobs	What is the first thing users do when a document fails to print? You guessed it—they send it again. So if there's any glitch in the printing process, the Print Queue tends to fill up with repeated print jobs. When this happens, the operator's first duty is to disable the queue from accepting print jobs.
	Delete jobs from the queue	The second job of an operator when a queue fills up is to delete the repeated print jobs sent by impatient users.
	Put print jobs on hold or reactivate jobs on hold	An operator may need to put a job on hold to change the paper to letterhead, or to realign ink jet cartridges.
	Schedule print jobs for later printing	Sometimes it's more efficient to save the really big print jobs for a time when nobody's around. The operator can schedule print jobs as needed.

Summary

P RINTING—IT'S THE NETWORK FUNCTION that's second only to file storage in importance, and Novell provides a simple yet elegant solution. You connect the printers where you want them. Then create, associate, and manage three objects in the Directory: the Print Queue, the Printer, and the Print Server.

If you have an HP JetDirect print server card, you should set up the JetAdmin software to configure and manage the card. Once you're finished, all that's left to do is manage the Print Queues.

TASK	PCONSOLE	NETWARE ADMINISTRATOR
When problems occur, stop users from repeatedly submitting print jobs.	Select Status, then Allow Users to Submit Print Jobs. Type **N.**	Click on (uncheck) the Allow Users to Submit Print Jobs check box. Click on OK.
Delete jobs from the queue.	Select Print Jobs. Select the job to be deleted, and press Del.	Select the Job List page. Select the Print Job and click on the Delete button.
Put print jobs on hold or reactivate jobs on hold.	Select Print Jobs. Select the job to be put on hold and press Enter. Highlight Operator Hold and press **Y.** Press **N** to reactivate print job.	Select the Job List page. Select the print job and click on the Hold Job button, then click on it again to reactivate the print job.
Schedule print jobs for later printing.	Select Print Jobs. Select the job to be deferred and press Enter. Highlight Defer Printing and press **Y.** Specify a time and date.	Select the Job List page. Select the Print Job and click on the Job Details button. Click on Defer Printing. Schedule a date and time.

Monitoring and Improving Server Operations

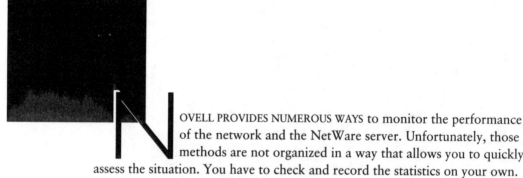

OVELL PROVIDES NUMEROUS WAYS to monitor the performance of the network and the NetWare server. Unfortunately, those methods are not organized in a way that allows you to quickly assess the situation. You have to check and record the statistics on your own. This chapter is organized into three sections:

- *General Server Maintenance:* Log files, early warnings, abend recovery options, alerts, and server settings.

- *Using Statistics to Monitor Basic NetWare Functions:* Disk errors, file system performance, and LAN performance.

- *Using Detailed Statistics:* Network protocol statistics, LAN driver statistics, and multiprocessor statistics.

General Server Maintenance
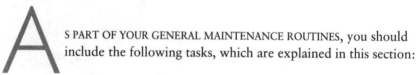

S PART OF YOUR GENERAL MAINTENANCE ROUTINES, you should include the following tasks, which are explained in this section:

- Manage and view the error log files, including the system error log (SYS$LOG.ERR), volume error logs (VOL$LOG.ERR), and TTS error log (TTS$LOG.ERR).

- Select the types of error messages you want displayed on the server console.

- Decide on the point at which you want the server to generate early warning alerts for low cache buffers and low volume space.

- Determine how you want the server to respond to abends.

This section also includes instructions for using MONITOR and SERVMAN, the utilities that help you set server parameters at the server console.

Setting Server Parameters Using MONITOR (NetWare 4.11 Only)

Although the MONITOR utility comes with all NetWare 4 versions, only the NetWare 4.11 version allows you to change server parameters. To set server parameters using the MONITOR utility, perform the following steps:

1. At the server console, type **LOAD MONITOR** and press Enter.

2. Highlight the Server Parameters option and press Enter.

3. Select the category of parameters you want to modify.

4. To change a parameter, move the cursor to the one you want to change and press Enter. Context-sensitive help is displayed in a window beneath your selection.

5. Supply the desired value and press Enter.

A sample MONITOR screen is shown in Figure 9.1. Table 9.1 gives an explanation of the General Information segment of the screen, and Table 9.2 describes the available options.

FIGURE 9.1
MONITOR's General Information screen tells you about your server's health and stress levels.

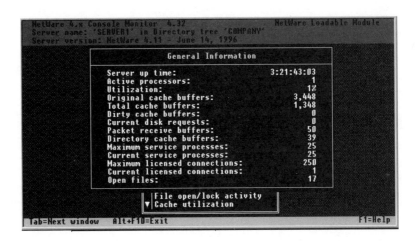

TABLE 9.1 Statistics on the Main MONITOR Screen	STATISTIC	EXPLANATION
	Server name	Server's name and Directory tree name.
	Server version	Version and release date of SERVER.EXE.
	Server up time	Length of time the server has been running since it was last booted.
	Active processors	Number of enabled processors on the motherboard.
	Utilization	On a single-processor server, the percentage of CPU cycles used in doing the server's work. This number is inversely related to the percentage spent in the idle loop process.
		On a multiprocessor server, the average utilization of all active processors. For utilization information about individual processors, select Multiprocessor Information.
	Original cache buffers	Number of cache buffers available from RAM when you booted the server (default size=4KB per buffer).
	Total cache buffers	Number of cache buffers (default size 4KB) available for file caching. This number has been reduced from original number of cache buffers since NLMs were loaded and needed memory.
	Dirty cache buffers	Number of cache buffers in memory waiting to be written to disk.
	Current disk requests	Number of disk requests waiting to be serviced.
	Packet receive buffers	Number of packet receive buffers available to handle workstation requests.
	Directory cache buffers	Number of buffers allocated to handle directory caching.
	Maximum service processes	Limit for number of task handlers. Server creates service processes to handle workstation requests. Once memory is allocated for service processes (4KB each), it remains allocated even when no longer required, until the server is restarted. To set this parameter, choose the Miscellaneous category.
	Current Service processes	Number of service processes currently allocated. If this number corresponds to the Maximum Service Processes value, no more can be allocated and performance may suffer.

	STATISTIC	EXPLANATION
TABLE 9.1 (continued) Statistics on the Main MONITOR Screen	Maximum licensed connections	Maximum number of licensed server connections possible. Corresponds to NetWare license you purchased.
	Current licensed connections	Number of active licensed connections, which count toward the limit on your NetWare license. For example, if you have a NetWare license for 250 users and there are currently 145 licensed connections, you have 105 unused connections. To see which users are occupying the current licensed connections, choose Connection Information on Available Options menu.
	Open files	Number of files being used by the server and workstations.

	MENU ITEM	DESCRIPTION
TABLE 9.2 MONITOR's Available Options (Main Menu)	Connection information	Lists Users connected and services advertised. Only Users are counted in the current connections statistic, not the services advertised. You can view files currently held open by a User or clear a User's connection.
	Disk Information	Each drive's status, size, and volumes.
	LAN/WAN Information	Each LAN driver's version, node number, network number, protocols bound to it, and packet statistics.
	System Module Information	Modules loaded on the server and resources allocated by each module (resource tags).
	Lock File Server Console	Locks/unlocks server console keyboard. Once keyboard is locked, you can't use it until you supply either the password that you used to lock the console or the Admin password.
	File Open/Lock Activity	Allows you to browse the file system to see who has a file open. Use this option to find out why an application or data file is unavailable to other users.

T A B L E 9.2 (continued) MONITOR's Available Options (Main Menu)	MENU ITEM	DESCRIPTION
	Cache Utilization	Shows disk cache statistics. This is a critical set of statistics affecting file system speed.
	Processor Utilization	Allows you to select an active process, an interrupt, and/or multiple processes and available interrupts to sample for a histogram. Tells you how busy the processor is and what processes are monopolizing it. (The idle loop process runs when the processor is not otherwise engaged. High idle-loop percentages indicate low processor utilization.)
	Resource Utilization	Shows memory statistics for tracked resources (resource tags) allocated by operating system and NLM programs. Especially useful is the Server Memory Statistics window.
	Memory Utilization	Shows modules and the memory they use.
	Scheduling Information	Allows you to view statistics for and change priority of CPU processes.
	Multiprocessor Information	Shows information about processors, threads, and mutexes (mutual exclusion locks) if you are running NetWare symmetric multiprocessing (SMP).
	Server Parameters	Allows you to set server parameter values and save them to the AUTOEXEC.NCF, TIMESYNC.CFG, and STARTUP.NCF files.

Setting Server Parameters Using SERVMAN

The version of SERVMAN that shipped with NetWare 4.10 is unpredictable. If you are using NetWare 4.10, download a newer version of SERVMAN.

To set any server parameters using SERVMAN, perform the following steps:

1. At the server console, type **LOAD SERVMAN** and press Enter.

2. Highlight the Server Parameters option and press Enter.

3. Select the category of parameters you want to modify.

4. To change a parameter, move the cursor to the one you want to change and press Enter. Context-sensitive help is displayed in a window beneath your selection.

5. Supply the desired value and press Enter.

Managing Error Log Files

The NetWare operating system sends information to three error log files.

ERROR FILE	CONTENT	LOCATION
SYS$LOG.ERR	Log of server errors and major server events, such as going down and restarting	SYS:SYSTEM
VOL$LOG.ERR	For volume errors	Root directory of each volume
TTS$LOG.ERR	Data backed out by the Transaction Tracking System	Root directory of the SYS volume

If you make a habit of viewing the error logs every day, you will find problems you might not have noticed otherwise. The logs also give clues to the causes of those problems.

Following is a sample from the system error log (SYS$LOG.ERR). Most of the entries are about closing and opening the bindery, a normal event associated with restarting a server. Notice, however, the cache memory shortage that occurred on 5-16-96.

```
5-13-96  12:43:22 pm:    DS-4.89-28
   Severity = 1  Locus = 17  Class = 19
   Bindery open requested by the SERVER

5-13-96  12:43:22 pm:    DS-4.89-26
   Severity = 1  Locus = 17  Class = 19
   Directory Services:  Local database is open

5-16-96   9:21:15 am:    SERVER-4.10-2324
   Severity = 5  Locus = 19  Class = 2
   Cache memory allocator out of available memory.
```

```
5-16-96  11:05:44 am:     DS-4.89-30
   Severity = 0  Locus = 17  Class = 19
   Bindery close requested by the SERVER

5-16-96  11:05:44 am:     DS-4.89-27
   Severity = 1  Locus = 17  Class = 19
   Directory Services:  Local database has been closed

5-16-96  11:05:44 am:     SERVER-4.10-2009
   Severity = 4  Locus = 7  Class = 19
   SERVER1 TTS shut down
because backout volume SYS was dismounted.
```

Following is a sample from the TTS error log (TTS$LOG.ERR). Again, most of the entries record normal mounting and dismounting of volumes. But notice the problem with the ROM files.

```
Volume SYS dismounted on Tuesday, April 30, 1996   5:41:26 pm.

Volume SYS mounted on Tuesday, April 30, 1996   5:42:08 pm.

Volume SYS mounted on Tuesday, May 7, 1996   8:05:20 pm.
Volume mount had the following errors that were fixed:
Problem with file 544FFEC4.ROM, length extended.
Problem with file 544FFEC4.ROM,  old length = 0, new length = 8454144

Volume SYS dismounted on Tuesday, May 7, 1996   8:10:31 pm.

Volume SYS mounted on Tuesday, May 7, 1996   8:14:30 pm.
```

Following is a sample from the volume error log (VOL$LOG.ERR). Notice the problem with the Q_ files. Apparently, the server allocated some disk space for the files, but the server had been shut down before the cleanup was done.

```
Volume SYS mounted on Friday, August 30, 1996   9:09:37 am.

Volume SYS mounted on Friday, August 30, 1996   9:14:59 am.
Volume mount had the following errors that were fixed:
Problem with file Q_00CB.SRV, (TTS file...was not changed)
  length kept = 0, had allocated = 65536
```

```
Volume SYS mounted on Friday, August 30, 1996   9:26:44 am.
Volume mount had the following errors that were fixed:
Problem with file Q_OOCB.SRV, (TTS file...was not changed)
   length kept = 0, had allocated = 65536

Volume SYS dismounted on Friday, August 30, 1996   9:27:36 am.
```

Setting Parameters for Log Files

As you can see, the error log files give valuable insight into the health of your server. They tend to grow large, though, so keep an eye on them. NetWare provides the settings shown in Table 9.3 to keep error log files from using too much disk space.

TABLE 9.3 Parameters for Managing Error Log Size	**SET PARAMETER SYNTAX**	**MEANING**	**VALUES**
	Server Log File State	What to do if the log file exceeds size limit	0–2 (default=1)
	Volume Log File State		0=nothing
	Volume TTS Log File State		1=delete file
			2=rename file
	Server Log File Overflow Size	Sets the limit for log file size	65536–4294967295
	Volume Log File Overflow Size		
	Volume TTS Log File Overflow Size		

You can use the MONITOR or SERVMAN utilities to set the log file parameters, or you can enter the parameters at the server console. It's easiest to use the utilities because they allow you to also check statistics. MONITOR and SERVMAN give you the added advantage of writing the changed parameters to the AUTOEXEC.NCF and STARTUP.NCF files, which is recommended. See "Setting Server Parameters Using MONITOR" and "Setting Server Parameters Using SERVMAN" in this chapter.

Displaying Alert Messages

You can control which alert messages are shown on the server console, and whether or not the server beeps. Start by selecting the Server Parameters option in either SERVMAN or MONITOR; then select Miscellaneous. (See upcoming sections on SERVMAN and MONITOR utilities.) Among other parameters, you'll see the display options shown below.

SET PARAMETER	VALUES	DEFAULT
Sound Bell for Alerts	ON or OFF	ON
Display Relinquish Control Alerts	ON or OFF	OFF
Display Incomplete IPX Packet Alerts	ON or OFF	ON
Display Old API Names	ON or OFF	OFF
Display Spurious Interrupt Alerts	ON or OFF	OFF
Display Lost Interrupt Alerts	ON or OFF	OFF

Setting Early Warnings

You can control the display of early warning messages for cache buffers and volume space. The number of cache buffers affects the performance of the server more than any other single factor; on the other hand, your volume is pretty useless if you run out of disk space. Therefore, you should set the limits for cache buffers and volume space according to your situation—and mind the alerts.

Cache Buffers

Use the Minimum File Cache Report Threshold parameter to set file cache alerts. This parameter is found under File Caching in SERVMAN or MONITOR. Its value determines how close to the minimum cache buffers the server gets before generating an alert. For instance, if the minimum cache buffers value is set at 20 and the Minimum File Cache Report Threshold is set at 20, you get an alert when the available cache buffers has fallen to 40.

Full Volumes

You'll want to get an early warning if a volume is approaching the maximum disk space available. Controls for this warning are found in the File System parameters, and consist of three interrelated settings:

- Volume Low Warn All Users causes the server to send a warning message to users when a volume is nearly full. "Nearly full" is defined by Volume Low Warning Threshold, and the point at which the warning stops is defined by Volume Low Warning Reset Threshold.

- Volume Low Warning Threshold sets the level (how many blocks remain free on the volume) at which the Volume Low Warn All Users will be issued. Block size may be up to 64KB.

- Volume Low Warning Reset Threshold specifies the level (the number of freed blocks on the volume) at which the Volume Low Warn All Users will be cleared.

For example, the Volume Low Warning Threshold might be set to 256 blocks (16MB with a 64KB block size) and the Volume Low Warning Reset Threshold set to 16 blocks. In this case, the server sends a warning when 256 blocks are left on the volume. The volume must then gain 16 blocks (for a total of 272 blocks of free space) before the warning message disappears.

Setting Abend Recovery Options (NetWare 4.11)

Before NetWare 4.11, you had very few abend (abnormal end) options. When the normal operation of the server halted, if you didn't know how Novell's programmers set up their debugger, you were stuck. If you were at home or at lunch, the server stayed stuck until somebody hit the reset switch.

With NetWare 4.11, there are some parameters available to let you control the handling of abends, including those shown in Table 9.4.

With the After Abend parameter set, the server lets you choose from the folowing options:

- S suspends running process, updates ABEND.LOG, and (if it's a software Abend) then tries to down the server.

- R resumes the running process, updates ABEND.LOG, and then attempts to down the server.

- X restarts server.

- Y copies diagnostic image to disk.

  - 1 = Automated server response to abends. Server chooses between an R or S response.

  - 2 = Restarts server.

TABLE 9.4 Parameters for Abends (NetWare 4.11)		

SET PARAMETER	MEANING	VALUES
Auto Restart After Abend Delay Time	Time in minutes after an abend occurs until the server restarts	2–60 (default=2)
Auto Restart After Abend	What the server does in the case of an abend	0, 1, 2 (default=1) • 0= Server displays error message and lets you choose from several options.

Using Statistics to Monitor Basic Network Functions

THIS SECTION COVERS the following topics:

- Checking for disk errors

- Maintaining efficient access to the file system

- Improving LAN performance

Checking for Disk Errors

Check for disk errors every week or so. If you find some, you should monitor the disk every day to see if they are multiplying. *A regular increase in errors can mean the disk is failing and needs to be replaced before a catastrophic failure and total data loss occur.*

When you create a volume, NetWare sets aside a certain number of blocks called the *hot fix* area. It keeps this area available for redirecting data from bad blocks found during read-after-write verification. Monitoring the hot fix feature tells you how many blocks NetWare had to redirect, giving you an idea of the drive's health.

Following are the steps to check the status of NetWare's hot fix redirection feature:

If the drive, rather than NetWare, redirects bad blocks, the following procedure won't work; check with the drive manufacturer for troubleshooting information.

1. At the server console, type **LOAD MONITOR** and press Enter.

2. Choose Disk Information from the Available Options menu.

3. From the System Disk Drives menu, choose the drive you want to check.

   The upper part of the screen shows statistics for the drive you selected, including hot fix and redirected blocks. An error-free drive has no redirected blocks.

Maintaining Efficient File System Access

This section covers the following topics:

- Assessing volume disk space and directory space

- Assessing server RAM

- Directory cache parameters

- File cache parameters

- File compression parameters

Assessing Volume Disk Space and Directory Space

You'll want to regularly monitor disk space and directory entry table (DET) space for each network volume. Checking these statistics can give you an idea of disk usage trends, allowing you to predict disk shortages in the future. Use NetWare Administrator for this task. Select the Volume you want to check and choose the Statistics page. You'll see a window similar to the one in Figure 9.2.

Notice that the Statistics page also displays file compression statistics, so you can tell how much disk space is being saved by the compression.

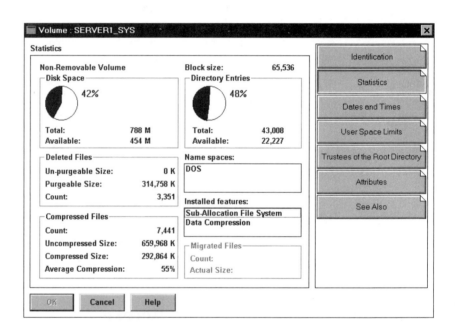

Assessing Server RAM

To know whether your server needs more RAM, you can view several statistics in MONITOR. Select a MONITOR category from the first column of Table 9.5, and then the option listed in the second column. Use the guidelines in the third column to evaluate the value displayed by the utility.

TABLE 9.5 MONITOR Options for Assessing Server RAM	MONITOR CATEGORY	OPTION	GUIDELINE
	Resource utilization	Cache Buffers	If below 20%, you should add RAM.
	Cache utilization	Long Term Cache Hits	If server has been in use more than two days and this value is under 90%, you need to add RAM.
	Cache utilization	Too Many Dirty Blocks	If this statistic increments rapidly, you need to add RAM.

Directory Cache Parameters

You can set the parameters shown in Table 9.6 using MONITOR (NetWare 4.11) or SERVMAN. In either utility, choose the Directory Caching category.

TABLE 9.6 Directory Cache Parameters Available in MONITOR and SERVMAN	SET PARAMETER SYNTAX	MEANING	VALUES
	Dirty Directory Cache Delay Time	How long the server keeps a directory table write request in memory before writing it to disk.	Increasing the parameter provides slightly faster performance, but may increase the chance of directory tables becoming corrupted. (Default=0.5 seconds)
	Maximum Concurrent Directory Cache Writes	How many write requests from directory cache buffers are executed at one time.	Increasing this value improves the efficiency of directory cache write requests, but decreases the speed of reads. (Default=10 seconds)
	Directory Cache Buffer NonReferenced Delay	How long a directory entry must be cached before it can be overwritten.	Increasing this value causes the server to allocate more directory cache buffers and thus accelerates directory access. (Default=5.5 seconds)

ACCELERATING DIRECTORY SEARCHES AFTER SERVER RESTART If
directory searches seem to be slow immediately after restarting a server, perhaps the server starts with too few directory cache buffers. You can increase the
Minimum Directory Cache Buffers parameter to improve this situation.

1. First, monitor the number of directory cache buffers usually allocated for
   directory caching. From MONITOR at the server console, select System
   Module Information.

2. Select NetWare Server Operating System.

3. Select Directory Tables. Write down the number in use.

4. Divide the number by the cache buffer size (4096) to get the number of
   directory cache buffers in use.

5. Using MONITOR or SERVMAN, select the Directory Caching category.

6. Set the Minimum Directory Cache Buffers parameter to the result of Step 4.

This provides enough directory cache buffers when your server is booted to
cover its normal workload. The server dynamically adds more if needed, up
to the Maximum Directory Cache Buffers setting. After the maximum is reached,
directory searches will slow down.

*Once a directory cache buffer is allocated, it can't be returned to file cache. Therefore, you
don't want to set the minimum higher than necessary, or it will affect file caching. You may also
need to reduce the value of the Maximum Directory Cache Buffers setting if file cache is low.*

File Cache Parameters

You can alter the settings for file caching in the File Caching category of
SERVMAN or MONITOR. The available parameters are listed in Table 9.7.

TURNING OFF READ-AFTER-WRITE VERIFICATION NetWare protects
your data by read-after-write verification. Most newer disk drives support this
in firmware, and this option is not needed. It can be disabled. However, some
older drives do not support read-after-write verification in firmware. In these
cases leave Read after Write verification on.

Here's how to disable it.

1. Using MONITOR, choose Disk Information.

2. Select the disk drive from the System Disk Drives menu.

TABLE 9.7	PARAMETER	DESCRIPTION	RATIONALE
File Cache Parameters	Dirty Disk Cache Delay Time	How long the server waits before writing a not-completely-dirty cache buffer to disk.	If value is low, server writes to disk more frequently but writes fewer requests each time. If value is high, server waits longer before writing to disk but executes more write requests with each operation. A higher value provides greater efficiency in writing to disk. Lower the value if network users frequently make many small write requests and server is slow to respond. (Default=3.3 seconds)
	Maximum Concurrent Disk Cache Writes	Maximum number of write requests that are serviced at one time	Decreasing this value improves the speed of reads, but may slow writes.

3. Select Read After Write Verify.

4. Select Disable Verify.

CHANGING THE TURBO FAT WAIT TIME   NetWare has a special feature to accelerate access to large files over 64 blocks. (Remember that block size is set when you create the volume and may be up to 64KB per block.) For files that contain more than 64 blocks, the server builds a Turbo FAT index for the file so that the information in the file can be accessed quickly.

To determine how long a Turbo FAT index remains in memory after the file is closed, the server relies on the Turbo FAT Re-Use Wait Time parameter. You can increase the value of this parameter so that Turbo FAT indexes remain in memory longer, allowing the file to be opened faster in subsequent accesses. Use MONITOR or SERVMAN to set the parameter.

1. Choose Server Parameters.

2. Choose File System from the Categories menu.

3. Select Turbo FAT Re-Use Wait Time.

4. Increase the value (maximum 1 hour, 5 minutes, 54.6 seconds) and press Enter.

CONTROLLING RESOURCE ALLOCATION WITH LOCKS Sometimes applications fail because they can't open enough files or records, usually due to the lack of file or record locks. Use the procedure below to increase the number of locks.

1. At the server console, load either SERVMAN or MONITOR.

2. Choose Server Parameters.

3. Choose the Locks category.

4. Increase the Maximum Record Locks and Maximum File Locks parameters.

5. To increase the number of file and record locks for each workstation, increase the Maximum Record Locks Per Connection and the Maximum File Locks Per Connection parameters.

File Compression Parameters

Each server uses a number of parameters for file compression. To access and set these parameters, use MONITOR or SERVMAN. Select the Server Parameters option, and then File System. The parameters are shown in Table 9.8 below.

Improving LAN Performance

You can use statistics to monitor and improve the performance of the network adapters and their associated drivers. If you have multiple network adapters in your server, you can balance the load among the adapters to reduce collisions and increase overall throughput. Use the following procedure to balance network traffic loads.

1. Choose a time when network traffic is at its highest.

2. Load MONITOR and select LAN/WAN Information.

3. Select each network adapter in turn, and write down the number of packets sent and packets received.

4. Repeat Step 3 at the end of the high-traffic period.

5. For each adapter, subtract the numbers of packets recorded in step 3 from the number recorded in Step 4. The difference is the packet traffic during the high-traffic period.

TABLE 9.8 File Compression Parameters	PARAMETER	DESCRIPTION
	Compression Daily Check Stop Hour	Hour when the compression program stops scanning files on compression-enabled volumes.
	Compression Daily Check Starting Hour	Hour when the compression program starts checking compression-enabled volumes (0=midnight).
	Minimum Compression Percentage Gain	Minimum percentage of file-space savings required before compression occurs.
	Enable File Compression	Allows compression to take place (OFF suspends all compression for all of this server's volumes).
	Maximum Concurrent Compressions	Maximum number of volumes that can be compressed at one time.
	Convert Compressed to Uncompressed Option	Determines the action taken to files when they are uncompressed: 0=leave the compressed version 1=leave the compressed version unless this is the second or subsequent access in the period set by the Days Untouched Before Compression parameter 2=leave the uncompressed version
	Decompress Percent Disk Space Free to Allow Compression	Prevents decompression if the available disk space falls below a certain percentage.
	Decompress Free Space Warning Interval	Time between warnings that amount of free space has dipped below required margin.
	Deleted Files Compression Option	For files that have been deleted yet remain salvageable: 0=don't compress 1=compress next day 2=compress immediately
	Days Untouched Before Compression	Files not accessed for this number of consecutive days become candidates for compression.

By comparing the statistics for each adapter, you can better see how to change the network cabling to put more users on the less-active network adapter. Table 9.9 contains a sample calculation for three adapters.

The examples in Table 9.9 show the disparity in load that can occur if you don't watch the statistics. Net 20 and Net 30 are handling about 20 times the load of Net 10. In this case, you would move some of the heavy users to the Net 10 cable segment.

You should also watch any statistics that indicate errors. Make sure, however, that you're watching an actual error statistic rather than a measurement of normal traffic. For instance, the statistic Send OK Byte Count Low may sound like the packets have too few bytes, but it is actually just a counter of transmitted packets that were okay.

TABLE 9.9 Sample Calculations of Network Traffic	**ADAPTER**	**BEGINNING VALUES**	**ENDING VALUES**	**DIFFERENCE**
	Net 30	Sent 286,950	Sent 329,805	Sent 42,855
		Received 231,615	Received 298,535	Received 66,920
	Net 20	Sent 3,656,210	Sent 4,408,895	Sent 752,685
		Received 2,928,635	Received 4,109,900	Received 1,181,265
	Net 10	Sent 1,543,100	Sent 1,987,805	Sent 444,705
		Received 1,984,095	Received 2,908,975	Received 924,680

ECB Available Count

Another statistic to watch is the No ECB Available Count. This counter increments when a packet is received at the network adapter but no packet receive buffer is available. The server allocates more packet receive buffers after each incident until it reaches its maximum limit (configured with a SET parameter).

If your No ECB Available Count is always 0, the server is allocating more packet receive buffers than you ever need, and you can reduce the minimum packet receive buffers.

If the No ECB Available Count is above 0 but seldom increments, then you have about the right amount of packet receive buffers. The system has spawned a few new ones since the server booted, but you haven't reached the limit.

If the No ECB Available Count is constantly incrementing, your server has allocated new packet receive buffers until it reached the maximum. You should increase both the minimum and maximum packet receive buffers and restart the server (during nonproduction hours, of course).

If you are using an EISA, PCI, or microchannel bus-master board (such as the NE3200), you will probably need to increase both the minimum and maximum number of packet receive buffers.

See "Detailed LAN Driver Statistics" in the following section for information on other LAN driver statistics.

Using Detailed Statistics

YOU PROBABLY WON'T USE the statistics in this section every day, but they can be helpful for troubleshooting the occasional problem. The first subsection covers network protocol statistics, including AppleTalk, IPX, and TCP/IP. The second subsection covers detailed LAN driver statistics. The third subsection covers symmetrical multiprocessor statistics.

Network Protocol Statistics

Of course, you'll only use the statistics for network protocols loaded on your network. Included in this subsection are AppleTalk, IPX, and TCP/IP.

AppleTalk Statistics

If you have loaded the AppleTalk network protocol, you can view statistics using ATCON at the server console. ATCON lets you observe and manage the AppleTalk protocol router on the server, and its relationship with other connected AppleTalk networks. The ATCON statistics are explained in Table 9.10.

	OPTION	PURPOSE
TABLE 9.10 ATCON Menu Options	AURP Information	(Statistics only available if AURP is enabled.) Shows the status of the IP Tunnel for AppleTalk Update-based Routing Protocol (AURP).
	Interfaces	View addressing information for interfaces directly connected to the AppleTalk router to see if they are seeded correctly. This option lists each known network with its address, type, port, status, and zones. The Status field tells you whether a router is seeded correctly.
	Log Files	Control which messages are committed to log files. You can choose from fatal errors, errors, warnings, informational messages, and verbose messages. You can also view the server's error log and volume log files.
	Lookup Network Entities	Detect which services are available on the AppleTalk network. This tells you whether other AppleTalk servers are communicating.
	Packet Statistics	View statistics maintained by the AppleTalk router, including packets sent and received, echoes sent and received, and dropped packets.
	Protocol Configuration	View the settings of the AppleTalk protocol stack. You can't actually change any settings using this screen.
	Routing Table	View the routing table, sorted by zone name or network. This tells you all the AppleTalk locations with their status, distance in hops, next router, and port.
	Zones List	View the list of zones known to this AppleTalk router. The same zones are displayed by the Macintosh workstation's Chooser program.

RP AND AURP ROUTING PROTOCOLS Routers use routing protocols to keep track of addresses so they can create a table with information about all the networks on the AppleTalk internetwork. The router uses this information to send packets by the best possible route. By learning its neighbors' routing information, a router gets information about the entire internetwork.

Routing Table Maintenance Protocol (RP). Routers use RP to exchange information needed to build and maintain each router's routing table. This allows routers to make contact and move packets from one point on an internetwork to another. AppleTalk routers on the internetwork that use RP *continually* maintain their routing tables by exchanging RP packets.

AppleTalk Update-based Routing Protocol (AURP) is new with NetWare 4.11 and an enhancement of RP. Update-based routing reduces the amount of bandwidth by sending updates to peer routers only when network routing information changes, rather than sending periodic broadcasts of the routing table. AURP also provides AppleTalk tunneling through TCP/IP (enclosing AppleTalk packets inside Internet packets). Tunneling allows two isolated AppleTalk networks to be connected by way of TCP/IP (a more common WAN protocol).

IPX Statistics (IPXCON and IPXPING Utilities)

The IPXCON utility allows you to monitor the IPX network protocol. You can run IPXCON each time you restart your servers by putting the command LOAD IPXCON in the servers' AUTOEXEC.NCF files.

IPXCON uses SNMP over IPX or UDP/IP to monitor remote servers, routers, or network segments on the internetwork, enabling you to view the following information:

- Links and routers

- Routing protocols

- Paths by which IPX packets can reach their destinations

- Services

- Number of IPX packets being sent, received, and forwarded by a router

- Networks

IPXCON uses IPXRTRNM.NLM and SNMP.NLM to retrieve its statistics from routers on the network.

- IPXRTRNM.NLM makes IPX, NLSP, and RIP/SAP Management Information Base (MIB) variables available. IPX routing statistics are provided through SNMP.NLM.

- SNMP.NLM is the NetWare SNMP Agent. It sends and responds to requests for management information.

The IPXPING utility sends an IPX ping request packet to an IPX target node (server or workstation) on the network. When the target node receives the request packet, it sends back a reply packet.

To run IPXPING, type **LOAD IPXPING** at the server console. Enter a network number and node number of a workstation or server. You can specify the number of seconds between pings. Press Esc to start sending packets, and press Esc again to stop sending packets.

IPXPING gives the following information:

- Number of requests sent

- Number of echoes received

- Highest response time

- Lowest response time

- Last response time

- Trend

TCP/IP Statistics (TCPCON and PING)

TCPCON. You can monitor configuration and statistics on the TCP/IP segments of your network with TCPCON. By default, TCPCON monitors and gathers information from the server. You can also set TCPCON to view statistics on any remote node that has SNMP instrumentation.

To start TCPCON, enter **LOAD TCPCON** at the server console.

TCPCON's main screen displays IP and TCP packet statistics for the selected node, including packets sent, received, and forwarded. It also allows you to view activity of the following TCP/IP protocols:

- EGP (External Gateway Protocol) messages received, invalid messages received, messages sent, and messages discarded due to resource limitations

- ICMP (Internet Control Message Protocol): 14 statistics on messages sent and received

- IP (Internet Protocol): Datagrams sent, received, forwarded, and delivered; discarded datagram errors

- OSPF (Open Shortest Path First): Advertisements originated, advertisements received, external link-state advertisements, and sum of link-state checksums

- TCP (Transmission Control Protocol): Statistics on segments and connections

- UDP (User Datagram Protocol): Datagrams delivered to UDP users, datagrams discarded due to no UDP user, invalid datagrams received, and datagrams sent

The main screen of TCPCON gives six general statistics on the selected node (default: server), as described in Table 9.11.

PING. If you have loaded IP on your server, you can get IP response time information by using PING. This utility sends echo request packets to an IP target node on your network. When the target node receives the request packet, it sends back a reply packet.

From the server console, type **LOAD PING**. Enter the host name or IP address of a workstation or server. You can specify the number of seconds

	STATISTIC	MEANING
TABLE 9.11 General TCP/IP Statistics Available in TCPCON	IP Received	Number of IP datagrams received from all interfaces.
	IP Sent	Number of datagrams sent to IP for transmission, not including datagrams forwarded by this host.
	IP Forwarded	Number of IP packets forwarded from one node to another.
	TCP Received	Number of TCP segments received.
	TCP Sent	Number of TCP segments sent, excluding those containing retransmitted data.
	TCP Connections	Number of currently established TCP connections.

between pings and the size of the packets. Press Esc to start sending packets. Press Esc again to stop sending packets.

PING gives the following information:

- Number of requests sent

- Number of echoes received

- Highest response time

- Lowest response time

- Last response time

- Trend

Detailed LAN Driver Statistics

You can view detailed LAN driver statistics using MONITOR. From the MONITOR menu, select LAN/WAN Information and then choose a LAN driver. A window shows you both the custom and generic statistics for the selected driver.

The custom statistics vary with the LAN driver loaded. See the network adapter's documentation for information on the custom statistics generated.

Generic statistics are created and maintained by two modules: a media support module (MSM) and a topology-specific module (TSM). MSM provides a standard generic interface among the LAN driver, the link support layer (LSL), and the operating system. The TSM is either ETHERTSM, RXNETTSM, TOKENTSM, or FDDITSM, depending on the topology in use. The TSM supports multiple frame types for a given topology.

The following tables give the general statistics maintained for LAN drivers:

Table 9.12: Generic LAN Driver Statistics

Table 9.13: Generic Statistics for Ethernet Drivers

Table 9.14: Generic Statistics for RX-Net Drivers

Table 9.15: Generic Statistics for Token Ring Drivers

Table 9.16: Generic Statistics for FDDI Drivers

TABLE 9.12 Generic LAN Driver Statistics	**STATISTIC**	**DESCRIPTION**
	Driver Name (seen as the heading to the statistics screen)	LAN driver name and configuration for hardware settings on the network adapter.
	Version	Current version of the LAN driver.
	Node Address	Address of the network adapter, usually configured by the manufacturer of the board.
	Protocols	Network protocols bound to the driver.
	Network Address	Network number (cable segment number) assigned to the LAN driver (IPX only).
	Total Packets Sent	Packets sent from the server via this LAN driver since the server was last booted.
	Total Packets Received	Packets received via this LAN driver since the server was last booted (includes file service requests, packets routed to another network, and packets sent to other IPX sockets in the server).
	No ECB Available Count	Times that a packet is sent to the server and no packet receive buffer is available (The server allocates more packet receive buffers after each incident until it reaches its maximum limit).
	Send Packet Too Big Count	Number of times the server tried to send a packet that was too big for the network adapter to handle.
	Receive Packet Overflow Count	Number of times the adapter's receive buffers overflowed, causing subsequent incoming packets to be discarded (the server received a packet that is too big to store in a cache buffer, normally 4KB). A new version of the LAN driver should clear this up.
	Receive Packet Too Big Count	Packets that are too big for the provided receive buffers.
	Receive Packet Too Small Count	Packets that are too small (RXNet only).
	Send Packet Miscellaneous Errors	Errors with "send" packets (packets to be transmitted).

TABLE 9.12 (continued) Generic LAN Driver Statistics	STATISTIC	DESCRIPTION
	Receive Packet Miscellaneous Errors	Errors with "receive" packets (packets accepted from the medium).
	Send Packet Retry Count	Packet transmissions that have failed because of a hardware error. (The server tries to send the packet again until either it succeeds or the retry setting is reached.)
	Checksum Errors	Number of times a checksum at the end of the packet does not equal the sum of the bytes contained in the packet.
	Hardware Receive Mismatch Count	Number of times a packet length received by the hardware and the length specified by the packet do not match (Ethernet only).
	Total Send OK Byte Count Low	Number of bytes, including low-level headers, successfully transmitted.
	Total Send OK Byte Count High	Upper 32 bits of the Total Send OK Byte Count Low counter. (This value is incremented by 1 every time the Total Send OK Byte Count Low counter reaches 4GB.)
	Total Receive OK Byte Count Low	Number of bytes, including low-level headers, successfully received.
	Total Receive OK Byte Count High	Upper 32 bits of the Total Receive OK Byte Count Low counter. (This value is incremented by 1 every time the Total Receive OK Byte Count Low counter reaches 4GB.)
	Total Group Address Send Count	Number of packets transmitted with a group or broadcast destination address.
	Total Group Address Receive Count	Number of packets received with a group or broadcast destination address.
	Adapter Reset Count	Times the adapter was reset because of internal failures.
	Adapter Operating Time Stamp	Time stamp of the last changed operational state (such as load, shutdown, or reset).
	Adapter Queue Depth	Number of transmit packets waiting for the adapter. (This indicates transmission overload.)

TABLE 9.13 Generic Statistics for Ethernet Drivers	STATISTIC	DESCRIPTION
	Send OK Single Collision Count	Frames involved in a single collision that are subsequently transmitted successfully.
	Send OK Multiple Collision Count	Frames involved in more than one collision that are transmitted successfully.
	Send OK But Deferred	Frames whose transmission was delayed because another station was transmitting.
	Send Abort From Late Collision	Transmissions that had a collision after 512 bits of the packet were transmitted. Often caused by faulty network adapters, hubs, terminators, or cables that are too long.
	Send Abort From Excess Collisions	Transmissions aborted because of too many collisions (due to very heavy traffic or a bad network adapter in the network).
	Send Abort From Carrier Sense	Transmissions aborted due to loss of carrier sense while transmitting without any collisions. Usually caused by a faulty network adapter on the network or faulty cabling.
	Send Abort From Excessive Deferral	Transmissions aborted because of excessive deferrals. Usually caused by a faulty adapter or repeater in the system that is jabbering on the wire. Can also occur under very heavy traffic conditions.
	Receive Abort From Bad Frame Alignment	Received frames that were not aligned (incorrect number of octets in the frame, or frame did not pass the FCS check). Usually caused by a faulty adapter on the network or a collision.

TABLE 9.14 Generic Statistics for RX-Net Drivers	STATISTIC	DESCRIPTION
	No Response To Free Buffer Enquiry	No response from the receiving node to a Free Buffer Enquiry.
	Network Reconfiguration Count	Number of network reconfigurations.
	Invalid Split Flag In Packet Flag	The Split Flag in the packet fragment is not the value expected (packet fragments received out of order).

TABLE 9.14 (continued) Generic Statistics for RX-Net Drivers	**STATISTIC**	**DESCRIPTION**
	Orphan Packet Fragment Count	A packet fragment has been received that is not a part of a previously received packet and therefore cannot be appended.
	Receive Packet Timeout	A received packet timed out while waiting for the rest of the packet fragments to arrive.
	Free Buffer Enquiry NAK Timeout	A transmit packet timed out while waiting for an acknowledgment to a Free Buffer Enquiry from the receiving node.
	Total Send Packet Fragments OK	Packet fragments sent successfully.
	Total Receive Packet Fragments OK	Packet fragments received successfully.

TABLE 9.15 Generic Statistics for Token Ring Drivers	**STATISTIC**	**DESCRIPTION**
	AC Error Counter	A ring station received a Standby Monitor Present MAC frame with the A/C bits in the Frame Status field equal to zero without first receiving an Active Monitor Present MAC frame.
	Abort Delimiter	A ring station transmitted an abort delimiter (a ring station received a frame in which token bit of access control field is set to show Token and not Frame; or an internal hardware error occurred).
	Burst Error Counter	A ring station detected the absence of 5 half-bit times (a burst-5 error).
	Frame Copied Error Counter	A ring station recognized a frame addressed to its specific address and detected that the FC field's A bits are set to 1, indicating a possible line hit or a duplicate address.
	Frequency Error Counter	Frequency of the incoming signal differs from the expected frequency by more than that specified in Section 7 of IEEE Standard 802.5-1989.
	Internal Error Counter	A ring station has generated a recoverable internal error.

TABLE 9.15 (continued) Generic Statistics for Token Ring Drivers	STATISTIC	DESCRIPTION
	Last Ring Status	See the IBM Token-Ring Network Architecture Reference for the status code, function, and meaning.
	Line Error Counter	A frame or token is repeated by the ring station (a Frame Check Sequence error has occurred or a code violation exists between the starting and ending delimiters of the frame).
	Lost Frame Counter	A ring station has transmitted a frame that does not return to the station.
	Token Error Counter	A station acting as the active monitor recognizes an error condition that needs a token transmitted.
	Up Stream Node High Dword	First 8 digits of the Up Stream node address of the next node upstream on the ring.
	Up Stream Node Low Dword	Next 4 digits of the Up Stream node address of the next node upstream on the ring.
	Last Ring ID	Local ring ID.
	Last Beacon Type	Last beacon type.

TABLE 9.16 Generic Statistics for FDDI Drivers	STATISTIC	DESCRIPTION
	Configuration State	Attachment configuration: 0=isolated 1=local_a 2=local_b 3=local_ab 4=local_s 5=wrap_a 6=wrap_b 7=wrap_ab 8=wrap_s 9=c_wrap_a 10=c_wrap_b 11=c_wrap_s 12=thru.
	Upstream Node Address	Upstream neighbor's MAC address (0 if unknown).
	Downstream Node Address	Downstream neighbor's MAC address (0 if unknown).
	Frame Error Counter	Bad frames that had not been detected by another MAC.
	Frames Lost Counter	Format errors detected during frame reception so that the frame was stripped.

TABLE 9.16 (continued) Generic Statistics for FDDI Drivers	STATISTIC	DESCRIPTION
	Ring Management State	Current state of the Ring Management state machine: 0=Isolated; 1=Non_Op; 2=Ring_Op; 3=Detect; 4=Non_Op_Dup; 5=Ring_Op_Dup; 6=Directed; 7=Trace.
	LCT Failure Counter	Consecutive times the link confidence test (LCT) has failed during connection management.
	LEM Link Reject Counter	Times a link was rejected.
	LEM Error Counter	Aggregate link error monitor (LEM) error count.
	Connection State	State of this port's Physical Connection Management (PCM) state machine: 0=Off; 1=Break; 2=Trace; 3=Connect; 4=Next; 5=Signal; 6=Join; 7=Verify; 8=Active; 9=Maint.

Monitoring SMP Performance

Once you install NetWare SMP on a server with more than one processor, MONITOR shows statistics to help you oversee your SMP server's performance. SMP statistics appear both in the MONITOR General Information window and in windows found under Multiprocessor Information.

The significance of SMP statistics depends upon many factors, including how many processors are installed, the amount of network traffic, the size of applications, and the suitability of applications for a multiprocessing environment. The SMP statistics that appear in the MONITOR General Information window are as follows:

- Active Processors: Number of processors detected by SMP (not including processors that are installed but not enabled)

- Utilization: Average utilization of all active processors

You can find utilization statistics under the Processor Utilization or the Scheduling Information options of the MONITOR menu. However, these statistics refer only to processor 0. To see utilization for multiple processors, select the Multiprocessor Information option.

After you install NetWare SMP, the Multiprocessor Information option in MONITOR becomes active. When you select this option, you see the Information for All Processors window and the Multiprocessor Options menu.

The Information for All Processors window contains general information about the SMP server (see Table 9.17).

To access the Help screens for the Information for All Processors window, press Tab to activate the window, and then F1 to see the Help screens.

If a sudden increase occurs in all of the Combined Lock Assertions, Combined Lock Collisions, *and* Maximum Lock Wait statistics, refer to the Mutex Information window to find out which application locks are causing lock wait times that are high, or numerous collisions. Then contact that application's manufacturer for help.

The Multiprocessor Options menu allows you to view information for each active processor, mutex information, and active threads information. For help with these options, press F1 to access the online help provided.

TABLE 9.17 SMP Statistics for All Processors	**STATISTIC**	**DESCRIPTION**
	Total Processors	Processors detected by SMP, including those installed but not enabled.
	Active Processors	Enabled processors.
	Combined Lock Assertions	Times that threads tried to acquire locks during the last update interval. Values greater than 50,000 can indicate application problems.
	Combined Lock Collisions	Times in the last update interval that locks were denied because requested resources were already locked.
	Maximum Lock Wait	Largest number of collisions for one lock during the last update interval.
	Combined Utilization	Average utilization of all active processors.

Summary

I T GOES WITHOUT SAYING that you'll want to keep a finger on the pulse of the server, so you know about any problems before they seriously affect server performance. In terms of your day-to-day routine, this means checking error log files and responding quickly to alerts and warnings.

You can control how NetWare warns you of shortages in disk space and cache buffers. You can also control how abends are handled, which alerts are displayed, and whether the server beeps when an alert condition occurs.

SERVMAN and MONITOR are your primary utilities for viewing and changing server settings. In NetWare 4.11, you can use them interchangeably. In NetWare 4.10, you can't use MONITOR—it only lets you view information— and you shouldn't use SERVMAN without installing the newer version available on NetWire.

You should follow the instructions in this chapter for monitoring disk errors. Today's drives last longer than they did in years past, but they still fail. Better to replace a failing disk before it becomes completely useless.

Study this chapter's information on directory caching and file caching, as well. The statistics you view and the settings you make can improve performance. Ditto on LAN driver statistics.

Finally, bear in mind that many of the detailed statistics are listed and described in this chapter as reference material. You probably won't use them unless you have a problem or install a special feature such as AppleTalk Filing Protocol or SMP.

Backing Up and Restoring Data

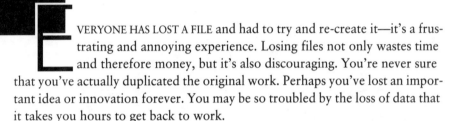

EVERYONE HAS LOST A FILE and had to try and re-create it—it's a frustrating and annoying experience. Losing files not only wastes time and therefore money, but it's also discouraging. You're never sure that you've actually duplicated the original work. Perhaps you've lost an important idea or innovation forever. You may be so troubled by the loss of data that it takes you hours to get back to work.

It's one of the tragedies of the information age. On one hand, you can be incredibly creative and productive with a mouse and keyboard; on the other hand, your brilliant creation can be instantly gone with a GPF. "The application has performed an illegal operation and will be shut down," says Windows 95 coldly.

Data loss can happen to an individual employee because of a buggy application, or it can happen to an entire geographic area because of an earthquake, tornado, or hurricane. Whether it's a badly behaving program or an unpredictable natural disaster that threatens the safety of your data, you need protection. That protection is a comprehensive plan to both avert and recover from data loss.

As with most network management duties, an ounce of prevention is worth a kilogram of cure. A stitch in time saves 9K.

Prevention Measures

MAKE A LIST OF POSSIBLE SCENARIOS involving data loss at your company. Put the possible situations in one column, and make a second column listing anything you could do to prevent or recover the loss. You'll probably be surprised at how few of the preventive actions you write down include backing up data onto tape. *Not to diminish the importance of tape backups*, but I believe administrators tend to focus too heavily on tape backups when trying to prevent data loss, and miss the concept of more comprehensive prevention. Table 10.1 is a sample list of data loss scenarios, with corresponding actions to prevent or recover the loss.

Looking at your own list, you'll probably discern that preventing data loss involves good planning (Chapter 2), conscientious server upgrading (Chapter 3) or installation (Chapter 4), using updated client software (Chapter 5), and generally meticulous administration (covered in the remaining chapters of this book).

The bottom line is this: To prevent data loss and recover from it, you need to do your job conscientiously every day. Then, when something catastrophic happens that defeats all your precautions, you can go to your backup tapes and restore your company's data.

Now let's see what to do when data loss really does happen.

Backing Up and Restoring Data

N A SENSE, NETWARE does some backing up for you. It keeps a copy of deleted files, so you can salvage them if needed. This "backing up" is done automatically, so you and your users only need to become adept at the salvaging (restoring) process.

In addition to knowing how to salvage deleted files, you'll want to implement a conventional backup/restore combination using Novell's Storage Management System (SMS). Normally, this calls for a tape drive on one of your servers.

SMS allows you to do much more than restore deleted files. You can selectively back up and restore workstations' local drives, the Directory, and the NetWare file systems of all the servers on your network.

Salvaging Deleted Files

When a user deletes a file, that file is not immediately erased unless you have done one of the following:

- Set the file's Purge attribute, or set the Purge attribute of the directory holding that file

- Used the SET command at the NetWare server to turn on immediate purging

TABLE 10.1 Sample Data Loss Scenarios	**SCENARIO**	**PREVENTIVE ACTION**
	A user closes an application without saving the work file.	Turn on the application's auto-save feature.
	A user's hard disk fails, destroying the applications, the data files, and the backup files.	1. Set the application preferences to save files to a network drive or other drive different from the normal working drive. For instance, if a word processor stores user files in the C:\OFFICE\MYFILES directory, have the auto-save feature store backups in the H:\BACKUPS directory. After you reinstall the application on a new hard drive, the user can open the backup data file on the network. 2. Back up workstation data to your server's tape drive.
	The backup software crashes the server.	1. Spend more money on better backup software. 2. Monitor memory statistics and buy more RAM, if necessary, to avoid crashes. 3. Check the server error log and the backup error log every day for errors that may foretell more serious problems. 4. Regularly look for software patches for any software that runs on your server. This includes the NOS, LAN, and disk drivers, and any NLMs (such as backup software). 5. Avoid running "point 0" software on the server, such as NOS version 4.0 or backup software version 5.0.
	A user accidentally unplugs the power cord of a remote hub. The workstations lose their connection to the network and need to be rebooted.	Use the latest version of client software, with its auto-reconnect feature.
	The server's drive fails.	1. Mirror drives to prevent downtime due to drive failure. 2. Check weekly for redirected blocks; replace the drive during off hours if redirected blocks are increasing. 3. Restore the drive's data from tape to a new drive.
	A fire burns down the business.	Keep backup tapes off site.

Until you deliberately take one of these steps, the file is still salvageable. Salvageable files are usually stored in the directory from which they were deleted. If the user deletes that directory also, the salvageable files are saved in a DELETED.SAV directory at the volume's root.

Deleted files are saved until the user or administrator purges them or until the NetWare server runs out of disk blocks on the volume. When the NetWare server runs out of disk blocks, it purges deleted files beginning with the oldest files (that is, the files least recently deleted).

Unless you tell them, users are not aware that NetWare has a utility that can restore deleted files. You can train some of them to use the FILER utility from DOS so they can restore deleted files on their own. Many users, however, would rather go to the administrator for help. So make sure they know that deleted files are salvageable, or they won't even think to ask for help.

This section will cover two methods for salvaging files: using FILER, and using the Salvage tool in NetWare Administrator.

Using the FILER Utility from DOS

The FILER utility is a DOS menu-driven utility available to all users in the SYS:PUBLIC directory. FILER offers many general file-maintenance functions, including deleting, copying, and moving groups of files and directories. Following are the steps to use FILER's salvaging feature:

1. At the DOS prompt, type **FILER**.

   The current context, volume, and path are shown in the upper-left corner of the screen.

2. From the Available Options menu, Select Salvage Deleted Files.

3. Choose one of the following:

   - To salvage files from an existing directory, choose View/Recover Deleted Files.

   - To salvage files from a deleted directory, choose Salvage Deleted Directories and select the volume that contained the deleted directory.

4. When prompted, type a filename or wildcard specifier to list the files you want to salvage.

   For example, if you want to list all files with the EXE extension, type *.**EXE**. If you don't specify anything, all files deleted from that directory will be listed.

5. Mark all files you want to restore by highlighting each file and pressing F5.

6. Press Enter.

If you salvaged files from an existing directory, the files are restored to that directory. If you salvaged files from a deleted directory, the files are restored to the volume's root.

Using the Salvage Tool in NetWare Administrator

NetWare Administrator also provides the file recovery function.

1. Using NetWare Administrator, click on the directory containing the files or directories you want to salvage.

2. Select Tools | Salvage.

3. Select the options appropriate to your situation:

   - Source (current directory or deleted directory)

   - Include (file name or wildcards)

   - Sort Options

4. Choose List to display the file names.

   The window displayed will look similar to the one shown in Figure 10.1. Notice that multiple versions of the same file are shown. Only one version may be salvaged, however. You'll normally want to salvage the most recent version.

5. Select the files you want to salvage. Pressing Ctrl as you click allows you to select multiple nonadjacent files.

6. Choose Salvage.

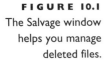

FIGURE 10.1

The Salvage window helps you manage deleted files.

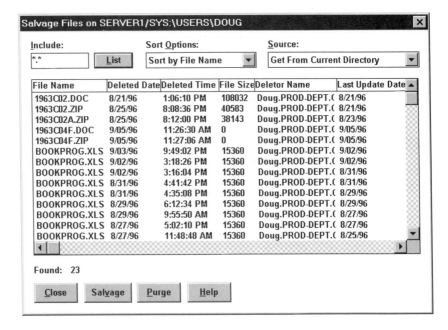

If you restored files from an existing directory, the files are returned to that directory. If you salvage files from a deleted directory, the files are restored to the volume's root.

Using a Backup Tape Drive on the Server

This section covers the conventional method of network backup and restoration using Novell's Storage Management Services (SMS) architecture.

What is the value you gain from spending the time to back up the network? If employees had to re-create all the data on the computers, how long would it take? Multiply the number of estimated hours by the average wage, and you'll have an idea how much your company's data is worth. Presumably, some of the data could never be re-created. Keep this in mind and mention it to your manager when evaluating backup hardware and software, and the time spent keeping it serviceable.

Regarding backup software, network administrators generally prefer third-party solutions to Novell's SBACKUP. The cost may be high for a piece of software, but the third-party vendors do offer greater functionality and ease of use.

That efficiency can translate into tangible value when the whole company is gathered outside your office waiting for you to save the server.

Someday you may need to restore the server data to a blank hard drive. Make sure you can locate all the backup tapes, Novell software, tape backup software, licenses, patches, and passwords. If there were a fire in the server room, would your tapes go up in flames with the server? Keep a full backup tape off site, just to be safe.

SMS and its utilities offer a wide range of backup and restoration capabilities, but these tools tend to be picky. That is, the proper modules must be loaded on the right computers in the recommended sequence or it doesn't work. And you usually aren't told very clearly why it doesn't work. So take some time to read the instructions in this book. As usual, be sure to document what you do. Then, if you get stuck, you can use Novell's excellent documentation (installed from the CD-ROM that accompanied your NetWare product) to get yourself out of trouble.

Overview of Storage Management Services (SMS)

NetWare's SMS lets you back up data to a server's tape drive, from workstations, from NetWare volumes, from other servers, and from the Directory. The data set that you want to back up is called a *target*. To make backups possible, you need to load a target service agent (TSA) on each of the machines to be backed up. Novell provides the following TSAs with NetWare 4.11:

DATA	TSA
Macintosh workstation	MacTSA
DOS/Windows workstation (VLM)	TSASMS.COM
DOS/Windows workstation (Client 32)	TSASMS.COM
Windows 95 workstation	W95TSA.EXE
OS/2 workstation	TSAOS2.EXE
NetWare server file system (4.0x)	TSA400
NetWare server file system (4.1x)	TSA410
NetWare server file system (3.11)	TSA311
NetWare server file system (3.12)	TSA312
NetWare Directory Services database	TSANDS

The TSA knows how to deal with the target data, in terms of getting it to the server for storage and retrieving it if necessary. The TSA must understand the name spaces, file and directory attributes, security privileges, and other elements particular to the target data.

The TSA on the target computer sends the data in a standard format to the Storage Management Engine (SME) on the server doing the backup. The SME included with NetWare is SBACKUP.NLM. Like many NetWare utilities, SBACKUP provides basic functionality—enough functionality for most small networks.

Other excellent SMEs are offered (at premium prices) by third-party manufacturers such as Cheyenne, Arcada, Palindrome, and Stac. Stac's SME, for instance, allows you to completely restore a server including its DOS partition, with just a couple of disks and a tape. With most third-party backup software, you can mount a tape drive as a NetWare volume and selectively restore the files you want using simple Copy commands.

The SME supplied with NetWare relies on the following support modules to do its job:

- Storage Management Data Requester (SMDR.NLM), an interface between the SME and TSAs

- Storage Device Interface (SMSDI.NLM) between the SME and the storage devices

- Device drivers for the backup hardware (host bus adapter and tape device)

- Workstation registry points (TSADOS and TSAPROXY), and the workstation manager (WSMAN.NLM) keeping track of the stations waiting to be backed up

SMS Tips and Precautions

Hardware:

- Make sure you have enough RAM in the server. SMS requires 3MB above the amount already needed for server operations.

- For the highest speed and reliability, install the tape drive on its own SCSI adapter, separate from the disk drives.

Software:

- Make sure you use an SMS-compliant backup engine. Only SMS-compliant engines can properly back up the Directory and NetWare file system trustee assignments.

- SMS software is constantly being updated. Make sure you have the latest versions of all software components.

Procedures:

- Unload SBACKUP (or other SME) *before* unloading the support modules and tape device drivers.

- If you have multiple NetWare servers, make sure the Directory is synchronized among the servers.

- Log in as Admin when performing a backup or restore operation. NDS requires the utmost in power and authority to handle everybody's data.

- You can back up the Directory by loading TSANDS on any server that holds a replica. In a small network with three or fewer servers, every server holds a replica, so you can load TSANDS on the server doing the backup.

- When denoting specific files and directories to back up, use the proper file-naming format for the target. *For a Macintosh,* use the following format: Volume::directory:directory:filename. *For all others,* use Volume:/directory/directory/filename.

- If you are restoring both Directory and file system data, restore the Directory first. This allows the trustee information to be coordinated with the file system.

- Use the proper case for non-DOS names. If you're not sure of the original capitalization, refer to your log file.

- Always test your backups by restoring a sample file.

- Always check the backup logs. Print them out and keep them in a binder in case they get corrupted or overwritten.

Detailed Backup/Restore Procedures

Complete the procedures in this section in the same order that are presented here.

1. Load the workstation registry points (TSADOS and TSAPROXY).

2. Load the TSAs on workstations and servers whose data you need to back up or restore.

3. Perform the backup or restoration.

If you try to perform a backup or restoration without the loaded TSAs, SMS will tell you there's nothing to back up. If you try to load the TSAs before the registry points, the TSAs won't register when loaded and you'll get the same error: nothing to back up.

The backup and restoration processes include loading drivers for the controller and tape drive. Again, this must be completed before starting SBACKUP or the process will fail.

LOADING THE WORKSTATION REGISTRY POINTS This procedure is unnecessary if you're only backing up servers and/or the Directory.

Before loading any workstation TSAs, you must load the workstation registry point(s). To back up DOS workstations, load TSADOS. For backing up other workstations, load TSAPROXY.

1. Use one of the following commands as necessary at the backup server console:

```
LOAD TSADOS
LOAD TSAPROXY
```

2. Add the appropriate command to the AUTOEXEC.NCF file based on the type of workstation you are backing up. To edit the AUTOEXEC.NCF file, type

```
LOAD EDIT AUTOEXEC.NCF
```

at the server console.

Or you can use a text editor from a workstation. The file is in the SYS:SYSTEM directory.

LOADING THE TSA ON A DOS/VLMS WORKSTATION You can configure the VLM client with the TSA by running the client installation program, INSTALL.EXE.

1. First make sure that you have updated the installation files on the server. You can download these files from `http://netware.novell.com/`.

2. Log in from the workstation, and change directories to the client installation directory.

3. Type **INSTALL,** and you will see an installation screen.

4. One of the options is as follows:

   ```
   Configure your workstation for backup by a NetWare server
   running software such as SBACKUP (Y/N?) No
   ```

   Highlight the word No and type **Y.**

5. Supply the following information:

   - SMS server name (this is the server with the tape drive)

   - A name for the workstation (you should write this down)

   - An optional password

   - The number of buffers available for the transfer (1–30); increasing the number accelerates the process but uses more RAM

   - Workstation hard drives to be backed up

6. After you have completed the options, press F10 and continue with the client software installation.

The TSA installation program adds TSASMS.COM to the workstation's STARTNET.BAT file. If you use a file other than STARTNET.BAT to load the client software, you can add TSASMS.COM manually to that file.

The installation program also puts the SMS options you specified into your workstation's NET.CFG file.

LOADING THE TSA ON A DOS/CLIENT 32 WORKSTATION You can configure a DOS/Windows computer for backups using the Client 32 installation program. The installation program has both an INSTALL.EXE version for DOS and a SETUP.EXE for Windows. Both work in a similar fashion. For the DOS version, change to the client installation directory and run INSTALL. Then continue with step 5 of the following procedure.

To run the Windows setup:

1. First make sure that you have updated the installation files on the server. You can download these files from `http://netware.novell.com/`.

2. Log in from the workstation and start Windows 3.1.

3. Select File | Run.

4. Browse to the network directory where the Client 32 for DOS/Windows 3.1 installation files are copied. Select SETUP.EXE and confirm OK.

5. After selecting the LAN driver, you are shown an Additional Options screen. Choose the TSA for SMS option.

6. A TSA for SMS Configuration screen appears. Supply the following information:

   ▪ SMS server name; this is the server with the tape drive.

   ▪ A name for the workstation (you should write this down).

   ▪ An optional password.

   ▪ Workstation hard drives to be backed up.

   ▪ The number of buffers available for the transfer (1–30); increasing the number accelerates the process but uses more RAM.

7. When you're done, click on the Next button and complete the client software installation.

The installation program adds TSASMS.COM to the workstation's STARTNET.BAT file. If you use a batch file other than STARTNET.BAT to load the client software, you can add TSASMS.COM manually to that file.

The installation program also puts the SMS options you specified into your workstation's NET.CFG file.

LOADING THE TSA ON A WINDOWS 95 WORKSTATION You can configure a Windows 95 computer for backups by using the following procedure.

1. Copy the files whose names begin with TSAW95 from the directory SYS:\ PUBLIC\CLIENT\WIN95\IBM_ENU to a directory on the Windows 95 workstation.

2. In the Startup program folder, add a shortcut to TSAW95.EXE (one of the files you copied).

3. Reboot the Windows 95 workstation. A TSA icon appears on the Windows 95 taskbar.

4. Double-click on the TSA icon. The TSA Information page appears, as shown in Figure 10.2.

5. Supply the following information:

- User name (the TSA picks up the workstation name from Windows 95).

- An optional password.

- Server (the one with the tape drive).

- Resources available to TSA (workstation hard drives to be backed up).

6. (Recommended) Click on the Auto Register check box to have the TSA automatically register with the server.

FIGURE 10.2
The TSA Information page helps you configure the Windows 95 workstation for backups.

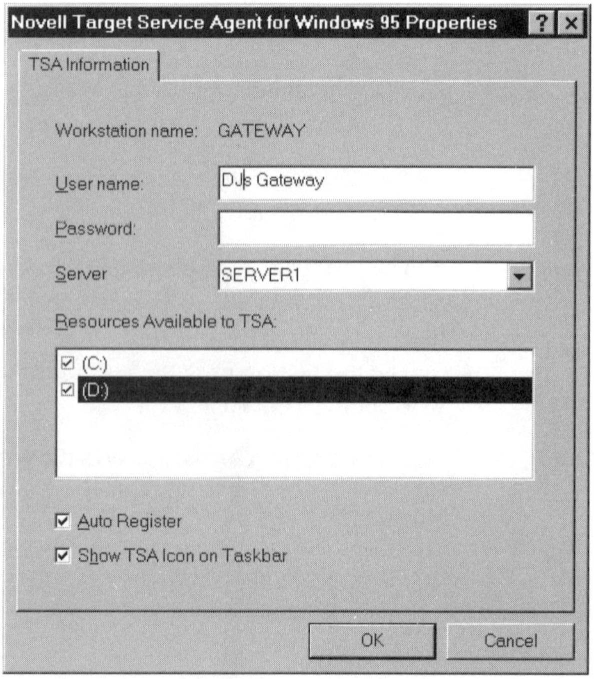

7. (Optional) Click on the Show TSA Icon on the taskbar if you want the TSA always available for configuration.

LOADING THE TSA ON A MACINTOSH WORKSTATION New with Net-Ware 4.11 is the NetWare Client for Mac OS software. Novell recommends using this client (requester) with System 7.5 or later. You can install the client from the NetWare 4.11 CD-ROM, or create installation disks from the server using INSTALL.NLM.

The new Client for Mac OS software is different from (better than) the old NetWare for Macintosh. NetWare finally gives Macintosh users the same access to NetWare and NDS that has been offered to DOS and Windows users.

During the installation of the Macintosh client software, make sure you select MaxIPX, which is the default for the easy installation method. The installation should also create a MacTSA folder containing the MacTSA application and the MacTSA Prefs file. After client installation, perform the following steps to load the TSA:

1. (Recommended) Place the MacTSA application in the Startup Items folder, so that the MacTSA starts when the workstation boots.

2. Restart the workstation.

3. Double-click the MacTSA Prefs application. The MacTSA Preferences dialog box is displayed.

4. Enter the following information in the MacTSA Preferences dialog box:

- MacTSA user name

- Optional password

- Host server (the one with the tape drive)

5. Open the Sharing Setup Control Panel and enter a Macintosh Name. This name appears in SBACKUP as an available backup target.

LOADING SERVER AND DIRECTORY TSAS If you are backing up data from a server, make sure you load the appropriate TSA at that server's console. You can add the LOAD command to that server's AUTOEXEC.NCF file to make the server available after you have rebooted it. The LOAD command is also required for the server with the tape drive that will run SBACKUP.

The various LOAD commands are as follows:

SERVER	LOAD COMMAND
NetWare 4.0x	LOAD TSA400
NetWare 4.1x	LOAD TSA410
NetWare 3.11	LOAD TSA311
NetWare 3.12	LOAD TSA312

For backing up the NDS Directory database, load TSANDS at the backup server's console.

BACKING UP DATA WITH SBACKUP The following procedure is performed at the host server—the one with the tape drive.

Before starting SBACKUP, make sure you have loaded the workstation registry NLMs if you are backing up workstations. Load TSAs at the computers you want to back up after you load the registry NLMs.

1. Insert a tape in the drive.

2. Load the drivers for your controller and tape drive. If you have a hard drive or CD-ROM drive mounted on the same controller as your tape drive, you have already loaded the controller driver.

   For example, the following LOAD commands are for the Adaptec 154x adapter and a SCSI-2 tape drive. Use the drivers recommended by the hardware manufacturers.

   ```
   LOAD SCSI154X.HAM
   LOAD SCSI2TP.CDM
   ```

3. Type the following command at the server console:

   ```
   SCAN FOR NEW DEVICES
   ```

4. At the server console, type

   ```
   LOAD SBACKUP SIZE=n BUFFERS=n
   ```

   and press Enter.

Replace the *n* specifiers with the size and buffer settings appropriate for your situation. The size of buffers is specified in KB and may be 16, 32, 64, 128, or 256 (default 64). The number of buffers may be from 2 to 10 (default 4). If you have plenty of RAM, increase the size and buffer parameters.

*To automate your backup process, you can put the commands required in steps 1 through 3 of the above procedure and LOAD TSA410 in an NCF file such as BACKUP.NCF. To create the file, type **LOAD EDIT BACKUP.NCF** at the server console, or create the text file in SYS:SYSTEM from a workstation. You might also want to load TSANDS, if you normally back up the Directory.*

5. The SBACKUP main screen appears, as shown in Figure 10.3. Select Backup, and you'll get a list of targets (TSAs) that are loaded on the network.

6. Select the target to back up.

   If you select a DOS workstation, you will be prompted for a user name. Type in **Admin** as the user name. You will then need to supply the Admin password.

7. Select a device (the tape drive or equivalent device on the server). If the tape is not labeled, you'll need to give it a label. You are also prompted to set or accept the default location of log and error files.

8. Select a type of backup, using Table 10.2 as a guide.

FIGURE 10.3
The SBACKUP
main screen

TABLE 10.2	TYPE	DESCRIPTION
Types of Backup	Full	Includes the entire target.
	Custom	You select specific data to include or exclude, such as certain files or directories.
	Differential	Includes all files and directories changed since the last full backup.
	Incremental	Includes all files and directories changed since the most recent full or incremental backup.

Don't mix differential backups and incremental backups. If you do, the differential backup won't contain all changes since the last full backup. Use a number of differential backups interspersed with full backups, or a number of incremental backups interspersed with full backups.

9. Start the backup (or schedule the backup for a later time).

Do not schedule a backup to occur at the same time a server's compression routine is running. Check and adjust the compression time using MONITOR | Server parameters | File system.

10. When the backup is complete, use SBACKUP to view the backup and error logs.

11. Restore a portion of the data to test the backup.

You may need to exit SBACKUP, unload the tape driver, then reload the tape driver and restart SBACKUP.

RESTORING DATA WITH SBACKUP You'll notice that the process for restoring data from a tape is very similar to backing it up. The following procedure is performed at the host server (the one with the tape drive).

Before starting SBACKUP, make sure you have loaded the proper workstation registry NLMs if you are restoring data to workstations. Load TSAs at the workstations to which you want to restore data.

1. Insert the tape holding the data in the server's tape drive.

2. Load the drivers for your controller and tape drive. If you have a hard drive or CD-ROM drive mounted on the same controller as your tape drive, you have already loaded the controller driver.

   For example, the following LOAD commands are for the Adaptec 2940 adapter and a Conner tape drive. Use the drivers recommended by the hardware manufacturers.

   ```
   LOAD AIC7870 SLOT=2
   LOAD TAPEDAI
   ```

3. Type the following command at the server console:

   ```
   SCAN FOR NEW DEVICES
   ```

4. At the server console, type

   ```
   LOAD SBACKUP SIZE=n BUFFERS=n
   ```

   and press Enter.

   Replace the n specifiers with the size and buffer settings appropriate for your situation. The size of buffers is specified in KB and may be 16, 32, 64, 128, or 256 (default 64). The number of buffers may be from 2 to 10 (default 4). If you have plenty of RAM, increase the size and buffer parameters.

5. Select Restore.

6. Select a target to which you want the data restored.

7. Choose to restore a session from existing log files (you will be prompted for the location of log files), or have a session log generated from the tape.

8. Select a storage device from which you want the data restored.

9. Select a type of restoration:

   - Single file or directory (good for checking the restoration process)

   - Entire session (good for recovery of catastrophic data loss)

   - Custom (the files, directories, or parts of the Directory you choose)

10. Start the restoration.

Summary

B ACKING UP AND RESTORING data involves more than having and using a tape drive. You also must make sure you have procedures in place for *preventing* data loss. Prevention is easier.

When you do make your tape backups, use NetWare's SMS architecture and a tape drive (or equivalent device).

Back up the NetWare file system, important data stored on workstations, and the Directory. Keep good logs and label your tapes. Test your backups. Store a full backup off site on a regular basis.

When somebody does need to restore deleted data, use the appropriate salvage utility if the data is on a functioning NetWare file system. Your last option for restoring data is the tapes created using NetWare's SMS architecture and SBACKUP or a third-party SME.

Synchronizing Time on Multiple Servers

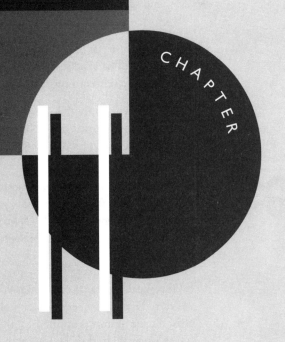

ETWARE'S TIME SYNCHRONIZATION service ensures that all your NetWare 4 servers agree on the time. Having synchronized servers gives you three important benefits:

- Third-party network applications will provide accurate time stamps to events. For instance, if you run GroupWise on a number of servers, the messaging and scheduling features will function properly. This means messages will be sorted in the right order, because their time stamps will be correct.

- If you use the SET_TIME ON command in login scripts, the workstations, too, will be synchronized to network time. This means local applications also use correct time stamps.

- NDS will apply the correct time stamps to NDS events. This is critical to the inner workings of NDS, since changes to the Directory must be accurately coordinated among all copies of the Directory on all servers.

If you have only one server, time synchronization is not an issue for your network. You can read this chapter for information, but you need not perform the procedures. If you have fewer than four servers and no WAN links, time synchronization sets itself up and usually runs fine. This chapter will be of help for troubleshooting and tuning purposes, however.

Whenever a change is made to a Directory object, that change is replicated to all NetWare 4 servers on the network. Since changes can originate at any of the servers, NetWare needs to keep changes in proper sequence. To accomplish this, a time stamp is applied to all NDS events. Time stamps are in Universal Time Coordinated (UTC), which is another name for the familiar Greenwich Mean Time. Using UTC ensures that servers in different time zones can be synchronized.

Time Synchronization Parameters

To ADJUST A SERVER'S TIME for the local time zone, time zone parameters are set at each server. The parameters are set when you run the installation program initially, and they are copied to the AUTOEXEC.NCF file so the adjustment is made whenever the server is booted. If you ever boot the server without running the AUTOEXEC.NCF file (by typing the command SERVER -NA), you get messages at the console saying the server is issuing synthetic time. This occurs because the server hasn't used the time zone parameters found in the AUTOEXEC.NCF file.

The time zone parameters are similar to the following:

```
set Time Zone = MST7MDT
set Daylight Savings Time Offset = 1
set Start Of Daylight Savings Time =
   (APRIL SUNDAY FIRST  2:00:00 AM)
set End Of Daylight Savings Time =
   (OCTOBER SUNDAY LAST  2:00:00 AM)
```

Don't worry about the abbreviations. The strings are generated from user-friendly questions during server installation.

Speaking of user friendliness, you should use MONITOR or SERVMAN to change the time zone parameters, rather than editing the AUTOEXEC.BAT file directly. If you change time synchronization parameters using MONITOR or SERVMAN, you can have some of the parameters saved to a file called TIMESYNC.CFG. NetWare 4 servers run TIMESYNC.NLM automatically when the server is booted, to control time synchronization. The TIMESYNC.CFG file in SYS:SYSTEM can contain parameters for TIMESYNC.NLM, if the default settings are not adequate. The server reads this file when it boots, just as it reads AUTOEXEC.NCF.

Another time synchronization parameter set in the AUTOEXEC.NCF or TIMESYNC.CFG file is time server type, as follows:

```
set Default Time Server Type = SINGLE
```

Time server type is a fairly complex issue. Don't worry about changing it, though, since the default works well.

Four time server types are available:

TIME SERVER TYPE	DESCRIPTION
Single Reference	Default type for first server. Issues time for the network.
Secondary	Default type for second and subsequent servers on the network. Accepts time from a Single Reference server.
Reference	Issues time for Primary server.
Primary	Receives time from Reference server. Issues time for selected Secondary servers.

In a small network, you have a Single Reference server and any number of Secondary servers. The Secondary servers get time from the Single Reference server. Reference servers and Primary servers are for networks with more than 20 servers or networks with servers separated by WAN links. They are not generally compatible with the default types.

Setting Time on a NetWare 4 Server

TO DETERMINE THE TIME on a NetWare server, type **TIME** at the server console. The console will display information similar to the following. The current time is shown on the last line of output.

```
Time zone string: "MST7MDT"
DST status:  ON
DST start:   Sunday, April 6, 1997   2:00:00 am MST
DST end:     Sunday, October 27, 1996   2:00:00 am MDT
Time synchronization is active.
Time is synchronized to the network.
Monday, September 23, 1996   6:57:27 pm UTC
Monday, September 23, 1996   12:57:27 pm MDT
```

To set time and date parameters on a server, bring it down and use the DOS commands **SET TIME** and **SET DATE**. Then reboot the computer.

If you reboot the server after setting time and date and you get incorrect time or date readings, you know you have a bad CMOS clock or battery on the motherboard. Contact the motherboard manufacturer for a remedy.

When you change a server's time, the server may display a message saying the network is out of synchronization. This occurs because network time is maintained separately from server time. On a Single Reference server, the server adjusts *network* time gradually, in small increments, until it agrees with the server time you set. When you change time on a Secondary time server, the *server* time is gradually adjusted to agree with network time.

Specifying a Different Single Reference Server

Y OUR FIRST NETWARE 4 SERVER is by default the Single Reference time server on the network. However, you may want to change to a server that keeps better time than the original. Here is the procedure to change time server types.

1. At the Single Reference server console, load MONITOR or SERVMAN.

2. Select Server Parameters.

3. Select Time. (To move quickly down the list of parameters, press **T**.)

4. Make the following time settings:

```
Timesync Type: SECONDARY
Default Timesync Type: SECONDARY
```

5. Select the following time synchronization actions from the same screen *in the order shown*:

```
Timesync Write Parameters (Confirm Yes)
Timesync Restart Flag (Confirm Yes)
```

Until you change another server to Single Reference type, the network will not be synchronized (since there is no reference server to synchronize *to*). That's what you do next.

6. At the server you want to be the Single Reference server, start MONITOR or SERVMAN and select Server Parameters.

7. Select Time. Remember, just press **T** to get through the list quickly.

8. Make the following time settings:

```
Timesync Type: SINGLE
Default Timesync Type: SINGLE
```

9. Select the following time synchronization actions from the same screen *in the order shown*:

```
Timesync Write Parameters (Confirm Yes)
Timesync Restart Flag (Confirm Yes)
```

Troubleshooting Time Synchronization

ANY TIME YOU NEED to determine the status of the time synchronization service on your network, perform the following steps:

I. At a server console prompt, type **LOAD DSREPAIR.**

2. Select Time Synchronization. Wait a moment for the utility to gather information from other servers. As you wait, a screen displays the status of time synchronization data collection.

The DSREPAIR log is displayed within a text editor. You can annotate or modify this log if you want to. The DSREPAIR log lists all NetWare 4 servers on the network, with data for each server as described in Table 11.1.

If you find that time is not synchronized in your network, before making adjustments evaluate the problem using the following simple guidelines:

- If the time is a few minutes out of synchronization, the time synchronization service will eventually adjust the clocks until they are synchronized.

- If the time difference amounts to hours or days, the time difference between servers is too great for automatic synchronization.

TABLE 11.1	FIELD	MEANING
DSREPAIR Log Statistics for Time Synchronization	DS.NLM version	The version of DS.NLM running on the server.
	Replica depth	The replica depth field reports −1 if no replicas are stored on the server or 0 if the server contains a replica of the [Root] partition. A positive integer indicates how many objects deep from the [Root] the first replica is on that server.
	Time source	The time server type. Normally this will be Single Reference for one server and Secondary for the rest. If you have more than one Single Reference server, you'll need to change all but one of these Single Reference servers to Secondary. (See the procedure in the previous section.)
	Time is in sync	The local time synchronization status on each server. This status should be Yes. It may be No if you have recently made some changes to time synchronization.
	Time +/-	The difference in time between the server from which you are running DSREPAIR and the selected server in the list. All servers should be within one second of each other. If the difference in time is more than a few minutes, it might indicate that you have recently made changes to time synchronization. See the troubleshooting suggestions in this section for more information.

Here are the steps to resynchronize if you find that it is indeed necessary:

1. Bring down the server using the **DOWN** command and exit to DOS.

2. Use the DOS **SET TIME** and **SET DATE** commands to correct the DOS clock.

3. Turn the computer off, then on again, to see if the settings are maintained. If they aren't, replace the CMOS battery on the computer.

4. Start the server. At the server console, type

```
SET TIMESYNC DEBUG = 7
```

The time synchronization service will then display its messages on the server console. The messages will show it contacting a Single Reference time server and calculating the time offset.

- If the server is not communicating with other servers, check network connections. Servers communicate time via Service Advertising Protocol (SAP). Make sure there are no bridges or routers between servers that filter SAP packets.

- Also make sure the time zone and daylight savings time options are correctly set for each server. An incorrect setting can throw the network out of synchronization.

5. When you are finished troubleshooting, type

```
SET TIMESYNC DEBUG = 0
```

at the server console.

Summary

TIME SYNCHRONIZATION IS BOTH a useful service for network applications and a critical one for NDS. Given its importance, you should have to deal with it rarely, if at all. NetWare automatically sets up your first server as a Single Reference time server, providing subsequent servers (which become Secondary time servers) with network time.

You can easily set a server's time or time server type using procedures in this chapter. Resetting may cause momentary loss of network synchronization, but NetWare automatically adjusts server time and/or network time to bring all servers back into synch.

If a server remains out of synchronization for hours or days, use the troubleshooting procedures in this chapter. The computer may have a bad CMOS clock, or you may have made an incorrect setting, or the servers may be having trouble communicating.

Internet and
Intranet Services

THIS CHAPTER DISCUSSES Novell's IntranetWare products, which support two significant operations in your company. They help you

- Connect your users to the Internet via the NetWare server.

- Create a company *intranet*. An intranet is a way of distributing company information that can be read with a Web browser—generally considered a way to increase internal communication and reduce paper usage.

The IntranetWare products offer these features for NetWare 4.10 and NetWare 4.11 servers. IntranetWare is available with NetWare 4.11 at no extra cost, or as a set of add-ons for NetWare 4.10.

Connecting Users to the Internet

THIS SECTION DISCUSSES the process of linking to the Internet via an Internet Service Provider (ISP), setting up a server for Internet access, and setting up workstations.

Linking to an Internet Service Provider

To establish your access account and physical connection to the Internet, you will need to work with both an Internet Service Provider (ISP) and a local telephone company. Two typical link options for small networks are ISDN and Frame Relay. Figure 12.1 shows these two configurations.

When you design your Internet connection, you'll be juggling three options: the WAN adapter, the link, and the ISP. All of these components must be compatible.

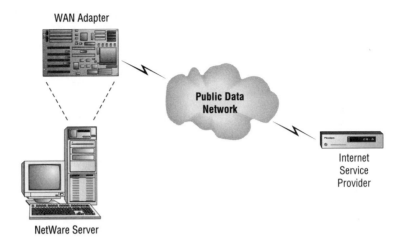

FIGURE 12.1
A typical Internet access configuration includes a WAN adapter, a wide-area link, and an Internet Service Provider.

WAN Adapter

Public Data Network

Internet
Service
Provider

NetWare Server

The sales representatives at the ISPs you contact can give you general information about the kind of service they provide, such as Primary Rate ISDN (or PRI), Basic Rate ISDN (or BRI), and Frame Relay. The representatives will also tell you about the cost of the services, names and information on the competing local phone companies, and even suggestions for what kind of adapter to buy.

Speaking of Adapters... *Since many manufacturers offer a wide variety of adapters, keep two important considerations in mind. (1) Match the adapter to both the ISP service available and the link provided by the local telephone company; and (2) Buy an adapter certified by the Novell Labs "Yes" program. Contact Novell Labs at* `http://labs.novell.com/` *for a list of WAN adapters certified for NIAS. Remember that the cost runs from a few hundred dollars up to a few thousand, and features vary greatly. Make sure you shop around.*

The ISDN Link

ISDN is an acronym for Integrated Services Digital Network. This kind of link offers channels for both voice and data through a digital network. ISDN replaces today's analog 28.8Kbps modem technology with digital transmissions yielding typical speeds of 64Kbps per channel before compression. These digital lines are virtually error free. Multiple devices can be in use at the same time for voice and data transmissions, and the lines can also be combined for higher data speeds. In most cases, the same copper wires used for modern telephone service can be used successfully for ISDN, so most homes and offices are ISDN ready.

Making Sense of the IntranetWare Components

With IntranetWare, you get four CD-ROMS:

- *NetWare 4.11 Operating System*, which includes the Web Server product, client software for accessing IP hosts, and Netscape Navigator

- *Online documentation* for IntranetWare

- *Novell Internet Access Server* (NIAS), which includes the IPX/IP Gateway, WAN Extensions, and MultiProtocol Router (MPR) products

- *FTP Services*, including NetWare UNIX Print Services

For your company's Internet and intranet solutions, you will use a sometimes-confusing mix of the products and subproducts on the IntranetWare CD-ROMs. Novell's documentation for the IntranetWare suite may be puzzling, as well. For instance, FTP Services is required for both Internet and intranet functions, but neither of the words *Internet* or *intranet* occurs in the Installation and Planning Guide that's on the FTP Services CD-ROM.

The reason for this confusion is that most of Novell's internetworking products were developed not with *the* Internet in mind, but rather for wide-area connectivity in general, or specifically for UNIX connectivity. Novell has yet to come up with a truly elegant Internet or intranet solution.

This chapter will help you navigate through the IntranetWare products to the functionality you're looking for. However, due to IntranetWare's poor usability, I suggest you wait for the next release of InternetWare or purchase a third-party Internet/intranet package if you can.

ISDN service includes data channels called B (bearer) channels, and a single D (delta) channel for signaling protocol. Two types of service are generally available, differentiated by the number of B channels:

- Basic Rate ISDN (BRI) offers two 64Kbps (or sometimes 56Kbit) B channels.

- Primary Rate ISDN (PRI) offers twenty-three B channels (56Kbps or 64Kbps). PRI service is equivalent to T1 speed.

A typical BRI connection costs about $200 per month, plus an installation fee that may run from $100 to several hundred dollars. For PRI service, you pay about $3,000 to set it up and $1,300 per month. The ISP will also charge you monthly for Internet access; charges depend on the bandwidth provided. These prices vary widely from area to area. You may find significantly lower costs.

The adapter you use for an ISDN connection should be a CAPI or AT type certified by Novell Labs. A BRI connection will need an integrated or separate NT1 adapter if it's not supplied by the local telephone company. For PRI service, a Channel Service Unit/Data Service Unit (CSU/DSU) is required, which may be separate or integrated with the adapter.

When considering ISDN adapters, you should check the following features. They must be compatible with your link to the ISP.

ADAPTER FEATURE	REQUIREMENT
Link type	BRI or PRI.
Number of ports	This is the number of lines to the ISP. You'll need only the number of ports you're paying for at the local telephone company and ISP.
Number of B channels	Adapters can support from 2 to over 100 channels per port. You'll need only the number of channels you're paying for at the local telephone company and ISP.
D channel protocol(s)	Get this information from the local telephone company.
Encapsulation	Point-to-point protocol (PPP) encapsulation.
Separate CSU/DSU device	Not needed if the adapter has an integrated CSU/DSU or NT1 adapter.

The Frame Relay Link

Frame Relay Service is a data network service that supports data transmission from 9.6Kbps to 1.544Mbps. Frame Relay operates in packet mode, using pre-established logical channel assignments (Permanent Virtual Circuits or PVCs) to route data over high-speed shared network facilities. This link provides a dedicated connection from the network interface at your location to the Frame Relay network.

Cost of a typical Frame Relay connection through the local telephone company starts at $500 per month. This provides from 56Kbps up to 1.544 Mbps (T1 speed). The ISP will also charge you monthly for Internet access (typically $300 for 56Kbps and $1,000 for T1). You'll need a WAN adapter ($700 for 56Kbps; $1,900 for T1). You may need a CSU/DSU if the WAN adapter doesn't have one built in. When setting up the link with the local telephone company, you will provide a circuit ID, which you get from your ISP.

The local telephone company generally charges for both ends of the link, plus a charge related to the data rate you need. If the distance to the ISP is very short, you may benefit from leasing a dedicated line. Leased lines cost more over a longer distance; Frame Relay connections, on the other hand, aren't charged by distance.

Setting Up the Server for Internet Access

Since the Internet uses TCP/IP, you need to do one of the following to accommodate this arrangement:

- Use TCP/IP on your workstations, either exclusively or in conjunction with IPX. If you choose to use IP exclusively on the LAN, you will maintain a list of IP addresses for each server and workstation on the network, and bind IP to each network adapter on the network.

- Use Novell's IPX/IP Gateway to translate between IP on the Internet and IPX (and/or IP) on the LAN. In this configuration, you only need an IP address for the NetWare server. The server automatically passes the appropriate Internet data to the workstations via IPX. The Windows 3.1 or Windows 95 workstations use Client 32 with a special WINSOCK DLL, and an HTML browser.

The IPX/IP Gateway

Installing an IPX/IP Gateway creates a new server object in the Directory tree called a Gateway Server. This object is actually a service (provided by IPXGW.NLM) added to the NetWare server. The name of the Directory object is the NetWare server's name with the characters -GW appended—for example, SERVER1-GW.

When using the IPX/IP Gateway, all IP traffic goes through the Gateway Server, which has control over user access to the Internet. This control can be configured by the network administrator using the familiar NetWare Administrator utility. Access control on the Gateway Server is switched on and off with the INETCFG NLM. When access control is switched off, all users have unlimited access through the gateway. When control is switched on but no access rights have been configured, then all users logged in have unlimited access rights.

Access control information is stored in NDS and can be configured for Organization, Organizational Unit, Group, and User objects. In addition, packet filtering allows you to control both inbound and outbound traffic, and to set limits based on services (Web or FTP, for example) and hosts. These restrictions apply to all users.

NetWare Administrator is extended to manage IP by the use of a snap-in DLL. The DLL adds buttons for IP service restrictions and host restrictions to the User, Group, Organizational Unit, and Organization objects. Before using NetWare Administrator, you must edit the appropriate NetWare Administrator INI file to install the snap-in.

The IPX/IP Gateway does not support the use of UDP or raw sockets by WINSOCK applications. The primary use of raw sockets is for ping functionality, so the Gateway replaces the ping function with an application named Winping.

Installing Novell Internet Access Server (NIAS)

Hardware requirements for NIAS are as follows:

HARDWARE	REQUIREMENT
Additional disk space	120 MB on the SYS volume.
Additional RAM	3MB, plus 500KB for each 100 TCP connections. Each user may have multiple TCP connections. Netscape Navigator, for example, uses four connections by default.
WAN adapter	Contact Novell Labs for a list of certified WAN adapters.

To install the NIAS software (which includes NetWare MultiProtocol Router, the IPX/IP Gateway, and WAN Extensions), follow these steps:

1. Modify the following parameters for the server, using SERVMAN or MONITOR.

SERVER PARAMETER	SETTING
▪ MINIMUM PACKET RECEIVE BUFFERS	▪ At least 400
▪ MAXIMUM PACKET RECEIVE BUFFERS	▪ At least 1000
▪ MAXIMUM PHYSICAL RECEIVE PACKET SIZE	▪ Set to largest value used by your topology plus 10: Ethernet=1542 4Mbps Token Ring=4540 16Mbps Token Ring=4540 FDDI=618

2. Insert the Novell Internet Access Server CD-ROM in the drive you will use for installation. You can use the CD-ROM in any of three ways; proceed to Step 3A, 3B, or 3C.

3A. Mount the CD-ROM as a NetWare volume on the server. (See Chapter 4, "Installing the Network.") Then proceed to Step 4.

3B. Load the CD-ROM driver from the server's DOS partition, and restart the server, accessing the CD-ROM as a DOS device (such as D:). Then proceed to Step 4.

3C. Insert the CD-ROM into a workstation and use RCONSOLE to perform the installation. For this option, complete Steps A through G:

A. Load RSPX and supply a password at the server console.

B. At the workstation, start RCONSOLE and select the server.

C. Display the RCONSOLE Available Options menu by pressing Alt+F1.

D. Select Transfer Files To Server.

E. Copy the RSPAWN.NLM and SPXS.NLM files from the CD-ROM's SUPPS\4X directory to the SYS:\SYSTEM directory on the remote server.

    F. Press Esc to return to the remote server console prompt.

    G. Type the following commands at the console:

```
UNLOAD RSPAWN

UNLOAD SPXS

LOAD RSPAWN
```

    and proceed to Step 4.

4. At the server console, type the following commands:

```
UNLOAD LIC_API
LOAD INSTALL
```

5. Select Product Options. The Other Installation Actions menu appears.

6. From the Other Installation Actions menu, select Install a Product Not Listed.

7. Supply the installation subdirectory of the CD-ROM.

- For a CD-ROM local to the server, press F3 and enter a drive letter and subdirectory (for example, **D:\NIAS\INSTALL**).

- For a CD-ROM mounted as a NetWare volume, press F3 and use the volume name and subdirectory (for example, **NIAS4:\NIAS\INSTALL**).

- For an RCONSOLE session, press F4 and enter the drive and remote installation directory (for example, **E:\RINSTALL**).

8. Take a break. The File Copy Status dialog appears, and a long (up to 30-minute) temporary file copying process begins.

9. When you're ready to continue, choose Install Product from the Installation options menu. A window displays the current server name.

10. From the Install To Servers menu, press Enter and confirm Yes to start the installation. If you are installing to servers other than the one whose console you are using, you will be prompted to log in as an administrator and supply a password.

11. When you are prompted to "Install configuration files?" select No.

When the installation of the Novell Internet Access Server product is complete, the following message is displayed:

```
Installation was successful. Bring down and restart each
server on which you installed the software to ensure that
it uses the newest NLM files.
```

In addition to updating NLM files, the installation program copies the client files to the SYS:\PUBLIC\CLIENT\WIN95 and SYS:\PUBLIC\CLIENT\WIN31 directories. The Netscape browser files are copied to the SYS:\NETSCAPE\32 and SYS:\NETSCAPE\16 directories.

12. Press Esc and confirm Yes to save changes.

13. Restart the server to load the new NLMs and server parameters.

After installing NIAS, you're ready to proceed to the task of enabling and configuring the link.

Enabling and Configuring the Link

MultiProtocol Router (MPR) handles the network protocols on the server that are required for the TCP/IP connection to the Internet. The tool for managing MPR is INETCFG, which you run from the server console. Perform the following steps to enable and configure MPR.

1. At the server console, type **LOAD INETCFG.**

2. You will be prompted to transfer commands out of AUTOEXEC.NCF. Choose Yes.

The LOAD and BIND commands originally entered into the AUTOEXEC.BAT file are transferred to a configuration file called NETINFO.CFG. After transferring the commands, INETCFG manages protocols via INITSYS.NCF and NETINFO.CFG. The following lines are put in the AUTOEXEC.NCF file:

```
; Network driver LOADs and BINDs are initiated via
; INITSYS.NCF. The actual LOAD and BIND commands
; are contained in INITSYS.NCF and NETINFO.CFG.
; These files are in SYS:ETC.
sys:etc\initsys.ncf
```

3. Do the following to enable IPX/IP Gateway:

A. Select Protocols.

B. Select TCP/IP.

C. Select IPX/IP Gateway Configuration.

D. Change the Gateway Status to Enabled and press Enter.

Several options now appear under the Gateway Configuration heading. Do not change any of these default values.

4. In the Name Server #1 field, enter the IP address of your primary DNS server (available from your ISP).

5. When prompted, enter the Admin object name and password, which are required to create the Gateway Server object in the Directory.

For ISDN connections, continue with the explanation in the following section, "Configuring for ISDN." For Frame Relay connections, skip to the section titled "Configuring for Frame Relay."

Configuring for ISDN

The following procedures apply generally to most adapters. You may need to modify the procedures somewhat to conform to the adapter you buy.

PERMANENT PPP CONNECTIONS Your permanent connection may use a leased line or a dial-up line. The leased line incurs a fixed cost whether you disconnect or not. The bandwidth of a leased line usually ranges from about 56Kbps to 2.048Mbps. In a permanent dial-up line interface, a modem keeps the permanent connection active. If the connection goes down, the modem reestablishes it.

To provide protection against unauthorized access, the PPP specification defines two optional protocols that authenticate inbound call attempts: the Password Authentication Protocol (PAP) and the Challenge Handshake Authentication Protocol (CHAP). These protocols ensure that the local system can accept calls only from authorized remote computers who know the user ID and password.

The main difference between PAP and CHAP is in their treatment of passwords. PAP sends the password string across the WAN in clear text. CHAP, on the other hand, provides greater security by using the password to encrypt a challenge string.

ON-DEMAND PPP CONNECTIONS Voice-grade telephone lines, ISDN lines, and switched data service such as switched/56 or switched/256 can be used for on-demand connections. However, network protocols generally expect each circuit to provide permanent connections to all remote systems. The reason is that the network protocols need to regularly exchange routing information and service updates.

To provide the required route and service information without tying up the on-demand connection, the MPR supplies static route and service databases. Each database is specific to the network protocol and contains a manually configured subset of the route and service information. Manual configuration eliminates the need for periodic maintenance updates because the required route and service information is already available in the static databases.

A single static route is also useful as a default route for IPX or TCP/IP hosts. In this way, only the routing information required by users to access a specified set of services crosses the link.

CONFIGURING ADAPTERS FOR RUNNING PPP OVER ISDN To configure adapters for running PPP over ISDN, you must first configure a physical WAN adapter. To configure a WHSMCAPI adapter, complete the following steps:

1. Load INETCFG.

2. Select Boards.

3. Press Ins to display the list of available drivers, and choose the WHSMCAPI driver.

4. Enter a name for the new adapter.

5. Press Enter to select CAPI Board Configuration. If prompted, elect to have the driver load automatically. The Select a CAPI Driver dialog appears.

6. Select a driver from the list. The CAPI Board Configuration dialog appears.

7. In the MAXPORTS field, enter the number of ports for the adapter. Press Esc.

8. From the CAPI Board Configuration dialog, select Driver Specific Configuration.

9. Press Ins. Type in the hardware configuration parameters and select Service Profile ID. Supply the origination address (OAD) and Service Provider Identification (SPID). When finished, press Esc and confirm Yes to save SPID information.

10. Press Esc until you return to the Internetworking Configuration dialog. Confirm Yes to save the changes.

Your next step is to configure either permanent or on-demand links.

CONFIGURING ISDN LINKS Following are the steps to configure a connection over a dial-up ISDN line.

To get descriptions of any field in the configuration dialogs, move to that field and press F1.

1. Select Network Interfaces. An interface is listed for each port of the adapter.

2. Select a network interface that has not been configured. The Select A Medium dialog is displayed.

3. Select PPP. For an ISDN configuration, point-to-point protocol (PPP) is the only available medium. Next up is the PPP Network Interface Configuration dialog.

4. In the ISDN Address field, enter the local phone number to which the interface is connected. Configure the following parameters:

   - In the Sync Type field, enter either **SYNC** or **ASYNC**. The SYNC type is defined as HDLC bit-synchronous, and ASYNC is defined as HDLC character-synchronous.

   - In the ISDN Address and Sub-Address fields, enter the numbers given to you by your ISP. If no ISDN Sub-Address has been supplied, leave this field blank.

   - In the Modem/DCE Type field, select ISDN (AT Controlled) as the adapter that uses AT commands. Otherwise, accept the None choice.

   - Under Authentication Options, select the authentication provided by your ISP. Authentication is required for dial-up connections, and recommended for permanent connections.

5. Press Esc to accept the remaining parameters and configure the remaining ports.

6. Press Esc to return to the Internetworking Configuration dialog.

7. Select WAN Call Directory. The Configured WAN Call Destinations dialog is displayed.

8. Press Ins to configure a new WAN call destination.

9. Enter a name for the call destination. You'll get a list of supported wide-area media. These are media available on previously configured interfaces.

10. Select PPP as the wide-area medium. The PPP Call Destination Configuration dialog appears next.

11. Select Interface Name, then choose an interface name from the pop-up dialog. This field allows you to choose the name of the configured WAN interface.

12. Specify a telephone number. If the data rate is 64Kbps, append the characters **p2** to the telephone number. If p2 is not entered for ISDN calls, the default is 56Kbps.

13. Specify a login script if the Internet service provider has provided one.

14. Select Outbound Authentication; then choose the appropriate authentication option from the pop-up dialog. This lets you specify the authentication protocol to use for an outbound connection. You can disable the authentication for a permanent call if the remote system does not require either authentication type. On-demand connections require authentication. If you choose *either* PAP or CHAP, PPP will provide CHAP authentication or PAP authentication, as appropriate.

15. Choose Select Password, and enter a case-sensitive password from your ISP. You can leave this field blank if no authentication is specified.

16. Select Local System ID, and enter a case-sensitive local system ID provided by the ISP.

17. Select Remote System ID, and enter a remote system ID. (TCP/IP host names are usually lowercase. Typically, this name is the remote system server name.)

When you configure the protocol you will use for an on-demand PPP connection, you must configure static routes and services. Some protocol stacks do not accept an inbound connection unless they have a configured static route or service to an identified remote system.

18. Leave all other parameters in the PPP Call Destination Configuration dialog at their default values. Press Esc to return to the Internetworking Configuration dialog, and confirm Yes to save changes.

19. *If prompted,* select Yes to synchronize the inbound authentication database. The inbound authentication database is made to agree with the outbound call authentication parameters in this WAN call destination configuration. This is useful if you also expect to receive calls from systems that you call.

20. Press Esc to return to the Internetworking Configuration menu.

21. Select Bindings and press Ins.

22. From the list of configured protocols, choose TCP/IP.

23. Select Network Interface, and choose a configured network interface from the list. The Binding TCP/IP to a WAN Interface dialog is displayed.

24. Select the WAN Network Mode field. The default, Numbered Point-to-Point, is displayed. Press Enter and select Unnumbered Point-to-Point.

Because Unnumbered Point-to-Point mode does not use IP addresses, you cannot select the Local IP Address and Subnetwork Mask of Connected Network fields. However, at least one WAN interface on each router must have an IP address.

25. Select WAN Call Destinations and choose a destination you've already configured.

26. Select Static Routing Table, and press Ins to add a new entry.

27. Give the new entry the following address:

    0.0.0.0

28. Press Esc to return to the Internetworking Configuration dialog; save your changes when prompted.

29. Bring the server down and restart it to enable the new configuration.

Configuring for Frame Relay

When you set up a Frame Relay link, you need to work with the ISP and local telephone company to get the following network service information:

- *Data-Link Connection Identifiers (DLCIs):* One DLCI denotes each end of a PVC.

- *Bc:* The committed burst size, or the maximum number of data bits. A network agrees to transfer at this rate under normal conditions over a measured time interval.

- *Be:* The excess burst size, or the maximum number of *uncommitted* data bits. The network *attempts* to deliver at this rate over a measured time interval.

- *CIR:* The committed information rate, or user information rate, in bits per second (bps). The network agrees to transfer data on a PVC at this rate.

- *AR:* The physical access rate of the user channel, in bits per second.

- *T:* The time interval used to measure rates.

For more information about NetWare Link/Frame Relay, refer to NetWare MultiProtocol Router 3.1 Concepts in the DynaText online collection.

Configuring a Frame Relay adapter involves choosing a driver for the adapter, assigning a name to the adapter, and specifying values for the adapter parameters. Here are the steps:

1. Load INETCFG.

2. Select Boards. The Configured Boards dialog is displayed.

3. Press Ins to display the list of available drivers. Select the driver that corresponds to the type of new LAN or WAN adapter you are installing in your system. You'll next see the Board Configuration dialog.

4. Fill in the parameters that apply to your adapter:

Board Name	Any name you want to use
Driver	Driver file
Int	Interrupt level (IRQ)
IOAddr	Base I/O port address
MemAddr	Base memory address
Slot	Number of the slot where the adapter is installed
Status	Enabled
Comment	Any remarks about the adapter or configuration

If the adapter driver has an .LDI file, the parameters you need to configure for the adapter are displayed as separate fields in the dialog.

If the adapter driver does not have an .LDI file, the Board Configuration Without A Driver Description File dialog is displayed. You must type the parameters into the Board Parameters field as required by the driver manufacturer, such as **PORT=340 INT=9**. These parameters are appended to the LOAD driver line.

INETCFG automatically manages frame types. Do not put a FRAME= option in the Board Parameters field.

5. Press Esc to return to the Configured Boards dialog. Confirm Yes to save changes. The Configured Boards dialog now shows the adapter you just configured.

6. Press Esc again to return to the main dialog.

7. Select Network Interfaces, and choose a port on a WAN interface adapter that has *not* been configured.

8. Select Frame Relay. The Frame Relay Network Interface Configuration dialog is displayed, showing the name you defined in the Configured Boards dialog. Configure the following parameters:

Interface Status field	Accept Enabled.
Physical Type field	Accept V.35 by pressing the Down Arrow key to skip to the next field, or press Enter to select a new value from the pop-up dialog. Possible physical interface types are RS-232, RS-422, V.35, or X.21. Select the one you are using.
Interface Speed field	Accept External, or press Enter to select a new value from the pop-up dialog. Internal speeds vary with the driver selected.
Data Encoding field	Accept NRZ, or press Enter to select NRZI from the pop-up dialog. This information should agree with the encoding at the ISP end of the link.

9. Select Expert Configuration. The Frame Relay Expert Configuration dialog is displayed. Configure these parameters:

User Data Size field	Enter a value representing the largest number of bytes in the user data frame that can be received on this link. This number should be smaller than the Maximum Physical Packet Receive Size value in the STARTUP.NCF file.
Send Queue Limit field	Enter a value representing the maximum number of outbound data packets that can be queued to this port for transmission. When the queue limit is exceeded, the most recently queued outbound packets are dropped.

10. Select the Parameter Group field. The available options are displayed in a pop-up dialog. Parameter groups LMI and Annex D both provide the same types of management but with different parameter settings. The only difference is that Annex D enables an unrequested status from the network, and the Point-to-Point Test lets you test two routers or servers using Frame Relay in a point-to-point test procedure.

11. Press Esc, confirm Yes to save your changes, and press Enter.

12. *If you use SNMP management,* press Enter in the Enterprise Specific Traps field to view or modify the SNMP traps. (If you don't use SNMP, you can skip this step.)

13. Press Esc to return to the Internetworking Configuration menu.

14. Select WAN Call Directory.

An empty Configured WAN Call Destinations list appears. You must create at least one permanent WAN call destination to use for the link by following Steps 14A through 14E.

A. In the Configured WAN Call Destinations list, press Ins to configure a new call destination.

B. Enter a name for the new destination. This name is used in other menus when a destination needs to be identified. A list of supported wide-area media is displayed. These media are available on previously configured interfaces. Note that Frame Relay won't be available if you have not yet configured a Frame Relay interface.

C. Select PPP as the wide-area medium and press Enter.

D. Select Interface Name and press Enter. The PPP Call Destination Configuration Dialog appears. Fill in the fields, using F1 if you need a definition for a particular field.

E. Press Esc, and confirm Yes to save the configuration. The WAN call destination you have configured now appears in the list of configured WAN call destinations.

15. To configure another WAN call destination, repeat Steps 14A through 14E.

16. Press Esc to return to the Internetworking Configuration menu.

17. Select Bindings and press Ins.

18. From the list of configured protocols, choose TCP/IP.

19. Select Network Interface, and choose a configured network interface from the list. The Binding TCP/IP to a WAN Interface dialog is displayed.

20. Set the WAN Network Mode to Numbered Single Point-to-Point.

21. Set the local IP address to the number supplied by your ISP for your router.

22. Set a subnetwork mask if assigned one by your ISP.

23. Press Esc to return to the Internet Configuration dialog.

24. Select WAN Call Destinations, and choose a destination you've already configured.

25. Select Static Routing Table and press Ins to add a new entry.

26. Give the new entry the following address:

```
0.0.0.0
```

27. Press Esc to return to the Internetworking Configuration dialog; save your changes when prompted.

28. Bring the server down and restart it to enable the new configuration.

Setting Up Workstations for Internet Access

Before you set up workstations with IntranetWare, you need to make some modifications to Directory objects and set some optional restrictions on access to the Internet. This involves editing properties of the Gateway, NetWare Server, and [Root] objects; and for access control, you'll edit the User, Group, Organization, and/or Organizational Unit objects.

Since you have enabled the IPX/IP Gateway and automatically created the Gateway Server object, you now need to insert a snap-in module to the NetWare Administrator configuration file. First, with a text editor, you'll edit the INI file for the version of NetWare Administrator you use.

▪ For NetWare 4.1, open NWADMIN.INI and add this line under the [Snapin Object DLLs] heading:

```
IPXGW.DLL=IPXGW.DLL
```

- For NetWare 4.11, open NWADMN3X.INI and add this line under the [Snapin Object DLLs WIN3X] heading:

```
IPXGW3X.DLL=IPXGW3X.DLL
```

Now proceed with the following steps to set up access restrictions:

1. Start NetWare Administrator and select the Gateway object.

2. From the Object menu, select Trustees of this Object.

3. Click on the Public object.

4. Among the object rights on the left, click on Browse.

5. Among the property rights on the right, click on Read and Compare for all properties. Click OK.

6. Select the NetWare Server object that has the gateway software running.

7. From the Object menu, select Trustees of this Object.

8. Click on the Public object.

9. Among the object rights on the left, click on Browse.

10. Click on Specific Properties.

11. Select the Network Address property and click on the Read and Compare property rights. Click OK.

12. Drag the Gateway object onto the [Root] object. Click OK.

13. (Optional) To configure access control, first select the object you want to configure. Then access the Details of that object and select the "IPX/IP Gateway Host Restrictions" button. You can fill in the desired restrictions on that page.

Setting Up Windows Workstations to Use the Gateway

To enable Windows clients to use the IPX/IP Gateway, you need to rename some files and run the client installation.

If you didn't install the client installation files during server installation, you can load INSTALL at the server console and select the Copy Files option. Then follow the instructions to copy client installation files to the server.

1. Before you run the client installation at each workstation, rename any WINSOCK.DLL and WLIBSOCK.DLL files on the workstation that are not in \NOVELL\CLIENT32 or the Windows directory. For example, you could rename WINSOCK.DLL to WINSOCK.OLD.

2. From Windows, start the client SETUP.EXE (found in subdirectories of SYS:\PUBLIC\CLIENT), and click on the NetWare IPX/IP Gateway check box to install the gateway client software.

For applications in Windows 3.1 and 16-bit applications in Windows 95, NOVGWP16.EXE is installed as the gateway support task. For 32-bit applications in Windows 95, NOVGWPRC.EXE is the gateway support task.

For Windows 3.1 users, an IPC/IP Gateway Switcher program item is installed in the NetWare Tools group. For Windows 95 users, a Gateway Switcher program is added to the Start | Programs | Novell folder. The Switcher allows users to select either the gateway or another installed WINSOCK interface. It renames the WINSOCK DLLs in the Windows and NOVELL\CLIENT32 directories. That way, a user can choose to dial out from a workstation using a modem with the existing WINSOCK DLL, or access the Internet (or intranet) via the server with the special gateway DLL.

When the IPX/IP Gateway Client is running, the Gateway task's icon appears minimized in Windows 3.1; for Windows 95, the icon appears on the taskbar. The Gateway task window can be maximized to display information related to the Gateway Server. (In Windows 95, the 32-bit Gateway task icon also appears in the tray. Hold the cursor over the icon to display the status of the connection to the Gateway Server.)

Normally, users shouldn't close the Gateway task window; they should minimize it and keep it running.

When the IPX/IP Gateway client is enabled, the filenames are

```
NOVELL\CLIENT32\WINSOCK.DLL
NOVELL\CLIENT32\WSOCK32.DLL
WINDOWS\WINSOCK.NO1
WINDOWS\SYSTEM\WSOCK32.NO1
```

When the IPX/IP Gateway client is disabled, the filenames are

```
NOVELL\CLIENT32\WINSOCK.NOV
NOVELL\CLIENT32\WSOCK32.NOV
WINDOWS\WINSOCK.DLL
WINDOWS\SYSTEM\WSOCK32.DLL
```

Under Windows 95, the renaming performed by the Gateway Switcher allows you to use the Novell Gateway when it's enabled, or Microsoft TCP/IP (if installed) when the Gateway is disabled. If it happens that the WINSOCK DLLs exist in both NOVELL\CLIENT32 and Windows—that is, if both sets have the .DLL extension—rename them manually as listed just above, depending on whether you want the Gateway enabled or disabled.

CONFIGURING THE WORKSTATION'S GATEWAY TASK USING NOVWS.INI The NOVWS.INI file contains the configuration data for Novell WINSOCK and the Gateway task. You can create your own NOVWS.INI file and copy it to clients' Windows directories, to eliminate the need for the Switcher or the Network Control Panel. The content of a NOVWS.INI file is as follows:

```
[stack]
gateway=x
ipxGateway=y
extension=n01
```

In the gateway= line, change *x* to 0 to disable the gateway, or to 1 to enable the gateway. In the ipxGateway= line, change *y* to the name of the Gateway Server (example: SERVER1-GW).

Setting Up the Server for Hosting an Intranet

TO SET UP YOUR COMPANY INTRANET, you'll need the following:

- A Web browser at each workstation (Netscape Navigator is included with IntranetWare).

- The Web Server software installed on a NetWare server. You can create a new NetWare server specifically for intranet service that runs a special copy of NetWare (called Runtime) and doesn't require a separate NetWare license.

- Web pages created in HTML (IntranetWare does not include an HTML authoring program). The Web pages may include databases, sound, complex graphics, video, hypertext links, and other features made popular on the Internet.

Preparation for Installing Web Server

Before you install Web Server, you need to do one of the following:

- Have TCP/IP running on the server and the workstations, or

- Have the IP/IPX Gateway running on the server, with a special WINSOCK running on the workstations

The preceding section gives instructions for loading the IP/IPX Gateway on the server. To load the TCP/IP protocol stack at the server, perform the following procedures:

- Binding the IP Network Protocol to the Server LAN Driver

- Loading NetWare IP at the Server

Binding the IP Network Protocol to the Server LAN Driver

Complete the following steps to load and configure TCP/IP on the server and workstation.

1. At the server console, load INETCFG.

2. Select Protocols.

3. Select TCP/IP.

4. Select the TCP/IP Status option to enable it. Leave all other parameters at their default values.

For a complete discussion of other TCP/IP parameters, see Novell's online Advanced Protocol Configuration and Management Guide.

5. Press Esc, confirm Yes to save the configuration, and press Esc again to return to the Internetworking Configuration menu.

6. Select Bindings.

7. Press Ins and choose TCP/IP.

8. Select the network adapter.

9. Type an IP address assigned to this interface (example: 111.22.3.4), and press Enter. *Write the number down. Each IP address on an IP internetwork must be unique. You can maintain this list in your Network Records binder.*

10. Type in the subnetwork mask of the network attached to this interface, and press Enter. *This number must match the mask used by the other nodes on the network. If you're not sure what to do here, leave the default.*

11. Repeat Steps 8 through 10 for each network adapter on the server.

12. Press Esc and confirm Yes to save changes.

13. Press Esc twice and confirm Yes to exit INETCFG.

14. At the console prompt, type **REINITIALIZE SYSTEM**.

15. Repeat Steps 1 through 14 for each server.

Loading NetWare IP at the Server

TCP/IP functionality in a NetWare 4.1*x* server is provided by the NetWare IP software. This software comes as an "installable product" with the core NetWare 4.11 operating system, so it is not generally considered part of the IntranetWare suite. This section gives the procedure for installing NetWare IP and all its services on a single server. If you want a more specific installation, with certain functions handled by individual servers, consult the Novell DynaText documentation.

DESIGNATING NAMES AND ADDRESSES Before running NetWare IP, you need to decide on the following names and addresses:

- DNS domain name. Typically this is the name of your company, with .com appended (example: lanservices.com).

- NetWare IP domain name. This is a subordinate of the DNS domain name (example: nwip.lanservices.com).

- Master DNS name server. This is another subordinate of the DNS domain name (example: server1.lanservices.com).

- Primary DSS server. If IP is only installed on one server, this name is the same as the master DNS name server (example: server1.lanserver.com).

- Server address. Four numbers separated by periods (example: 1.2.3.4).

Once you have documented your name and address decisions, you can install NetWare IP as follows:

1. At the server console, stop all services using PKERNEL, by typing **UNISTOP**.

2. Type **LOAD INSTALL**.

3. Select Product Options.

4. Press Tab to access the list of products, and select Install NetWare IP.

   After the program files are copied, the installation program displays a message indicating that NetWare IP has been successfully installed. Press Esc to continue.

5. Exit INSTALL and type **LOAD NWIPCFG**.

   NWIPCFG sends a DHCP request to get NetWare IP configuration parameters. If a DHCP server responds to the request, you are prompted to confirm the parameters.

6. Select Configure DNS Client.

7. Enter the name of the DNS domain to which this server belongs (example: **lanservices.com**).

8. Enter the IP address(es) of the DNS name server(s) this server should contact to resolve DNS queries. If this server is the only server running TCP/IP on the network, give the IP address of this server (example: **1.2.3.4**).

9. Exit the DNS Client Access form by pressing Esc.

10. Select Configure NetWare IP Server, and enter the following information:

    A. Enter the name of the NetWare IP domain (example: **nwip.lanservices.com**). This name must be different from the DNS domain name.

    B. In the Preferred DSSes field, enter the name of the DSS server (example: **server1.lanservices.com**).

C. To configure the NetWare IP server as a *forwarding gateway* (see the sidebar, "What Is a Forwarding Gateway?") choose Forward IPX Information to DSS, press Enter, and confirm Yes. (If you have only the IP protocol on your network, you can skip this step.)

D. Press Esc and confirm Yes to save changes.

11. Exit NWIPCFG. *Do not start the NetWare IP server at this time.* You need to launch the DNS and DSS services first.

12. Load the UNICON utility at the server console. You'll see a login form with the server name filled in.

13. Supply the password for User Admin as required.

14. Select Manage Services.

15. Select DNS.

16. Select Initialize DNS Master Database, and answer the prompts.

A. When prompted for the DNS domain name, enter a fully qualified DNS domain name or choose the default. Press Esc. The DNS Domain field now shows the current host name, similar to the following: lanservices.com.

B. When prompted for name servers, accept the default or specify another known name server.

C. Specify whether you want DNS to service specific sub-networks. If you're not sure whether you have sub-networks, answer No. If you choose Yes you are prompted to specify which sub-networks you want DNS to service.

D. Confirm Yes to initialize the DNS database.

To link to an existing DNS hierarchy, such as an Internet server, refer to the NetWare IP Administrator's Guide using DynaText.

17. Press Esc to return to the Manage Services menu.

18. Select NetWare IP.

19. Select Configure Primary DSS, and specify the following:

    A. Supply the NetWare IP Domain name. This is *not* the DNS Domain name supplied in Step 16A. Enter the same NetWare IP domain name specified in Step 10A (example: **nwip.lanservices.com**).

    B. Supply the fully qualified host name of the DSS server (example: **server1.lanservices.com**).

    C. Supply a unique IPX network number for the cable segment. This number (up to eight characters in hexadecimal) must be different from the numbers already used in BIND commands for network protocols.

    D. Accept the other parameters and press Esc to continue. A DSS configuration reminder is displayed, indicating that the DNS database should specify your DSS host.

20. Return to the main menu and select Start/Stop Services. In the Running Services list, the DNS Server should appear.

21. Press Ins and select Domain SAP/RIP Server.

22. Press Ins again and select NetWare IP Server.

23. Press Esc and exit UNICON.

Installing the Web Server Product

Once you've completed the preparations described in the preceding sections, you're ready to install Web Server.

1. Load INSTALL at the server console.

2. Select Product Options.

3. Press Tab to move to the product menu, and choose Install NetWare Web Server.

4. When prompted, supply the server name and management password.

5. When prompted, restart the server.

What Is a Forwarding Gateway?

A forwarding gateway connects separate IP and IPX networks, providing both IP and IPX clients with access to services on either network. This type of gateway forwards packets between the two networks, performing protocol conversion as required.

You should create a forwarding gateway if you want to connect a group of TCP/IP-only workstations with IPX-only services and vice versa. In addition to translating packets and passing them from one network segment to another, the forwarding NetWare IP gateway also translates service and routing information between IP and IPX.

On an IPX network, services and routes are advertised using SAP and RIP broadcasting. The forwarding gateway accepts the IPX SAP and RIP broadcasts through its IPX interface and uploads them directly to the DSS server. This enables NetWare IP servers and clients to learn about services and routes on the IPX network.

Similarly, the forwarding NetWare IP gateway downloads SAP/RIP information for the IP network segment from the DSS server. Then, to advertise the IP services and routes, the gateway broadcasts the SAP and RIP information it downloaded from the DSS server to the IPX network. This enables NetWare servers and clients on the IPX network to learn about services and routes on the IP network.

The Web Server installation program inserts commands in AUTOEXEC.NCF. These commands set the maximum "receive" buffers to 1,000. They also call UNISTART.NCF, which contains the following commands:

```
LOAD NETDB.NLM
LOAD HTTP.NLM -D SYS:WEB
LOAD BASIC.NLM -D SYS:WEB
LOAD PERL.NLM
```

These NLMs handle the basic functions of Web Server, including interpretation of Perl/CGI and BASIC scripting languages. HTTP.NLM provides a console status dialog for viewing HTTP activity.

Web Server Directory Structure

During installation of Web Server, a WEB directory is created at the root of the SYS volume. The subdirectories of WEB are as follows.

- \WEB\CONFIG contains server configuration files, including ACCESS.CFG and SRM.CFG. The ACCESS.CFG file contains access control information for each subdirectory in the WEB directory and designates which users can access files in your WEB directory through Web browsers.

- \WEB\DOCS is the directory for HTML documents and multimedia files. Scripts can refer to the HTML files in this directory.

- \WEB\LOGS contains Web Server log files. These logs document the frequency of user access to server-specific files.

- \WEB\MAPS contains image map files. An image map file contains maps of active images that produce results depending on which region of the graphic is clicked by the user.

- \WEB\SAMPLES contains LCGI and RCGI files.

- \WEB\SCRIPTS contains BASIC scripts and the subdirectory for Perl scripts (\WEB\SCRIPTS\PERL).

- \WEB\LCGI\NETBASIC contains NetBasic scripts.

User Access Control

You can use the WEBMGR utility to restrict user access in one of three ways:

- Restrict access to all valid Users

- Restrict access using individual User names

- Restrict access using Groups

The administration utility (WEBMGR.EXE) does not support user comments in CFG files. If you manually edit these files and add comments as lines preceded with a pound sign (#), these lines will be deleted when you run the WEBMGR utility.

1. From Windows, start the SYS:\PUBLIC\WEBMGR.EXE utility. (You may want to create a program item for the utility.)

2. To set access restrictions, click on the User Access tab. Then use one of the following options:

- Click on the All Valid Users check box.

- Type in the NDS context and select no more than 25 users.

3. To set the context for intranet Users, edit the ACCESS.CFG file, supplying the proper context in the following line:

```
AuthGroupMethod nds .OURCO
```

Users outside the specified context will need to supply a distinguished User name such as .Amy.ACCT-DEPT.OURCO when starting intranet access. To enable a certain Group to access the intranet, add the following line:

```
Require group .WEBUSERS.OURCO
```

Setting Up Workstations for Accessing Your Intranet

To ACCESS THE COMPANY INTRANET, the workstations need to use either the IPX/IP Gateway or the TCP/IP protocol stack. Setting up and using the Gateway is described in the earlier sections entitled "Enabling and Configuring the Link" and "Setting Up Workstations for Internet Access."

For a Windows 3.*x* workstation to use the TCP/IP protocol stack, you need to run the client installation program. From the Additional Options dialog, enable the TCP/IP and NetWare IP check boxes. You'll need to supply the information required by the configuration dialog shown in Figure 12.2, and then the information for the NetWare IP configuration as shown in Figure 12.3.

The information you provide in these configuration dialogs is recorded to the NET.CFG, RESOLV.CFG, and STARTNET.BAT files. TCP/IP programs and utilities are also copied to the workstation.

To install Netscape Navigator, change to the SYS:\NETSCAPE\16 or SYS:\NETSCAPE\32 and run SETUP.EXE.

FIGURE 12.2
The TCP/IP
Configuration dialog
requires these
parameters.

TCP/IP Configuration

Client IP Address:

Default Router Address:

Subnetwork Mask:

DNS Domain Name:

Domain Name Server Address:

< Previous   Next >   Exit   Help

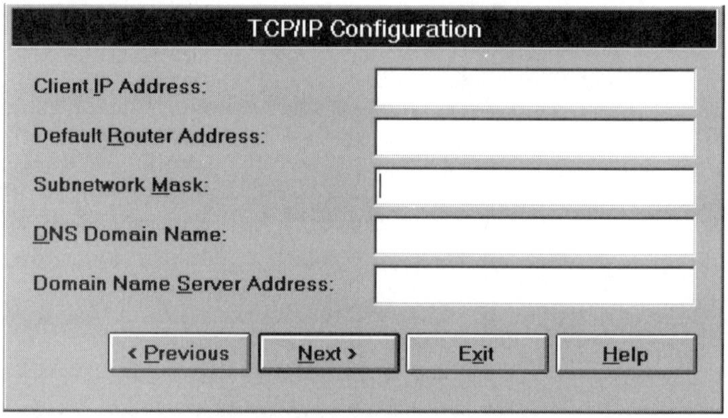

FIGURE 12.3
The NetWare IP
Configuration dialog
requires these
parameters.

NetWare/IP Configuration

NetWare/IP Domain Name:

Preferred DSS:

Nearest NWIP Server:

< Previous   Next >   Exit   Help

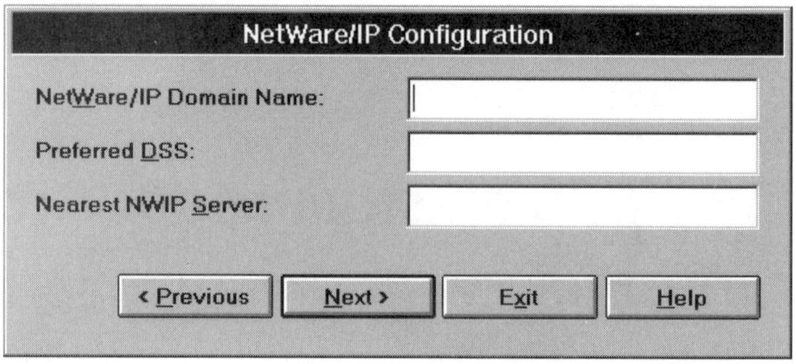

Creating Documents for the Intranet

THE NETWARE WEB SERVER publishes both static and dynamic documents. The Dynamic Web Page Programmer's Guide is an HTML document describing how to create dynamic documents and publish them on the Web Server. It includes information on creating dynamic Web pages using BASIC and Perl scripts, NLMs written to the Remote Common Gateway Interface (RCGI), and NLMs written to the Local Common Gateway Interface (LCGI). The guide is available on the NetWare Operating System CD at the following location:

```
/products/webserv/diskl/web/docs/online/wpguide/index.htm
```

Maintaining and Troubleshooting the Server

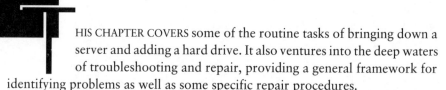

THIS CHAPTER COVERS some of the routine tasks of bringing down a server and adding a hard drive. It also ventures into the deep waters of troubleshooting and repair, providing a general framework for identifying problems as well as some specific repair procedures.

This chapter does *not* include procedures for general PC troubleshooting and repair, a subject that deserves a book of its own. Here we will focus on NetWare-specific problems and solutions.

Bringing Down a Server

BRINGING DOWN A SERVER is a fairly straightforward task. You just type **DOWN** and then **EXIT** from the server console.

To restart a server without going to DOS, you can type **DOWN** and then **RESTART SERVER.** If you want to reboot a server from a remote location, such as a workstation on the network or a computer at home, it gets a bit more complicated. Here's a typical procedure:

1. Make sure the remote modules are loaded in the AUTOEXEC.NCF file. That way you can establish a remote connection again after the server boots. For example, add the following commands:

   ```
   LOAD REMOTE MYPASS
   LOAD RSPX
   ```

2. Create a batch file in the SYS:SYSTEM directory. You can use any text editor and name the file anything you want, as long as the file name extension is NCF (for example, REBOOT.NCF). Put the following commands in the NCF file:

   ```
   UNLOAD DOS
   DOWN
   ```

3. To reboot the server remotely, access the server console through RCONSOLE and type the name of the NCF file (in our example, **REBOOT**). You will lose your remote connection, but the server will restart. Then you can establish the remote connection again if desired.

The REBOOT.NCF file will execute a "warm" boot, similar to pressing Ctrl+Alt+Del. Resetting a SCSI controller may require a "cold" boot (also called a "hard" boot), which means shutting off power to the server. You cannot accomplish a cold boot with an NCF file.

Extended Down Time in a Multiserver Network

When a server is down for an extended period and you have other servers on the network, those other servers will try to contact the missing server to update its copy of the Directory. Also, if the missing server has been acting as a Single Reference time server, the remaining servers will try to contact it for time synchronization.

If you're going to take a server down for a week or more, you can remove its replica of the Directory and change its time server type. Following are two procedures for this task, one for NetWare 4.10 and one for NetWare 4.11.

NetWare 4.10

The following procedure ensures that the server you remove does not have a replica, that another server has a Master replica, and that another server is a Single Reference time server.

1. Start NetWare Administrator, and select Tools | Partition Manager.

2. Select the [Root] object on the browser.

3. Choose Replicas. All servers that contain a replica of the Directory are listed.

4. If the server you will be removing has a Master replica, select a *different* server's replica and choose Change Type. Change the type to Master and confirm OK. This automatically changes the other server's replicas to Read/Write.

5. Highlight the replica on the server you will remove.

6. Click on the Delete Replica button and confirm OK.

7. If the server you will remove is a Single Reference time server, continue with the remainder of this procedure. (Otherwise, you can stop here.) Access the console of a server that you will remove, either directly or via RCONSOLE.

8. Load SERVMAN and select Server Parameters.

9. Select Time. (You can quickly move down the list of server parameters by typing **T**.)

10. Highlight Timesync Type and press Enter.

11. Backspace over the word SINGLE and type **SECONDARY**.

12. Highlight Timesync Write Parameters and press Enter.

13. Highlight Timesync Restart Flag and press Enter.

14. Access the console of a server that will stay up, either directly or via RCONSOLE.

15. Load SERVMAN and select Server Parameters.

16. Type **T** to move quickly down the list of server parameters, and select Time.

17. Highlight Timesync Type and press Enter.

18. Backspace over the word SECONDARY and type **SINGLE**.

19. Highlight Timesync Write Parameters and press Enter.

20. Highlight Timesync Restart Flag and press Enter.

NetWare 4.11

NetWare 4.11 has a new, separate utility called NDS Manager for managing replicas.

1. Create a program item for NDS Manager (NDSMGR.EXE in the SYS:PUBLIC directory).

2. Start NDS Manager. A window similar to the one shown in Figure 13.1 will appear.

3. Select the [Root] object in the browser on the left. The browser on the right will list all servers that contain replicas of the [Root] partition.

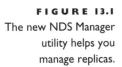

FIGURE 13.1
The new NDS Manager
utility helps you
manage replicas.

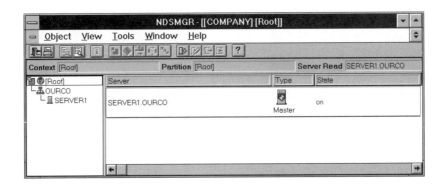

4. If the server you want to remove has a Master replica, select a *different* server's replica. Select Object | Replica and choose Change Type. Change the type to Master and confirm OK. This automatically changes the other server's replicas to Read/Write.

5. Right-click on the server you will remove.

6. Select Delete and confirm OK.

7. If the server you will remove is a Single Reference time server continue with the remainder of this procedure. (Otherwise, you can stop here.) Access the console of a server that will be removed, either directly or via RCONSOLE.

8. Load SERVMAN or MONITOR and select Server Parameters.

9. Select Time. (You can quickly move down the list of server parameters by typing **T**.)

10. Highlight Timesync Type and press Enter.

11. Backspace over the word SINGLE and type **SECONDARY.**

12. Highlight Timesync Write Parameters and press Enter.

13. Highlight Timesync Restart Flag and press Enter.

14. Access the console of a server that will stay up, either directly or via RCONSOLE.

15. Load SERVMAN and select Server Parameters.

16. Type **T** to move quickly down the list of server parameters, and select Time.

17. Highlight Timesync Type and press Enter.

18. Backspace over the word SECONDARY and type **SINGLE**.

19. Highlight Timesync Write Parameters and press Enter.

20. Highlight Timesync Restart Flag and press Enter.

Creating a Replica in a Multiserver Network

If you have removed a server's replica in order to bring it down for an extended time, you'll need to create a new replica when you bring the server back on line. Following are two procedures for this task, one for NetWare 4.10 and one for NetWare 4.11.

NetWare 4.10

For NetWare 4.10, you will use the NetWare Administrator utility.

1. Start the server.

2. Start NetWare Administrator, and select Tools | Partition Manager.

3. Select the [Root] object on the browser.

4. Choose Replicas. All servers that contain a replica of the Directory are listed.

5. Click on the Add Replica button.

6. Browse in the Servers box and select the restored server.

7. Select Read/Write and confirm OK.

NetWare 4.11

For NetWare 4.11, you will use the NDS Manager utility.

1. Start the server.

2. Start NDS Manager.

3. Select the [Root] object.

4. Select Object | Add Replica.

5. Using the Browse button, select the recovered server.

6. Click on Read/Write and confirm OK.

Permanent Server Removal from a Multiserver Network

To remove a server from the network permanently, you need to first make sure it holds no replicas and is not a Single Reference time server. To do so, follow the procedure "Extended Down Time in a Multiserver Network" above.

You then need to remove NDS from the server. This deletes the NetWare Server object from the Directory tree and downgrades the server's volumes to bindery volumes. Trustee assignments and all NDS information are lost. It is assumed that your intention is to completely remove this server from the network forever, and that any data that you want from its volumes has been moved to other servers.

If you installed this server into the wrong container, it isn't necessary to remove NDS. Use the NetWare Administrator utility to move the Server object to the correct container.

1. At the server console, type **LOAD INSTALL.**

2. From the Installation Options menu, select Directory Options (Install NetWare Directory Services).

3. From the Directory Services Options menu, select Remove Directory Services from this Server. Confirm Yes. You will be required to enter the password for Admin.

INSTALL removes NDS and deletes the Server object and associated Volume objects from the Directory.

4. Bring down the server. It may take a few minutes before the Server and Volume objects disappear from the NetWare Administrator view of the Directory tree.

Rebuilding a Server after Catastrophe

THIS SECTION IS FOR THOSE INSTANCES when a catastrophe has caused the loss of your SYS volume: the volume that contains the Directory, your configuration files, and perhaps all your data. This is equivalent to losing your server, with the possible exception that other volumes may have been saved.

Take a deep breath. If you've been making backups of the file system and Directory, things aren't as bad as they may seem.

First, if the DOS partition is still available, see if the SYS volume can be repaired. Type **SERVER** to start the server, then type **DISMOUNT SYS** and **LOAD VREPAIR** and try to fix the volume. If VREPAIR fixes some errors but not all of them, run VREPAIR again. VREPAIR has been known to fix the most critical errors on the third or fourth pass.

If your SYS volume really is lost, you can rebuild the server entirely, using the same hardware or a completely new system (with at least as much disk space). Follow these steps.

1. Boot the server using the licensed disk that came with the NetWare product.

2. Create the DOS partition using the FDISK utility on the licensed disk, and make the partition bootable.

3. Format the DOS partition using the **FORMAT** command on the licensed disk. Use the /S option to copy the system files to the new DOS partition.

4. Using the EDIT utility on the license disk, create the AUTOEXEC.BAT and CONFIG.SYS files on the DOS partition. Include the drivers to use the CD-ROM drive from DOS.

5. Copy the CD-ROM drivers to the DOS partition.

6. Reboot the server and insert the NetWare 4 Operating System CD-ROM into the CD-ROM drive.

7. Change to the CD-ROM drive (typically D).

8. Type **INSTALL** and create the new server using the following parameters:

   - Give the server the same name and context as the old server.

   - If this is the only server on the network, use the same Admin container and password that existed when the last backup was created.

   - Create NetWare partitions of the same size as on the old server.

   - Create volumes of the same size (or larger) and with the same names as on the old server.

9. If this is the only server on the network, load the backup software (including TSANDS) and restore the Directory from tape.

10. Load the backup software (including TSA410) and restore the file system from the last full backup.

11. Restore any partial—differential, incremental, or custom—backups made since the last full backup, in the same order that they were made.

12. Reboot the server to load any NLMs and patches included in the restored AUTOEXEC.NCF file.

You should now have a server that is up-to-date as of the last backup you made. If you have been diligent in making daily backups, this is as recent as the previous evening!

Third-party products may provide an easier solution for a dead server. Stac's Replica product can totally recover a lost SYS volume to a blank hard disk with two floppies and the tape. It recovers the DOS partition as well. It costs about $750 (street price) for a server, but you'll find it well worth the expenditure.

Adding Hard Drives to a Server

T HIS SECTION DESCRIBES the temporary shutdown that is normally required for any hardware changes you make to the server. But first, a word of caution about adding RAM.

Adding RAM? Watch Out!

If you're downing the server to add a hard drive, you'll probably need to add RAM, too. You'll probably need the RAM for caching the added files and directory entries. But the seemingly benign procedure of adding RAM gives rise to more problems than you would think.

Several things can go wrong, because NetWare exercises RAM in ways unimaginable to those familiar with DOS and Windows. Many PC users adding RAM to a computer will reboot the computer and, upon seeing the power-on self-test count up all the RAM, will assume the RAM is good. But this is not necessarily so for NetWare.

You might imagine that running HIMEM /TESTMEM:ON from a CONFIG.SYS file would verify the quality of the RAM. Again, not necessarily so. You add the RAM to a Windows 95 machine, load up the computer with applications, and it works fine. The RAM should be okay for NetWare, right? Maybe not. Let's say you've added RAM to the server. If the memory is bad, you'd expect a message saying something like "You have installed bad RAM in the server. Replace the SIMM in slot 2." Sorry, not in NetWare. You could get *any* error message, although the most common ones are Page Fault Processor Exception and Non-Maskable Interrupt. If you added a hard drive at the same time you added RAM, you don't know if the errors are the result of the drive, the controller, the driver, or the RAM.

The bottom line is this: Don't add RAM at the same time you add a hard drive. Add the RAM first, boot the server, and let it run for a day on the new RAM. Look for Page Fault Processor Exception or Non-Maskable Interrupt errors. If the server runs error free for a day, then go ahead and add the hard drive.

Procedure for Adding the Hard Drive

Assuming you have enough RAM for the added hard disk space, here are the steps to add the hard drive.

1. Bring the server down. Type **DOWN**, then **EXIT**.

2. If you are installing a new controller, copy the configuration software and drivers to the server's DOS partition.

3. Shut off the power.

4. Install the new drive into the computer. If it's a SCSI drive, make sure the termination and unit ID are correct. If it's an IDE drive, make sure the master/slave setting is correct.

5. Turn on the server.

6. Run any configuration software necessary for the drive. If it's a SCSI drive, you'll need to run a SCSI BIOS setup program.

7. If you've added a controller, add the controller's driver to the STARTUP.NCF file. For example:

```
LOAD AIC7870 SLOT=2
```

or

```
LOAD IDEATA.HAM INT=F PORT=170
```

The controller drivers should detect the new drive. If you haven't added a controller, the new drive should be automatically detected by the controller driver.

8. Type **SERVER** from the proper DOS directory (usually C:\NWSERVER).

9. When the server has started, type **LOAD INSTALL** from the console prompt.

10. From the Installation Options menu, select Disk Options.

11. Select Modify Disk Partitions or Hot Fix.

12. Select the new drive from the Available Disk Drives menu.

13. Select Create NetWare Disk partition, and accept the default partition and hot fix sizes.

14. Once the partition is created on the new drive you have three options:

   - **Mirror the drive to another.** Select the option for mirror/unmirror disk partitions; then choose the existing partition and in turn select the new disk partition.

   - **Create a new volume.** Press Esc to return to the Installation Options menu and select Volume Options. Press Ins to get the Volume Disk Segment list. Follow the instructions for creating a new volume.

- **Add the new drive space to existing volumes.** Press Esc to return to the Installation Options menu and select Volume Options. Press Ins to get the Volume Disk Segment list. Follow the instructions for adding the free space to existing volumes.

15. If you have created a new volume, use NetWare Administrator to create directories and grant the proper objects (containers, Groups, or Users) trustee rights to those directories. Then modify login scripts to automatically map drives to directories on the new volume.

Troubleshooting the Network

M ANY, MANY THINGS CAN GO WRONG with a network. Considering the thousands of interrelated hardware components in a single PC, not to mention the entire network, and the millions of lines of interrelated software code in O/Ss, NOSs, and applications, it's hard to imagine a network working at all.

Still, some NetWare servers have been known to run for years without a failure, which is longer than the average tenure of a network administrator. If you're reading this chapter, you're probably not so lucky.

Network troubles tend to come in two varieties. One variety is the single problem that manifests itself in many different ways. Maybe a workstation loses connections intermittently, or a user can't log in, or a workstation tells you "File Server Not Found." So you replace a network adapter and the problem happens less frequently—but it still happens. You install the latest patches to the client software, and the problem still occurs. By the time you finally fix the problem, which happens to be in the workstation's motherboard, you've used 40 hours over a month's time and unnecessarily replaced $250 of hardware.

The second variety of network trouble is centered around major software or hardware changes. Let's say you have installed a new Macintosh graphics application for your company's technical illustrators. You followed the installation instructions perfectly, yet it takes a couple of weeks of troubleshooting to get the rights and login scripts working, the printers working, and the Mac file name support in place.

Rectifying both kinds of trouble requires a combination of deductive reasoning, intuition, and troubleshooting tools. This section, covering the basics of fault isolation and common repair strategies, will help you develop those skills.

Fault Isolation

Network faults sometimes manifest themselves as some sort of machine "hang" that requires restarting of the application, or restarting Windows, or rebooting the workstation. Other times, you see an error message.

For workstations, you should be able to diagnose a machine hang using standard PC fault-isolation procedures or troubleshooting software. A hang is seldom the result of a networking component per se. Check for interrupt and memory port conflicts first. If you find no hardware conflicts, you might try reloading the application software. Finally, call the manufacturer of the software that is running when the hang occurred. Be sure to have specific hardware and software information in hand when you call, so that you and the support person can quickly identify known incompatibilities in hardware/software and software/software.

If you see an error message, you will normally be able to discern the source of the message from its header or content. For instance, "LOGIN-4.10-100: Access has been denied." leads you directly to networking components. Once you have followed the error message's clues to isolate the problem, you can use the System Messages manual or Novell's support database to determine the cause—and maybe even the solution. (The next two sections of this chapter give you more information about the System Messages manual and the support database.)

For server hangs, you can isolate the problem using your specific configuration, some deductive logic, and Novell's support database. Say you get the error "Page Fault Processor Exception running module SMSDI..." After restarting the server, you avoid loading SMSDI and immediately retire to a workstation with a modem to search Novell's support database. You enter a search string:

```
"Page Fault" SMSDI hang
```

The database returns a list of ten documented problems. Moving through the list, you see a software/hardware combination similar to yours. Eureka!

Novell's support database normally includes a recommended solution for each problem.

Using the System Messages Manual

When Novell developed NetWare 4.0, a companywide effort was initiated to isolate, label, classify, and document error messages. The major impetus for the project came from internationalization: the process of separating language-specific data from code for translation purposes.

Novell's engineering and documentation managers have been diligent in documenting error messages that help you, the administrator. This documentation has been converted to Standard Generalized Markup Language (SGML) and presented as an online manual in the DynaText set that comes with your software. You can read the documentation CD-ROM from any workstation with a CD-ROM drive. For speed and portability, you can load the documentation collections on a laptop computer's hard drive.

As mentioned, earlier, each error message begins with an identifying code consisting of the following elements:

- The software module that originated the message (for example, LOGIN or SERVER), including the software version or platform. This module is not necessarily the *cause* of the problem—only the one that *encountered* it.

- The message number.

- (Sometimes) an error code.

Depending on the type of error and the engineer who wrote the error message, there is some diversity in the way error messages are formatted; you can generally count on at least a module name and message number. To search for an error message in the DynaText online manual, you can enter a text string in the Find form at the bottom of the window, or follow this procedure:

1. Begin by starting the DynaText viewer. (You'll find a SETUP program for the viewer on the documentation CD-ROM.)

2. Double-click the System Messages book to select it.

   In NetWare 4.10, the book is in the NetWare 4.1 collection. In NetWare 4.11, the book is in the NetWare 4.11 Reference collection.

3. In the Book menu, choose Search Forms. The Search History dialog appears.

4. In the Search History dialog, use the Search Form drop-down list to choose Messages by Module (see Figure 13.2).

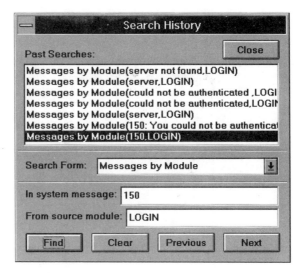

5. In the In System Message box, type the message number or part of the message text.

6. In the From Source Module box, type the software module name.

7. Click the Find button.

8. Click on the Close button.

You are returned to the System Messages manual, where all instances of your search string have been found for that module and highlighted in the window on the right. To move to the next or previous instance of the string, click on the Forward or Reverse arrow button at the top of the screen. See Figure 13.3.

The explanations and actions presented by the DynaText viewer range from quite helpful solutions to somewhat feeble advice, like "Contact your network supervisor." The error codes used in the viewer will further assist you in fault isolation, and are documented in Appendix A of the System Messages manual.

Using Novell's Support Web Site

As an administrator, you undoubtedly have a modem and an Internet account to access Novell's support site on the Web, at

`http://support.novell.com/home/`

FIGURE 13.3

Error message
documentation typically
includes explanations
and actions.

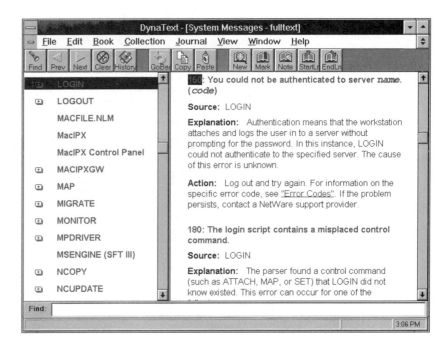

FIGURE 13.3

Error message documentation typically includes explanations and actions.

This home page currently has over 60 links to more specific support pages, grouped by product. Each specific support page has a "What's New" link, a frequently asked questions (FAQ) link, and a search dialog.

If you've had a problem loading new software or resolving some incompatibility between networking software/software or software/hardware, the FAQ link will often take you to the solution. It stands to reason that Novell has already addressed the most common incompatibilities, and has figured out a way around them. Chances are you'll find information here about your own situation.

Many issues can be resolved by using the search dialog to get to a Technical Information Document (TID). These TIDs may not have the precise scenario documented that you encounter, but it'll be close enough that you can figure it out yourself. Following is an excerpt from a TID:

```
SYMPTOM

The 3.12 server would abend with a GPPE loading
NFSSERV.NLM if manually registering 64 meg of additional
memory. If they didn't register the extra 64 meg,
NFSSERV would load fine.
```

CAUSE

This problem initiated when trying to upgrade the memory in the server from 64 meg to 128 meg. The server wouldn't auto register the new memory. All it showed was the original 64 meg. The Dell box would count up the 128 meg upon bootup. They had to manually register the additional 64 meg.

SOLUTION

The customer didn't know that he had to run the Dell EISA configuration to add the additional memory. After doing that,the problem went away. The server would auto register the additional memory and NFSSERV.NLM loaded fine.

Of particular interest for troubleshooting is the Web page

```
http://support.novell.com/home/server/nos/faq.htm
```

This page gives links to such topics as the following:

- What are the recommended baseline patches?

- How do I register memory in NetWare 3.*x* and 4.*x*?

- What do "Error-621 FD93" and "Transaction Tracking Disabled" indicate?

- What are the top server support issues?

- What recommendations do you have for troubleshooting abends?

- What should I do if I can't create a directory, or I can't create a file in certain directories?

- What is the maximum number of files I can create on a volume?

- Are there compatibility problems between NetWare and the PCI technology?

- What should I do if my server is abending?

- What is the first step to resolving critical server issues?

- What can I do if my server is dropping connections when utilization is high?

Log Sheet Strategies

If you've been keeping your log sheets up to date, you can use those logs for isolating trouble on your network. You'll have ammunition ready for resolving those problems, as well. Log sheet strategies fall generally into two categories: detecting what changes were made to the network before a problem occurred, and checking to see if the problem has happened before.

What Changed?

If the network was running fine for some time before the problems started, the log can tell you what happened in the meantime. For a server, you'll need to remember when the server was healthy and then examine the log for all entries made from that time to the point at which errors started occurring.

For a workstation, you'll need to question the user of that workstation. When was the last time you used the workstation successfully? When was the first time it failed? You'll need to find out what happened in between. Whenever you work on a workstation, you can use diagnostic software such as Win CheckIt to create a baseline configuration after you're done. Win CheckIt records hardware and software settings in its own log file. The next time a user has a problem with the workstation, you can run Win CheckIt again; it will show in a bright red font every setting that has changed since the last time Win CheckIt was run.

Has This Happened Before?

It's likely that many of your users have similar workstations and use similar software; therefore, you'll probably see some repetition in the problems users have. If you use a log to record errors and solutions, you may be able to use that log to find the last time a specific error occurred. Then you can skip all the fault isolation steps and implement the solution recorded in the log.

This strategy won't work every time, since any given error may have more than one cause. But it works enough of the time to make trying it a good bet.

At What Time Does the Problem Occur?

Some errors seem intermittent, but with some study can turn out to be periodic. That is, they may happen at a specific time every day or every week. Your logs can help you determine whether errors are periodic or truly intermittent.

The first time a server goes down at 2:15 A.M. on a Monday morning, you might not have the slightest idea why. The second time it happens, you're likely to have a better clue. Periodic errors occur, obviously, as a result of periodic events. Do your backups start at 2:00 A.M. every day or every week? Have you set compression to occur at 2:00 A.M.? The answers to these kinds of questions can lead you to a diagnosis of periodic events.

Another kind of periodic event is the ebb and flow of a company's workday or workweek. The server may periodically go down during peak usage at 10:30 A.M. or 2:30 P.M., or it may go down (heaven forbid) every second Thursday while paychecks are being printed. Being able to track and identify periodic errors gives you an enormous advantage in fault isolation.

Diagnostics for Intermittent Errors

Clearly, you'll be making extra work for yourself if you fail to identify a periodic error and instead assume the error is intermittent. But if you've gone through the error logs and been unable to determine that there is a rhythm to the errors, it's time to set your sights on a truly intermittent problem.

Intermittent errors are the hardest to troubleshoot. To use an example from the real world, consider intermittent windshield wipers. Of course, you know that they really are *periodic* windshield wipers in most cases. That is, you turn them on and they wipe the windshield at consistent intervals until you change the interval or turn them off.

I have an old pickup truck that has *truly* intermittent windshield wipers. When I turn them on, they may or may not wipe, and there's no discernible way to determine if or when they will. This makes driving my truck in the rain more exciting, but your users can probably do without such melodrama when it comes to earning a profit for the company.

Intermittent errors are best handled by using the System Messages manual and the Novell support Web site. As already mentioned, however, these resources sometimes give vague or otherwise useless information for your situation. Sometimes you need to dig into the lower-level workings of NetWare to see what's causing the problem.

Using TRACK ON

The TRACK ON console command is generally for multiserver networks, although you can use it for watching packets from workstations when they first attach to the network. When you type **TRACK ON** at the server console, the RIP Tracking screen appears. This screen shows the Router Information Protocol (RIP) traffic. Following are sample IN and OUT packets:

```
IN [00000020:0000F209A9DB] 02:21:08am 00000010 1/2
   0000200 3/4
OUT [00000200:FFFFFFFFFFFF] 02:23:00am 0000200 1/2
   00000010 3/4
```

The IN packet comes from the server at node address 0000F209A9DB on network address 00000020. The packet was sent at 2:21 A.M. The remaining numbers in the IN line are network numbers that the sending server knows about. For example, 00000010 and 00000040 are the network numbers recognized by the server. The numbers 1/2 and 3/4 indicate routing information about that network. In these fraction-like numbers, the 1/ and 3/ indicate the *hop count* (number of gateways or routers) from the sending server to this network. A hop count of 1 indicates the server is cabled directly to that network segment. The /2 and /4 indicate the number of ticks (1/18th of a second) that it took for a packet to reach this network from the sending server.

The OUT packet is a broadcast packet (node address FFFFFFFFFFFF) advertising a virtual TCP/IP network segment.

When a client loads networking software, a Get Nearest Server request is broadcast on the network to which the station is cabled. You'll see this request at the RIP Tracking Screen:

```
IN [00000020:0040000945BB43] 02:21:08am SPECIFIC ROUTE
   REQUEST
```

A server will normally respond to the message with a Give Nearest Server response, similar to this one:

```
OUT [00000020:0040000945BB43] 02:21:09am 3184114F 1/2
```

To terminate the Rip Tracking screen, type **TRACK OFF** at the server console.

Using NDS TRACE

In a multiserver network, you can use NDS TRACE (a SET parameter) to see whether the Directory is synchronizing across servers. You can also diagnose miscellaneous NDS errors, which may occur when you are managing Directory objects with the administration utilities. NDS-related system messages are numbered as follows: –601 through –699, and F966 through F9FE.

To start NDS TRACE, type the following command at the server console:

```
SET NDS TRACE TO SCREEN = ON
```

Or, if you would rather copy NDS TRACE messages to a file, type

```
SET NDS TRACE TO FILE = ON
```

The messages will be copied to the file DSTRACE.DBG in the SYS:SYSTEM directory.

What you want to see is the message All processed = YES, as shown in Figure 13.4. If the network is having trouble synchronizing the Directory, you'll see All processed = NO for an extended time. In this case, you should run DSREPAIR to fix the Directory (see the upcoming section, "Repairing the Directory").

FIGURE 13.4
If Directory synchronization is completing normally, you'll see "All processed = YES."

Repair Utilities

NetWare has included the repair utilities DREPAIR and VREPAIR for its most substantial features—namely, the file system and NDS.

Running either DREPAIR and VREPAIR will affect your users, so it's best to wait until nonproduction hours to run these utilities.

Repairing a Corrupted File System

You can repair a corrupted volume by running VREPAIR. This utility requires that you unload the affected volume, so you'll want to have all users log out first. Obviously, if you can wait until nonproduction hours, you should do so.

To run VREPAIR, unload the corrupted volume from the server console. Let's say you're concerned with the SYS volume. You'd type **UNLOAD SYS** to unload it. Then start VREPAIR. Since you've unloaded the SYS volume, you run VREPAIR from the C:\NWSERVER directory. Your command would be

LOAD C:\NWSERVER\VREPAIR.

You will be presented with an Options screen. The default options work fine, so press Enter to continue with the repair. You may need to run VREPAIR a number of times to fix all corrupted files and directories.

Repairing the Directory

If NDS is having trouble synchronizing the Directory among multiple servers, it's usually because of a communication problem. Therefore, you should troubleshoot communications problems first. Since NDS uses Service Advertising Protocol (SAP) packets for Directory synchronization, check the routers on the network to make sure they are not filtering SAP packets.

If you have brought down a server or physically removed it from the network, make sure it isn't the one that contains the Master replica of the Directory. If it does, then you'll need to follow the steps in this chapter's section, "Extended Down Time in a Multiserver Network."

In a small network, all servers should hold a replica. Therefore, when a server is brought back on line, make sure you add a Read/Write replica to that server. See "Creating a Replica in a Multiserver Network" in this chapter.

If your servers are up and communicating, you can use DSREPAIR to check all the Directory objects and repair any problems if possible. Simply select Full Unattended Repair from DSREPAIR's main screen.

Summary

THIS CHAPTER GIVES YOU PROCEDURES for some routine network maintenance tasks, such as bringing down a server for a short time, adding hard drives, or permanently removing a server. Also included are procedures for the more dire circumstances, such as a catastrophic server loss.

The troubleshooting section focuses on specific Novell-related problems, not general PC troubleshooting. You'll want to get familiar with the System Messages manual, as well as Novell's support Web page. Don't forget to keep and use log sheets; they are sure to be of help in discovering what changes might have caused a network problem.

You can use the TRACK ON and NDS TRACE screens at the server console to observe routing packets, and Directory synchronization at a base (and user-unfriendly) level.

For repair of the file system, use the VREPAIR utility. To repair the Directory, you can use DSREPAIR.

For a more exhaustive look at troubleshooting, you might try Logan G. Harbaugh's Troubleshooting NetWare Systems *(Sybex, 1996).*

NetWare
Utilities for the
DOS and OS/2
Command Lines

APPENDIX

A

THE UTILITIES LISTED IN THIS INDEX can be run from the DOS command line. Some can also be run from the OS/2 command line. To get help with a command-line utility, simply type the utility name followed by a /? option. Some of the utilities listed here are character-based menu utilities. For help while using those utilities, press F1.

You can get additional information on most utilities from the Utilities Reference manual in the online DynaText manual set.

3C589MGR.EXE Novell has included this 32-Bit ODI utility from 3Com, for use in configuring the 3Com EtherLink III LAN PC Card (3C589A/B/C).

ADDICON.EXE Use ADDICON in a login script or from the DOS prompt to add program items to Windows 3.1 workstations. Here's an example of a login script using ADDICON:

```
IF MEMBER OF "123USERS" THEN
#ADDICON /EXE=K:\TOOLS\123WXMAC.EXE /DESC=Macro Editor
/WORK=K:\TOOLS/GROUPFIL=LOTUSAPP.GRP
END
```

ADDICON cannot create a new program group; nor does it replace an existing program item with a new one.

ATOTAL.EXE Use ATOTAL to create a summary of accounting information. This utility comes in both DOS and OS/2 versions. ATOTAL works only if you have enabled accounting on your system. You must either run ATOTAL from the SYS:SYSTEM directory, or have a search drive mapped to it. You must also have the Supervisor object right to the NetWare Server object.

ATOTAL uses the accounting data file NET$ACCT.DAT. The following summary information is included in the report for each day:

- Connect time

- Blocks read

- Blocks stored per day

- Server requests

- Blocks written

The following command runs ATOTAL and redirects its output to a text file:

```
ATOTAL  /C >G:\NETUSAGE.TXT
```

AUDITCON.EXE AUDITCON is a character-based menu utility for a network auditor. A *network auditor* is a user whose job is to monitor network transactions. Auditors can view information about network events, such as who logs in and when and who opens a file; but they cannot open or modify files other than the audit data and audit history files. Auditing may be enabled at a volume level for file-system activities or at a container level for NDS activities. Options available from AUDITCON include the following:

- Auditing directory services

- External auditing

- Changing current server

- Enabling volume auditing

BREQUEST.EXE, BREQUTIL.EXE, BROLLFWD.EXE These utilities are part of the Btrieve database record-management system. See the Btrieve Installation and Operation manual in the online DynaText set for descriptions.

CAPTURE.EXE Use CAPTURE in login scripts or from the DOS command line to redirect print streams from local printer ports to network Print Queues or Printers. This utility comes in both DOS and OS/2 versions.

Following is an example of a CAPTURE command:

```
CAPTURE Q=ADMINQ /L=2 /TI=1 /NB /NFF
```

Remember to precede the command with a # if you are using it in a login script. Use a relative queue name or an alias when referring to a Print Queue outside the workstation's current context.

COLORPAL.EXE This character-based menu utility allows you to modify the color palette of NetWare text utilities. The palette is saved as IBM_RUN.OVL in the SYS:\PUBLIC directory. You probably won't ever have to use this utility, since the default colors work fine. However, on a *really* boring day it might be entertaining.

CPQCFG.EXE This utility is provided by Compaq and Xircom for initializing PCMCIA network adapters. Use this utility only when instructed to by the adapter manufacturer.

CX.EXE CX is available in both DOS and OS/2 command-line versions. Use CX to list container objects or to change a workstation's current context. In the following example, a workstation's current context is changed by giving a distinguished container name:

```
CX .PROD-DEPT.OURCO
```

When you use CX without specifying a container, a list of containers is displayed.

Following are some options of CX that can help you navigate the Directory tree.

CX OPTION	DESCRIPTION
/R	Lists containers at the [Root] level, or changes context in relation to the root.
/T	Lists containers below the current context or below a specified context in a tree structure.
/CONT	Lists containers at the current context or at a specified context, in a vertical list with no structure.
/A	Includes all objects at or below the context. Use with /T or /CONT.

CXCFG.EXE This utility is provided by Xircom for initializing PCMCIA network adapters. Use this utility only when instructed to by the adapter manufacturer.

DOSGEN.EXE To use a remote boot PROM on a network adapter to boot a workstation, you need to run the DOSGEN utility. DOSGEN uploads the workstation's boot files into a remote boot image file, NET$DOS.SYS, in the server's LOGIN directory. To use DOSGEN:

1. Create a boot disk for the workstation by formatting a floppy disk with the /S option to copy hidden and system files.

2. Create AUTOEXEC.BAT, CONFIG.SYS, and NET.CFG files for the work-station, including the commands required to load the networking software. Copy these files and all software to the disk that is required for logging in.

3. Type the command **DOSGEN A:** from your workstation. The boot files will be stored in the SYS:LOGIN directory.

For more information on booting from a remote boot PROM, see the NetWare Client for DOS and Windows User Guide in the online DynaText collection.

DOSNP.EXE DOSNP is client software that provides support for Named Pipes client/server applications.

FILER.EXE Filer is a character-based menu utility for managing files and directories. It also provides options to view volume information, to salvage deleted files, and to purge files that have been deleted.

FLAG.EXE NetWare includes both DOS and OS/2 versions of the FLAG utility. Similar to the DOS ATTRIB command, the FLAG utility allows you to view or change attributes of files and directories. For instance, to change all EXE files on the SYS volume to Read-Only and Shareable, type

```
FLAG SYS:\*.EXE RO SH /S
```

HRMIB.EXE HRMIB is the Host Resources manager, an executable file that is part of the NetWare VLM client software. HRMIB collects information about client workstations that are running DOS on the network for Simple Network Management Protocol (SNMP) management.

INSTALL.EXE INSTALL.EXE files are provided as subdirectories of SYS:PUBLIC, to install the following client software:

- VLM
- Client 32
- OS/2 Requester
- VLMIP
- Windows 3.1

LOGIN.EXE LOGIN is provided as both a DOS and an OS/2 utility for logging in from the command line. The typical format of a login command is LOGIN *name*, where *name* is the name of a User object. The LOGIN utility looks in the workstation's current context for the User object, and then in the server's context. You can specify a distinguished or relative name for the User object if the User does not exist in either the server context or the workstation's current context.

LOGIN options are as follows:

LOGIN OPTION	DESCRIPTION
/NS	Prevents login scripts from running. You may need to use this while debugging bad login scripts.
/NB	Suppresses the NetWare banner during the login process.
/S *path*	Specifies a login script file to run.
/S *object name*	Specifies an *object name* whose login script you want to run.
/B	Specifies a bindery-style login.
/PR=	Specifies a Profile object script to run.
/NOSWAP	Prevents LOGIN from swapping to disk or to extended or expanded memory.
SWAP=*path*	Swaps memory to this path when external commands are executed.
/TREE	If you have multiple Directory trees on the network, use this option to specify which one.

LOGOUT.EXE This utility closes your connection with the network. Versions of LOGOUT.EXE are provided for both DOS and OS/2 workstations. To log out from NDS but keep your bindery connections, type

```
LOGOUT /T
```

To close a single bindery connection only, specify a server name, as in

```
LOGOUT SERVER1.
```

MAP.EXE Versions of MAP.EXE are provided for both DOS and OS/2 workstations. MAP is both an internal and an external command, so you can use it from the command line or from login scripts without the # character.

MAP is typically used to create a new drive letter and associate it with a path you specify. See "Mapping Drives Using the MAP Command" in Chapter 5 for instructions on using this utility.

MENUCNVT.EXE, MENUEXE.EXE, MENUMAKE.EXE, AND MENURSET.EXE

These commands, along with the NMENU command, comprise a system for creating and converting character-based, customized menus for your users. The menu system is included in NetWare 4.10 but has been dropped from subsequent NetWare releases and replaced by NetWare Application Launcher (NAL).

For instructions on using the menu system, refer to Supervising the Network in the online DynaText collection.

NCOPY.EXE NCOPY is available in both DOS and OS/2 versions. Similar to the DOS COPY command, NCOPY allows you to copy files and directories. The following options are available:

NCOPY OPTION	DESCRIPTION
/A	Copy only files with the archive bit set, leaving the archive bit unchanged.
/C	Copy only DOS information.
/F	Copy sparse files.
/I	Inform with a message during the copy operation when non-DOS file information will be lost.
/M	Copy only files with archive bit set, then clear the bit.
/R	Retain compression on supported media.
/R/U	Retain compression on unsupported media.
/S	Copy subdirectories.
/S/E	Copy subdirectories including empty directories.
/V	Perform a read-after-write verification of data copied to local drives (applies only to DOS workstations).

NCUPDATE.EXE NCUPDATE.EXE is provided in both DOS and OS/2 command-line versions. This utility is used in login scripts to automatically update users' NET.CFG files. For each container you move, you should edit the login script of the alias left behind to include lines similar to these:

```
IF LOGIN_ALIAS_CONTEXT = "Y" THEN
    MAP INS S1:=SERVER1/SYS:PUBLIC
    #NCUPDATE /NP
    MAP DEL S1:
END
```

NDIR.EXE NDIR is available for both DOS and OS/2. Similar to the DOS DIR command, NDIR allows you to list files and directories. The following options are available:

NDIR OPTION	DESCRIPTION
/[NOT] *attribute*	Displays files with or [without] a specific *attribute*. Attribute options are Ro, Rw, Sy, H, A, Ds, X, T, P, Sh, I, Ci, Di, Ri, Co, Ic, Dc, Cc, Dm, and M.
/[REV] SORT *option*	Sorts [or sorts in reverse] the output by *option* specified. Options are AC=last accessed date, AR=last archived date, CR=date created or copied, OW=owner, SI=size, UP=date of last update.
/C	Scroll output continuously.
/COMP	Shows compression information.
/D	Shows detailed file information.
/DA	Shows date information.
/DO	Lists only directories.
/FI	Displays location of a file in search drives.
/FO	Displays only files.
/L	Shows long file names.
/MAC	Shows Macintosh files.

NDIR OPTION	DESCRIPTION
/option [NOT] operator value	Restricts files and directories listed, based on specified *option* and *operator* with *value*. Available *options* include AC=last accessed date, AR=last archived date, CR=date created or copied, OW=owner, SI=size, UP=date of last update, NAM=name space. Available *operators* include LE=less than or equal to, GR=greater than, EQ=equal to, BEF=before, AFT=after.
/R	Shows filters, rights, and file attributes.
/S	Lists files in all subdirectories.
/SPA	Displays directory space information.
/VOL	Displays volume information.

NDSSCH.EXE This utility updates the NDS schema with rules contained in a script file.

NDSSCH.EXE is called from other utilities supplied by Novell, and should not be used by network administrators.

NETADMIN.EXE This character-based menu utility offers most of the functionality of NetWare Administrator without Windows. It allows you to browse the Directory tree, manage trustee assignments, and edit properties of Directory objects.

NETBIOS.EXE An optional client module that provides compatibility with IBM's NetBIOS peer networking applications. These applications are only for IBM PC networks and IBM Token-Ring networks. Before setting up and configuring client workstations for a NetBIOS connection, you need to install and load a NetBIOS application on a server.

NETUSER.EXE This is a character-based menu utility for users. It lets users

- Change printer port capturing for their workstations

- Send messages to Users and Groups (and allow/reject receiving of messages)

- Create new drive mappings, including search drive mappings

- Edit their own login scripts (if they have the Write right to their own Login Script property)

- Change their passwords (if they have the rights)

- Change the workstation's current context

NIOS.EXE NIOS.EXE is the core executable file of Client 32 software for DOS and Windows 3.1*x*. The Client 32 software for Windows 95 doesn't use NIOS.EXE, but instead has a NIOS virtual device driver (VXD).

NLIST.EXE NLIST.EXE comes in both DOS and OS/2 versions. This command-line utility provides very complex options to list Directory objects and their properties.

Typing **NLIST** without any options displays the help screen. Available options are as follows:

NLIST OPTION	DESCRIPTION
/A	Lists active Users or servers.
/B	Displays bindery information.
/C	Scrolls output continuously to the end.
/CO *context*	Lists objects in a specified context.
/D	Shows detailed information.
/N	Shows only the object name.
/R	Lists objects at the [Root].
/S	Lists objets in all subordinate contexts.
/TREE	Lists Directory trees.
object class	Lists objects of the *object class* specified.
SHOW *"property"*	Displays the specified *property* of objects selected.
WHERE *"property" operator "value"*	Displays only objects where the *property value* meets the specified test. Available *operators* are EQ=equal, NE=not equal, LT=less then, EXISTS=property exists, LE=less than, TE=greater than, NEXISTS=property does not exist.

NLSLSAPI.EXE NLSLSAPI is a workstation TSR for NetWare Licensing Services. This TSR must be loaded before you run the DOS client application that uses the licensing service.

NPATH.EXE The NPATH utility is provided in both DOS and OS/2 versions for troubleshooting problems with NetWare executable files that can't find the proper message files. NPATH provides information similar to the following:

```
Based on the following workstation information:
      Current working directory: G: = CN=SERVER1_SYS: \
      Utility load directory: Z: = CN=SERVER1_SYS: \PUBLIC
      NWLANGUAGE=English
      PATH=Z:.;C:\DOS;C:\WINDOWS;C:\PKZIP;C:\NOVELL\
  CLIENT32;D:\NETSCAPE\WINSOCK;Y:.

The search sequence for message and help files is:
      G: = CN=SERVER1_SYS: \
      Z: = CN=SERVER1_SYS: \PUBLIC\NLS\ENGLISH
      Z: = CN=SERVER1_SYS: \PUBLIC
      Z: = CN=SERVER1_SYS: \PUBLIC
      C:\DOS
      C:\WINDOWS
      C:\PKZIP
      C:\NOVELL\CLIENT32
      D:\NETSCAPE\WINSOCK
      Y: = CN=SERVER1_SYS: \APPS\PKZIP
      Z: = CN=SERVER1_SYS: \PUBLIC\NLS\ENGLISH
```

NPRINT.EXE NPRINT.EXE comes in both DOS and OS/2 command-line versions. It is similar to the DOS PRINT command, allowing you to send text files or print-stream files to network Printer or Print Queue objects. NPRINT options are as follows:

NPRINT OPTION	DESCRIPTION
B=*banner name*	Specifies a banner to print before the print job.
C=*number*	Allows you to print multiple copies of the job.
F=*form*	Allows you to specify a form or form number.
FF	Includes a form feed at the end of the job.
filename	The name of the file you want to print.
HOLD	Sends the print job but puts it on hold.

NPRINT OPTION	DESCRIPTION
J= *configuration*	Name of the print job configuration.
NAM=*name*	Specifies the name to print on the banner page.
NB	Prevents the banner page from printing.
NFF	Disables the form feed at the end of the print job.
NNOTI	Disables user notification when the job is completed.
NOTI	Notifies the user when the print job is completed.
Q=*Print Queue name*	Destination of the print job.
S=*NetWare bindery server name*	Specifies the bindery server that has the print queue.
T=*number*	Specifies the number of spaces assigned to a tab.

NPRINTER.EXE Versions of NPRINTER.EXE are included for both DOS and OS/2 command lines. This port driver allows network users to print to printers attached to workstations. For NPRINTER to work, you must have a Printer object created in the Directory. Options for NPRINTER are as follows:

NRPINTER OPTION	DESCRIPTION
/B=*number*	Number of KB to use as buffer (range: 3–60).
/S	Shows the status of a loaded NPRINTER.
/T=*number*	If your workstation is bogging down due to printing, use this " tick" option to increase the timing interval. Higher tick settings mean faster overall workstation performance but slower printing performance. A tick value of 2 takes twice as long to service a job as a tick value of 1 (range: 1–9).
/U	Unloads the NPRINTER utility.
printer	Name of the Printer object you have created in the Directory.
printserver number	Name of the Print Server that services this Printer, and the printer number associated with that Print Server. Use these parameters in place of the Printer name.

NVER.EXE NVER.EXE is provided as both a DOS and an OS/2 command-line utility. Use this utility to determine the version of the NOS and workstation software. Information similar to the following is displayed:

```
DOS:      V6.22

LAN driver:  LINKSYS ETHER16 series Ethernet Driver
    v3.18 (950823) ETHERNET_802.2 Version 4.00
              IRQ 10, Port 200

IPX API version:       3.32
SPX API version:       3.32

VLM: Version 32.00 Revision A  using Extended Memory

Attached file servers:

Server name:  SERVER1
Novell NetWare 4.11 (August 22, 1996)
```

NWDETECT.EXE Use NWDETECT in login scripts to determine the version of network client software. Syntax is as follows:

NWDETECT [*name*] [*version1*] [*version2*] /*options*

where *name* is the name of the software to detect; and *version1* and *version2* are the beginning and ending version stamps to detect (see also NWSTAMP). Available *options* are listed in the following table.

NWDETECT OPTION	DESCRIPTION
/C *netcfgname*	Specifies the NET.CFG file (including path).
/DT	Sets the default action to be FALSE or 0.
/NS	Detects if there is no stamp set in NET.CFG.
/P *prompt-text*	Specifies message to be displayed when the client is detected.
/T *clienttype*	Specifies type of NetWare client: NETX or VLM.

NWIPMAP.EXE For networks running NetWare/IP, NWIPMAP provides functions similar to the MAP utility. NWIPMAP, however, maps drives to servers in other IP domains, called remote domains. For example, you might want to connect to a NetWare/IP server at another company over the Internet.

You'll need the following information to use the NWIPMAP utility:

- Fully qualified name of the remote NetWare/IP domain

- Name of the NetWare/IP server in the remote domain

- Volume (and directory if desired) on the remote server

Also, a DSS server in the remote NetWare/IP domain must be accessible through DNS, and you must have permission to attach to the server.

Syntax for the NWIPMAP command is as follows:

NWIPMAP *drive:=servername\vol:path@domain*

For *domain*, substitute the fully-qualified domain name of the remote NetWare/IP domain, such as nwip.company.com.

NWIPMAP provides file access only. Services in the remote NetWare/IP domain that rely on SAP/RIP broadcasting, such as print services, are not available.

NWLOG.EXE The NWLOG utility lets you append a log entry to a log file. To use it, type **NWLOG /F** *filename* **/M** *message* where *filename* is the name of the log file and *message* is the text you want appended.

NWSTAMP.EXE Use NWSTAMP in login scripts to apply a name and version "stamp" to client NET.CFG files. Syntax for the NWSTAMP command is as follows:

NWSTAMP *name version /options*

For *name* and *version,* indicate what you want stamped in NET.CFG. See also NWDETECT.EXE. Here are the available *options*:

NWSTAMP OPTION	DESCRIPTION
/B *backupname*	Specifies the name of the backup NET.CFG file (including path).
/C *netcfgname*	Specifies the name of the NET.CFG file (including path).

NWUNPACK.EXE Use NWUNPACK to decompress files from installation media. Compressed files usually have the underscore (_) as the last character in the file name extension. You can use NWUNPACK with a specific file name or with wildcards. Examples:

```
NWUNPACK WSSNMP.VL_
NWUNPACK *.??_
```

If the unpacked version already exists, you are prompted to overwrite it.

PARTMGR.EXE The PARTMGR utility is the character-based menu utility that helps you manage partitions and replicas. You can accomplish the following tasks with PARTMGR:

- Create or modify partition boundaries

- Delete a server that has been permanently removed from the network

- List replicas stored on a server

- List servers that hold replicas of a partition

- Merge a partition with its parent

- Change replica types

- Delete replicas from a server

PCONSOLE.EXE PCONSOLE is the character-based menu utility for printing management. You can to create and manage Printers, Print Queues, and Print Servers.

PING.EXE With PING you can test TCP/IP connectivity from the workstation. This utility sends ICMP echo packets (ICMP ECHO_REQUEST) to the remote host you specify, and records the time it takes the host to respond to the packets.

You can either specify one size for all packets or vary the size. You can also tell the utility to display the IP addresses and host names of the IP routers along the path of the packet between your workstation and the destination host. Syntax for the PING command is

PING *hostname /option*

with these available *options:*

PING OPTION	DESCRIPTION
/R	Show trace route information.
/RN	Show trace route IP addresses without host names.
/T*n*	Specifies the destination response timeout value (*n*) in seconds; default is 2.
/N*n*	Specifies the number (*n*) of packets to send; default is 1.
/P*n*	Specifies the number (*n*) of seconds after a packet is sent before another packet is sent. Use 0 for a continuous stream.
/L*n*	Specifies number (*n*) of bytes in the ICMP packets (12 to 8192); default is 12.
/S*n*	Specifies the starting packet size (*n*) for variable-sized packets(12 to 8192); default is 12.
/I*n*	Specifies the number of bytes (*n*) to increment between variable-sized packets; default is 1.

PRINTCON.EXE PRINTCON is a character-based menu utility for creating and editing print job configurations.

PRINTDEF.EXE PRINTDEF is a character-based menu utility for editing, importing, and exporting printer devices and forms.

PSC.EXE The PSC utility comes in both DOS and OS/2 command-line versions. Use it to monitor and control Print Servers and Printers. Syntax is
   PSC PS=*printserver* P=*printernumber* S=*binderyserver* /*option*
with available *options* as follows:

PSC OPTION	DESCRIPTION
FF	Execute form feed on printer.
PAU	Pause a printer.
STAR	Start a printer.
STO	Stop a printer.
AB	Abort a printer.

PSC OPTION	DESCRIPTION
STAT	Get a printer's status.
M	Mark top of form on printer.
MO=*formnumber*	Mount a form on a printer.
PRI	Make a remote printer private.
SHA	Make a remote printer shared.

If you have issued a Down command to a Print Server and you want to cancel the command, use **PSC PS=***printserver* **CD.** To check the status of all printers, type **PSC PS=***printserver* **P=ALL STAT.** To list all printers, type **PSC PS=** *printserver* **L.**

PURGE.EXE This utility is provided in both DOS and OS/2 command line versions. Use PURGE to eliminate deleted files from the file system. You can use it with specific file names or wildcards. To purge files in all subdirectories, append the /A option to the command. Examples:

```
PURGE *.TMP /A
PURGE CONTACTS.IDX
PURGE *.* /A
```

RCONSOLE.EXE RCONSOLE is the character-based menu utility for accessing a server console. RCONSOLE gives you the following options:

- View console screens
- Run console commands
- List files on the server's DOS partitions
- Copy files to the server's DOS partitions

To use RCONSOLE, you must have REMOTE.NLM loaded at the server, along with a remote driver such as RSPX.NLM or RS232.NLM.

RENDIR.EXE RENDIR helps you rename network directories. You can use volume names or drive letters to specify the directory you are renaming. Examples:

```
RENDIR USERS EMPLOYEE
RENDIR Z:\USERS EMPLOYEE
RENDIR SYS:\USERS EMPLOYEE
```

RIGHTS.EXE RIGHTS.EXE is provided in both DOS and OS/2 command-line versions. It lets you track trustee assignments to the file system, as well as create or change trustee assignments. To show your effective rights to the current directory, type **RIGHTS** without optional parameters. Following is the general form of the RIGHTS command. (Be sure to note the exceptions, indicated just below.)

RIGHTS [*path*] [[+ | –]*list*] /*options*

where *path* is a directory and/or file specification, and *list* is a list of rights to be changed. The plus sign (+) adds the right but does not alter other rights assigned. The minus sign (–) revokes a right but does not alter other rights. If you don't use either the plus or minus sign, all rights are revoked except those in the list. Here are the available *options*:

RIGHTS OPTION	DESCRIPTION
/C	Scroll output continuously.
/F	Create/modify the IRF.
/I	Display inheritance to the specified path.
/NAME= *object*	Indicate Directory object to which the rights assignment applies.
/S	Apply the operation to subdirectories.
/T	Display trustees of the specified path.

Exceptions: There are exceptions to general usage for RIGHTS. To view trustees of a directory or file, type **RIGHTS** *path* /T without a rights list. To remove a trustee, type **RIGHTS** *path* REM /**NAME**=*object*. To view how inheritance has made the effective rights, type **RIGHTS** *path* /**NAME**=*object* /**I.**

SEND.EXE SEND.EXE is included in both DOS and OS/2 command-line versions. SEND delivers a message to another User, to all Users in a Group, or to all Users in a container. The general format of the command is
SEND *"message" user*
To send to bindery objects, you can precede *user* with a server name (for example, SERVER1/ED).

You can also control message reception at a workstation. Type **SEND** /*option* using one of the following options:

SEND OPTION	DESCRIPTION
/A=*x*	Defines which messages to accept, where *x* is one of the following letters: A (all messages), C (only console messages), N (no messages), or P (accept messages only when polled).
/P	Poll server for stored messages.
/S	Show message settings.

SETPASS.EXE The SETPASS.EXE utility is for changing passwords. Type **SETPASS** without options to change your password. Type **SETPASS** *user* to set someone else's password (assuming you have the rights). You are prompted to enter the new password.

SETTTS.EXE SETTTS.EXE comes in both DOS and OS/2 command-line versions. Use **SETTTS** to specify the logical and physical record-lock thresholds for database applications. Syntax is as follows:

SETTTS *logical physical*

For instance, you might type **SETTTS 6 9** to limit logical locks to 6 and physical locks to 9. To reset limits to the normal value, type **SETTTS /N,** and to disable the logical and physical locks type **SETTTS /D.**

SYSTIME.EXE DOS and OS/2 command-line versions of SYSTIME.EXE are available. Type **SYSTIME** to synchronize your workstation's time with the network's time.

UIMPORT.EXE UIMPORT.EXE is provided in both DOS and OS/2 command-line versions. You can use UIMPORT to create or modify User accounts in a batch process.

Before using UIMPORT, you must first create a control file and a data file. The control file specifies the format of information in the data file. The data file contains User names and other information about the Users you will add. You can create the data file with a text editor, or export data to the data file from a database or spreadsheet application.

There are many tips and caveats for using UIMPORT, so you should consult the Upgrade manual in your NetWare manual set.

VLM.EXE VLM.EXE is the program that loads Virtual Loadable Modules (VLMs) in DOS/Windows client software (before Client 32). Use VLM with any of the following options:

VLM OPTION	DESCRIPTION
/C=[*path*]*filename*	Specifies the configuration file (default is NET.CFG).
/D	Display VLM diagnostics.
/MC	Use conventional memory.
/ME	Use expanded memory (EMS).
/MX	Use extended memory (XMS).
/PS=*server*	Specifies preferred server name.
/PT=*tree*	Specifies preferred Directory tree name.
/U	Unload VLM.EXE from memory.
/V*n*	Specifies the progressive level of message display, where *n* is one of the following: 0 = Display copyright and critical errors only 1 = Also display warning messages 2 = Also display VLM module names 3 = Also display configuration file parameters 4 = Also display diagnostic messages

WHOAMI.EXE WHOAMI.EXE comes in both DOS and OS/2 command-line versions. Type **WHOAMI** to get information on your current connection to the network. A sample output of WHOAMI is as follows.

```
Current tree:  COMPANY
Other names: DJones

User ID:    DOUG
Server:     SERVER1  NetWare 4.11
Connection: 4 (Directory Services)
```

WSUPDATE.EXE Use WSUPDATE to update files on a workstation. You'll normally use WSUPDATE from a login script. This utility compares the version of the file you specify with the version of the same file on the workstation. If the specified file is newer, it is copied to the workstation.

Syntax for WSUPDATE is as follows:

WSUPDATE *sourcefile target /option*

where *sourcefile* is the file name, including a path; you can't use wildcard characters. For *target*, use a drive letter and optionally a path (to search all local drives, use the /LOCAL option). Subdirectories of the drive and path are searched. Here are the available *options:*

WSUPDATE OPTION	DESCRIPTION
/ALL	Search all mapped drives.
/C	Copy the new file over the old one without creating a backup of the old one.
/CON	Scroll the output continuously.
/E	Erase the existing log file (use with /L option).
/F=*file*	Specifies a text file that contains a list of target files to update.
/L=*file*	Specifies the name of a log file.
/LOCAL	Search all local drives.
/N	Create the directory specified by the target drive and path.
/O	Update all files, including Read Only files.
/P	Prompt the user as to whether to proceed with the update.
/R	Rename the replaced file with the .OLD extension.
/S	Search all subdirectories of the target path.
/V	Update the CONFIG.SYS file in the root directory with the line LASTDRIVE=Z:

WSUPGRD.EXE Use WSUPGRD, usually in a login script, to upgrade a pre-ODI LAN driver to ODI. Syntax is as follows:

WSUPGRD *file /option*

where *file* is the file to be upgraded (default: IPX.COM). Include a full path to the file. Available *options* are as follows:

WSUPGRD OPTION	DESCRIPTION
/C	Exit with error level 1 if no upgrade is performed. An error level 3 is generated if there is any other error in the process. By default, no error code is generated, whether an upgrade is made or not. Setting an error code allows a batch file to perform conditional steps if the replacement fails.
/N	If the old driver and new driver have different names, do not delete the old driver. (If they have the same names, the old driver is deleted anyway.)
/E0	Do not change the AUTOEXEC.NCF file.
/E1	In the AUTOEXEC.NCF file, delete the line that loads the old driver and add lines to load LSL, the ODI driver, and the IPX driver.
/E2	In the AUTOEXEC.NCF file, delete the line that loads the old driver and add a call to a new batch file, NWSTART.BAT. This batch file is created with commands to load the LSL, ODI driver, and IPX.
/S	Suppress the generation of a NET.CFG file from the information in the IPX driver's configuration table. Note: If an LDC file is present with the ODI driver, a NET.CFG file may be generated even when this switch is present.
/I	Print out the hardware ID in the master configuration table of the ODI driver. Note: You cannot use this option with any other option. If this switch is specified, no upgrade is performed.

Educational Opportunities

APPENDIX

B

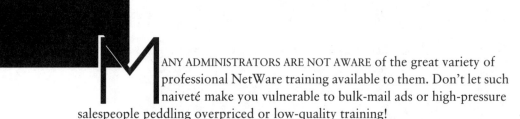

ANY ADMINISTRATORS ARE NOT AWARE of the great variety of professional NetWare training available to them. Don't let such naiveté make you vulnerable to bulk-mail ads or high-pressure salespeople peddling overpriced or low-quality training!

If you want more NetWare education and would like to know more about the excellent opportunities available to you, read on.

Training: Novell-Authorized or Not

Novell has an entire profit-making segment of its business: Novell Education. This division sells manuals and other training materials to authorized education centers and offers certification testing for a fee.

Novell Education also encourages purchase of the company's software (another Novell profit center) by promoting Novell products in class. Certified Novell Instructors (CNIs) agree in writing to "...conduct business in a manner which reflects favorably at all times on the products, goodwill and reputation of Novell..."

Instructors are themselves required to be certified, and they each pay $500 for their final instructor evaluations from Novell. Novel Authorized Education Centers (NAECs) and independent instructors also pay a yearly fee for the privilege of providing authorized instruction.

Obviously, Novell has a vested interest in its educational products. But the question is, do you? To help you decide, Table B-1 compares some aspects of Novell-authorized training versus other training. When you have decided which avenue is better for you, look in your telephone directory under Computers - Networking, or Computers - Training for local NetWare instruction providers. NAECs display a special logo.

TABLE B.1 Comparison of Novell-Authorized and Other NetWare Training	TRAINING ASPECT	NOVELL-AUTHORIZED	OTHER
	Quality	More consistent. NAECs and NAEPs must use Certified Novell Instructors (CNIs), must use Novell training materials, and must meet classroom equipment requirements.	Less consistent. Each training company can use instructors, materials, and classroom arrangements of their liking.
	Objectivity	Less objective. CNIs are not allowed to disparage Novell or its products. Still, most will admit that more "challenges" exist with some products than with others.	More objective. Instructors are not bound to Novell. They may, for instance, recommend a non-Novell gateway, application server, or groupware product that you can run on your network.
	Cost	Generally more. Suggested retail training prices are set by Novell (although the prices are almost always discounted).	Generally less. Non-Novell instruction is the underdog in the training market, and it is priced accordingly.

Education Centers and Partners

Novell has two main branches of its education business: Novell Authorized Education Centers (NAECs) and Novell Authorized Education Partners (NAEPs).

NAECS NAECs are local businesses, franchises, or branches of larger corporations that sell Novell training. The classes offered by NAECs generally occupy from one to five full-day sessions. Some NAECs offer evening and weekend classes.

NAECs provide Novell software and student manuals. They follow Novell course plans with Novell-defined course objectives. The instructors are Novell-certified (CNIs), meaning they have taken the classes they teach, have passed a certification test at a higher level than CNAs or CNEs (see "Are You Certifiable"), have passed an instructor evaluation, and have signed a contract with (and paid dues to) Novell.

Following are some of the courses that might interest a NetWare 4 administrator:

- *Course 200, Networking Technologies.* Three days for about $900.

- *Course 520, NetWare 4.1 Administration.* Five days for about $2,000.

- *Course 525, NetWare 4.1 Advanced Administration.* Four days for about $1,200.

- *Course 526, NetWare 3.1 to NetWare 4.1 Update.* Four days for about $1,600.

- *Course 532, NetWare 4.1 Design & Implementation.* Three days for about $1,000.

- *Course 605, NetWare TCP/IP Transport.* Two days for about $800.

- *Course 801, NetWare Service & Support.* Five days for about $2,000.

- *Course 804, NetWare 4.1 Installation & Configuration.* Two days for about $800.

NAEPS NAEPs have many of the same quality standards required of NAECs. They must use CNIs as instructors; they must encourage Novell certification of their students and reflect well on Novell and its products; and their classrooms must meet the same minimum hardware and software requirements extended to NAECs.

Beyond these standards, Novell has gone to great lengths to make sure NAEPs sell to a different customer base and therefore don't compete with NAECs. Following are some unique characteristics of NAEPs:

- All Novell courses are taught as part of a two- or four-year degree or certificate program that requires an equivalent of one year (minimum) full-time attendance at a scholastic institution.

- All Novell courses are taught in the school's standard format. Duration of an individual Novell course may not be less than one academic quarter or semester in length. For example, eight consecutive hours of Novell training per day (which you can receive at an NAEC) is not permitted under the NAEP program.

- NAEPs are not permitted to conduct Novell training at locations off campus.

- NAEPs may not schedule Novell courses as stand-alone courses. As mentioned previously, all Novell courses must be part of an overall degree or certificate program.

- The school must be a two- or four-year degree-offering college or university that is accredited at both state and regional levels.

- Private or public vocational schools must be accredited at both state and regional levels, must function as nonprofit organizations, and must charge a state-regulated tuition.

If you're already employed and can't take two years off to go to school, the NAEP route is not for you. However, if you like network administration and want to make it a career, you might consider full-time school. Traditional scholarships, loans, and grants may be available to help you financially. Visit Novell's education Web site at

```
http://education.novell.com/
```

or call Novell at 1-800-233-EDUC to find an NAEP in your area.

Are You Certifiable?

Novell offers Certified Novell Administrator (CNA), Certified Novell Engineer (CNE), and Master CNE (MCNE) designations. To achieve these certification levels, you need to pass some tests and enter into a contract with Novell.

Novell's certifications may look good on a resume, but employers are generally more interested in what you can *do* than in whether or not you've passed a test. If you begin a certification quest, you should do so knowing that hands-on experience in solving problems is your greatest guarantee of employment—not the certification itself.

NetWare classes generally focus on hands-on training and allow you to install or manage a network in the classroom. Furthermore, authorized NetWare classes correspond to specific certification tests; and course objectives correspond with test questions.

Attendance at Novell classes is not required for certification. You can buy a book at the bookstore, such as the *CNE-4 Study Guide* from Sybex's Network Press; study and try things on your own network; and pass the tests (while saving a few thousand dollars in the meantime).

Most CNAs, CNEs, and MCNEs have chosen a mix of classwork and outside study. For information on certification testing in your area, call either of the following centers:

- Sylvan Prometric, 1-800-RED-EXAM or 1-612-820-5706

- Sylvan Technology Centers, 1-800-RED-TEST or 1-410-880-8700

College Credit for Novell Classes

You can get college credit for attending Novell classes and passing tests. The number of credits you earn for attending an NAEC will vary, depending on the educational institution that sponsors you. To obtain credits, you must complete the following steps:

1. Attend an approved, full-length Novell authorized course at a Novell Authorized Education Center (NAEC).

2. Pass the corresponding Novell certification test at a Sylvan Prometric Testing Center.

3. Request a college credit transcript. For a college transcript from a participating NAEC, you must specify each course and test you want included in your transcript and present the NAEC with an original standard Novell Education course certificate, as well as an original, embossed test score report indicating a passing score. Suggested list price is $30 for the initial transcript, and $5 for each additional copy made at the time of the initial request.

The NAEC will print your transcript and forward it to the school(s) of your choice.

Bear in mind that, as with all transferring credit, the college or university evaluates your transcript prior to awarding any college credits. You should contact your school's admissions office for more information. The college or university may award some or all of the corresponding college credits, or it may not award any credits at all. For more information on the subject, call these numbers at Novell:

1-800-233-3382

1-801-222-7800 (select option 3)

1-801-429-5363 (request fax-back document 1104)

Glossary

GLOSSARY

10base2 Ethernet

A popular cabling scheme for Ethernet networks. This system uses coaxial cable in a bus configuration.

10baseT Ethernet

A common cabling scheme for Ethernet networks. This system uses twisted-pair cable in a star configuration, and all devices are attached to a central hub.

abend

NetWare's term for a server crash (short for abnormal end). An application (NLM) writing to an area of memory that belongs to the operating system frequently causes an abend.

Access Control List (ACL)

The property of an NDS object that contains the list of *trustees* or other objects that have rights to the object.

across-the-wire migration

One of the two possible migration strategies from NetWare 3.1*x* to NetWare 4. In the across-the-wire strategy, a new NetWare 4 server is connected to the same network as the NetWare 3.1*x* server, and data is copied over the network.

alias object

An object that represents, or points to, another object in the NDS tree. Alias objects can be created to make a resource in a different context available in the local context. NetWare can create aliases automatically when an object or container is moved.

AppleTalk

A networking system developed by Apple for use with Macintosh computers. The software for AppleTalk connectivity is built in to the Macintosh operating system. NetWare for Macintosh allows connectivity between AppleTalk and NetWare networks by emulating AppleTalk services on the NetWare server.

attributes

Attributes are stored for each file and directory on a server's file system. File attributes are used for security purposes and for status information for the file. For example, the Read Only attribute prevents a file from being written to or erased, and the Can't Compress attribute indicates that NetWare was unable to compress the file.

NDS objects also have attributes. For clarity, these attributes are usually referred to as *properties*.

auditing

A NetWare 4 service that allows a user, or auditor, to monitor activities on the network. The auditor can monitor the file system or an NDS container. You use the AUDITCON menu utility to monitor activities.

auditor's password

A password that is set when you begin an audit on a volume or NDS container. The auditor should change this password when the audit begins. The password is required for all auditing activities, including ending the audit.

backbone

A portion of a network that connects network segments together, often between buildings. High-speed networking systems such as FDDI and ATM are ideally suited for backbones.

backup engine

An application, such as Novell's SBACKUP, that provides backup services under the SMS (Storage Management Services) system.

bandwidth

A general term for the amount of traffic that can be carried over a network, measured in Mbps (millions of bits per second).

banner

In NetWare 4 printing, a page that is printed at the beginning of a print job to identify the job and the user who sent it. Banners can be turned on or off with options of the CAPTURE command.

base schema

The NDS base schema defines the structure of NDS—which objects are possible, which properties an object can have, and so forth. The NDS base schema is written to the server when NDS is installed. Third-party applications can extend, or add to, this schema using the NetWare API.

batch file

A file containing a list of commands to be executed. DOS batch files have the extension .BAT. Examples include AUTOEXEC.BAT, which executes when the workstation is booted, and STARTNET.BAT, which is used to attach to the network. NetWare command files (NCF) provide a similar feature for server commands.

bindery

The database used to store information about users, printers, and other network objects in NetWare 3.1x and earlier versions. The bindery is a simple, flat database that is stored separately on each server. NetWare 4 replaces the bindery with NDS.

bindery context

The context that will be provided as a simulated bindery by *Bindery Services*. You can set up to 16 separate contexts to serve as bindery contexts; these will be combined into a "bindery" that bindery-based clients can access.

Bindery Services

NetWare 4's service that allows the simulation of a bindery. This enables clients using older client software, such as the NetWare *DOS Shell*, to access the network. A branch of the NDS tree, the bindery context, is used as a simulated bindery.

binding

A link between a protocol, such as *TCP/IP* or *IPX*, and a network card. You can create a binding with the BIND command at the server or via the NET.CFG file at a workstation.

browsing

The process of navigating the Directory tree, usually using the NetWare Administrator (NWADMIN) utility.

bus

One of the types of network topology. In a bus topology, all nodes are connected to portions of a continuous bus. A break anywhere in the bus can disrupt the entire network.

cache buffer

NetWare sets aside a portion of the server's memory as cache buffers. These buffers cache information for the file system. The number of cache buffers depends on the available memory.

caching

A technique NetWare servers use to increase disk performance. Data read from the disk drive is stored in a block of RAM memory, or *cache buffer*. When clients request this data, it can be read directly from the cache, avoiding the use of the disk. NetWare provides both read and write caching.

child object

In NDS, an object that is under a *container object*. The container object is referred to as the *parent object*.

client

Any device that attaches to the network server. A workstation is the most common type of client. Clients run client software to provide network access. A piece of software that accesses data on a server can also be called a client.

client-server network

A server-centric network in which some network resources are stored on a file server, while processing power is distributed among workstations and the file server.

colon prompt

The prompt at the server console where you can enter server commands. The prompt displays the server's name followed by a colon. This is also referred to as the console prompt.

common name

In NDS, the least significant portion of an object's name. This is the name given to the object when it is created. The common name is abbreviated CN in typeful naming.

compile

In the NetWare 4 menu system, the process of converting a *menu source file* into a *menu data file* that the NMENU program can use. You use the MENUMAKE program to compile menus.

concentrator

A device, also called a hub, that is used at the center of a network with a star topology. All nodes in the network connect to a port on the concentrator.

container administrator

An administrator who is given rights to a *container object* and all the objects under it. A container administrator can be *exclusive,* meaning that no other administrator has access to the container.

container object

In NDS, an object that contains other objects. Container objects include Organization, Organizational Unit, and Country objects. The [Root] object is a specialized kind of container object. Objects within a container can be other container objects, or *leaf objects,* which represent network resources.

container security equivalence

See *Implied Security Equivalence.*

context

In NDS, an object's position within the Directory tree. The context is the full path to the *container object* in which the object resides.

current context

The current position in the Directory tree, maintained for a workstation connection. By default, objects are assumed to be in this context unless you specify the full *distinguished name*. The current context is also called the *default context*.

data migration

A system where infrequently used data is moved to a high-capacity storage device, such as a jukebox. The *High-Capacity Storage System* (HCSS) is the NetWare 4 service that handles data migration.

de-migrate

The process of moving data back from a high-capacity storage system to which it was migrated. This occurs when a user attempts to access the file that was migrated.

dedicated server

A server that serves no other purpose—it cannot be used as a workstation. All NetWare 3.1*x* servers and most NetWare 4 servers are dedicated. NetWare 4 provides a non-dedicated option through NetWare Server for OS/2.

default context

See *current context*.

Directory

In NDS, the database that contains information about each of the objects on the network. The Directory is organized into a tree-like structure, the Directory tree, with a *[Root] object* on top and *leaf objects* at the bottom. To distinguish it from disk directories, the NDS Directory always starts with a capital *D*.

directory map

A special NDS object you use to map directories in the file system. The MAP command can specify the name of the Directory Map object rather than the exact directory name. The directory name is contained in a property of the Directory Map object.

Directory tree

See *Directory*.

disk partition

See *Partition (disk)*.

distinguished name

In NDS, the full name of an NDS object, which includes the object's *common name* and its *context*, or location in the *Directory* tree. Also referred to as the *full distinguished name*.

distributed database

A database that is contained in multiple locations. NDS is a distributed database that is contained on multiple NetWare 4 servers.

divisional implementation

One of the methods of implementing NDS in a network. Each division is moved to NDS separately, with its own Directory tree. This is similar to the *departmental implementation*.

divisional organization

A type of NDS organization that divides the Directory tree into branches for each division or department within an organization. This is often a practical way to organize since members of a department or division often require access to the same set of resources.

drive mappings

Client software uses drive mappings to link DOS drive letters to directories on network volumes. The MAP command is used for this feature.

DynaText

The online documentation system included on CD-ROM with NetWare 4. You can use this system from the CD-ROM drive or install it on the network or a workstation. You use the DynaText Viewer to read and search the documentation. DynaText replaces Electrotext, used by NetWare 3.1*x* and earlier versions.

effective rights

The rights a user (or other *trustee*) has in a file system directory or NDS object after all factors—*explicit rights, inherited rights,* the *Inherited Rights Filter (IRF),* and *security equivalences*—-are considered.

environmental variable

In DOS, a named value that can be set and used by software. The SET command sets environmental variables in DOS; these can also be set with the DOS SET command within a login script.

exclusive container administrator

A special type of *container administrator* who is given rights to a container and the objects within it. The *Inherited Rights Filter (IRF)* prevents other administrators from having rights in the container.

explicit rights

In NDS or the file system, any rights that are given directly to a user for a directory or NDS object. Explicit rights override *inherited rights.*

explicit security equivalence

In NDS, a method of giving one *trustee* the same rights as another. Explicit security equivalence can be assigned with group membership, an Organizational Role, or the trustee's Security Equal To property.

extension

In DOS, OS/2, Windows 95, and NetWare file systems, a three-letter section at the end of a file name that denotes the file's type.

file

An individual unit of storage on a disk, usually corresponding to a single document. The file system in NetWare supports file storage.

file attributes

See *attributes*.

file name

In DOS, NetWare, and other file systems, a name given to a file. The name may include an *extension* to denote the type of file.

file server

A NetWare server. This name is used because file storage is one of the primary purposes of the server.

file system

The NetWare file system defines how files can be stored on disk volumes. Files are stored in a hierarchy of directories and subdirectories. NetWare's file system is similar to that of DOS.

frame types

Specifications for the method in which data is transmitted over the network. Clients and servers must support the same frame type in order to communicate.

full distinguished name

See *distinguished name*.

Greenwich Mean Time (GMT)

See *Universal Coordinated Time (UTC)*.

hybrid organization

An NDS organization strategy that combines two or more of the other methods—*locational*, *divisional*, and *workgroup*. Hybrid organizations are most useful for larger companies.

implied security equivalence

In NDS, an object is security equivalent to (receives the rights of) the object's parent object and its parents, leading up to the [Root] object. This is also called *container security equivalence*. The *Inherited Rights Filter* (IRF) does not affect this process.

in-place migration

A method for migrating NetWare 2.*x* to NetWare 4. This involves converting the file system to the NetWare 3.1*x* format and upgrading to NetWare 4 with the installation program.

inherited rights

In NDS or the file system, inherited rights are rights a *trustee* receives for an object because of rights to the object's parent (a *directory* in the file system or a parent object in NDS). Inherited rights can be blocked by an explicit assignment or by the *Inherited Rights Filter* (IRF).

Inherited Rights Filter (IRF)

In the file system, the IRF is the list of rights a user can inherit for a Directory from Directories above it. An IRF also exists for each NDS object and lists the rights a *trustee* can inherit from the object's parents. In NetWare 3.1*x*, the IRF was called the Inherited Rights Mask (IRM) and applied only to the file system.

internetworking

The process of connecting multiple *local area networks* (*LANs*) to form a *wide area network* (*WAN*). Internetworking between different types of networks is handled by a *router*.

IPX (Internetwork Packet Exchange)

The principal protocol used in NetWare 4. This is a connectionless protocol that sends data along the network until the appropriate device receives it.

IPX external network number

A number that represents an entire network. All servers on the network must use the same external network number.

IPX internal network number

A number that uniquely identifies a server to the network. Each server must have a different internal network number.

LAN

See *local area network*.

leaf object

An object that cannot contain other objects and that represents a network resource. Leaf objects include User, Group, Printer, Server, Volume, and many others.

local area network (LAN)

A network that is restricted to a local area—a single building, group of buildings, or even a single room. A LAN often has only one server but can have many.

locational organization

A method of organizing the Directory tree that divides it into Organizational Units for each geographical location of the organization. This strategy is often the best for network communication.

logging in

The process of entering a username and password to gain access to the network. NetWare 4 allows you to log into a Directory tree rather than a single server.

logical ports

Ports the CAPTURE command used to redirect a workstation printer port to a network print queue. The logical port has no relation to the port to which the printer is actually attached, or *physical port*.

login script

A set of commands that are automatically executed when a user logs in. NetWare 4 includes Container, Profile, User, and Default login scripts. Up to three of these can be executed for each user.

login script commands

Special commands that make up the *login script*.

login security

The most basic form of network security. A username and password are required in order to log in to the network and access resources.

master replica

The main replica for a *partition*. The master replica must be available when major changes, such as partition merging and splitting, are performed. Another replica can be assigned as the master if the original master replica is lost.

memory allocation

The system NetWare 4 uses to provide memory for use by applications (NLMs) on the server. Memory is allocated from an allocation pool.

menu data file

A file used to run a menu, using the NMENU program. The data file is the result of *compiling* the menu source file using the MENUMAKE utility. Menu data files have the .DAT extension.

menu source file

The file you write, using menu commands, to create a user menu. This file must be compiled into a *menu data file* using the MENUMAKE utility before it can be used. Source files typically have an .SRC extension.

merging Directory trees

The process of combining two Directory trees into a single tree. The objects in the source tree are combined into the destination or target tree. You use the DSMERGE utility to merge trees.

merging partitions

The process of combining an NDS partition with its parent partition, resulting in a single partition. The master replica of the partition must be available for this process.

message file

A file that provides prompts and messages for a NetWare workstation or server utility. Message files are provided for each supported language (English, French, Italian, German, and Spanish).

multi-valued property

In NDS, a property that can have multiple values. For example, a User object's Telephone Number property can store multiple telephone numbers.

Multiprotocol Router (MPR)

The software that provides *routing* capabilities for a NetWare 4 server. This allows communication between different types of networks.

name conflict

A situation in which names conflict with each other. This typically happens in *Bindery Services* or when using *NetSync*. All users in the *bindery context* must have unique common names.

name space

A service you can install on a NetWare 4 server volume to allow different types of file names to be used. Name spaces are available for OS/2 NFS and Macintosh naming. The default NetWare 4 name space supports DOS file names only.

NDS

See *NetWare Directory Services*.

NDS schema

See *Base Schema*.

NetSync

The software that allows NetWare 3.1x servers to be managed through NDS utilities. You accomplish this by using the NETSYNC3 NLM at the NetWare 3.1x servers and the NETSYNC4 NLM at the NetWare 4 server.

NetSync cluster

A NetWare 4 server and a group of NetWare 3.1x servers it can manage using NetSync. Each NetWare 4 server can manage up to 16 NetWare 3.1x servers.

NetWare Directory Services (NDS)

The system NetWare 4 uses to catalog objects on the network—users, printers, volumes, and others. NDS uses a *Directory tree* to store this information. All of the NetWare 4 network's resources can be managed through NDS.

NetWare DOS Requester

The client software that is used on a DOS workstation to access the NetWare 4 network and NDS. The DOS Requester replaces the *DOS Shell* in previous NetWare versions. Use the VLM.EXE program to load the DOS Requester.

NetWare Loadable Module (NLM)

An application or program that executes on the NetWare server. NLMs are used for device drivers, *local area network* (*LAN*) drivers, and applications such as backup software. A variety of utility NLMs are provided with NetWare 4, and others are available from third parties.

NetWare OS/2 Requester

The client software used to access a NetWare 4 server and NDS from an OS/2 workstation. The OS/2 Requester provides the same benefits as the DOS requester.

network address

A unique address that identifies each node, or device, on the network. The network address is generally hardcoded into the network card on both the workstation and server. Some network cards allow you to change this address, but there is seldom a reason to do so.

network-centric

The architecture used in a NetWare 4 network, in which objects are created for the entire network rather than for a single server. This feature is one of the benefits of NDS.

network client software

The software used to interface between a client and a NetWare server. Client software is available for DOS, Windows 3.1, Windows 95, Windows NT, OS/2, and UNIX.

Network Interface Card (NIC)

A device that is installed in a computer (either a client or server) to interface between the computer and the network wiring. Network cards are also called LAN cards.

network nodes

Devices (clients or servers) that are connected to a network are referred to as network nodes.

Network Operating System (NOS)

The software that runs on a file server and offers file, print, and other servers to client workstations. NetWare 4 is a NOS. Other examples include NetWare 3.1*x*, Banyan VINES, and IBM LAN Server.

network-aware

A type of application that directly supports networking. Such applications may support network printing, file sharing and locking, and other features.

NIC

See *network interface card.*

NLMs (NetWare Loadable Modules)

Programs that run on a NetWare server. These may be drivers for devices or system utilities. You can run these by typing **LOAD** followed by the name of the module at the server prompt.

non-dedicated server

A server that can also act as a workstation. NetWare 2.2 provided this capability, and NetWare 4 provides it through NetWare Server for OS/2. This is not possible under NetWare 3.1*x*.

object

In NDS, any resource on the network. Users, printers, and groups are examples of *leaf objects*. Another type, *container objects*, is used to organize other objects.

object trustee

See *trustee.*

occupant

A user who has been assigned to an Organizational Role object. Each Organizational Role can have multiple occupants, stored in the Occupants property of the object.

Organization object

Usually the highest-level container object used. Organizations are created under the [Root], or under the Country object if it is used. This object usually represents an entire organization or company. You can use multiple Organization objects in the same Directory tree.

Organizational Role object

An object that represents a role—an administrator or other specialized user who requires access to certain NDS objects or files. This object is often used for container administrators. See also *occupant*.

Organizational Unit object

The lowest-level container object. You can use Organizational Units to divide locations, divisions, workgroups, or smaller portions of the Directory tree. You can further subdivide Organizational Units with additional Organizational Units.

packet

A unit of data transmitted over the network. Different network types use different packet configurations. A packet includes data along with a header that refers to the network address of the destination node.

Packet Burst protocol

A streamlined protocol available in NetWare 4 and as an addition to NetWare 3.1*x*. In this protocol, several packets (a burst) are sent, and a single acknowledgment is sent back. If there is an error, only the packets that were not received correctly need to be re-sent. This eliminates most of the process of sending acknowledgments back and forth.

packet receive buffers

Areas of memory that NetWare sets aside for receiving packets over the network. Packets are stored in *buffers* until the server is able to process them.

parent object

In NDS, an object that *contains* another object—a container object. This is a relative term; a parent object also has parent objects of its own and is considered a child object from that perspective.

partition (disk)

NetWare uses disk partitions to divide a hard disk. A disk can contain a single NetWare partition, which you use to hold one or more NetWare volumes. In addition, a disk can have a DOS partition, used to boot the server and hold the SERVER.EXE program.

partition (NDS)

A branch of the NDS tree that can be replicated onto multiple servers. The partition includes a container object and the objects under it and is named according to the name of that object. By default, a single partition—the [Root] partition—exists.

path

In DOS, the list of directories that are searched to find an executable program or command. NetWare expands this through the use of search drives.

peripherals

Non-computer devices, such as printers and storage devices, that are attached to the network, to a server, or to a workstation.

physical port

In NetWare 4 printing, the port to which a printer is actually attached. This differs from the *logical ports* used in the CAPTURE command for printer redirection.

port driver

A component of NetWare 4 printing. The port driver accepts data from the print server and sends it to the printer. The port driver can be NPRINTER.EXE on a workstation, NPRINTER.NLM on a server, or a hardware device.

primary time server

One of the four types of time servers. A primary server communicates with other primary servers and reference servers and negotiates or "votes" to determine the correct time.

print job

A file that has been sent by a client for printing. See also *print queue*.

print job configuration

A set of parameters for network printing. These are similar to the parameters in the CAPTURE command. Print job configurations can be set for User and *container objects*.

print queue

The area that holds the list of print jobs that are waiting to print. The print queue is managed through the Print Queue object in NDS. Print jobs are sent from the print queue to the *print server* one at a time.

print server

A device that is used to manage printing. The Print Server NDS object is used to configure the print server. The print server itself can run on a NetWare 4 server (PSERVER.NLM) or in a hardware device. NetWare 3.1*x* included PSERVER.EXE, which ran on a DOS workstation; this is not supported in NetWare 4.

printer forms

Configurations that allow you to use specific paper types or send special codes to a printer. These are defined with the PRINTDEF utility.

printer redirection

The process of mapping a logical printer port in the workstation to a network printer. The user can then print to the port as though it were an actual printer, and the print job will be sent to the print queue. You use the CAPTURE utility to start redirection.

printer sharing

NetWare's feature that allows multiple users to send data to a printer. A print queue is used to store each print job, and they are sent to the printer one at a time.

Profile object

A special NDS object for assigning the same *login script* to a group of users. The Profile login script is executed after the container login script and before the user login script.

properties

In NDS, all the possible information that can be entered for an object. The properties of a User object include login name, full name, and telephone number. See also *values*.

protocol

A method of communicating between NetWare servers and clients. The protocol is the "language" used for sending data. Data is divided into *packets* specified by the protocol. IPX is the typical protocol for NetWare networks.

[Public] trustee

A special NDS trustee you can use to assign rights to all users in the network, including those that are not logged in. This allows users to browse the Directory tree before logging in. You should avoid assigning rights to this trustee.

reference time server

One of the four types of *time server*. The reference server provides an authoritative source of time. It is often attached to an external clock or a modem or radio link to a time source. One or more *primary time servers* must be used.

registry

In Windows 95, a special file that stores configuration information for the operating system and installed applications. You use the REGEDIT utility to manage the registry.

relative distinguished name (RDN)

A shortened version of an object's full *distinguished name* that specifies the path to the object from the current context. Relative distinguished names do not begin with a period. You can use periods at the end of the RDN to move up the Directory tree.

remote printer

See *workstation printer*.

repeater

A device that connects segments of a network together, allowing greater distances. This device amplifies the signal and outputs it.

replica

In NDS, a copy of a partition stored on a server. At least one replica, the master replica, is required for each partition. Other replicas include read/write and read-only replicas.

replication

The process of keeping copies of the NDS information on separate servers. Each *partition* in NDS has a set of replicas. These include the master replica (the original *partition*) and optionally read/write and read-only replicas.

root directory

In the DOS or NetWare file system, the highest location in the directory hierarchy. Files can be stored in the root directory or in subdirectories underneath it.

[Root] object

The ultimate NDS container object. The [Root] object is created when NDS is installed and contains all other objects. You cannot delete, rename, or move this object.

router

A device that connects two dissimilar networks and allows packets to be transmitted and received between them.

routing protocols

Protocols that send information to manage routing. The routing protocols supported by NetWare 4 are RIP (Routing Information Protocol) and NLSP (NetWare Link Services Protocol).

same-server migration

One of the methods for upgrading NetWare 2.*x* to NetWare 4. This requires that the server running NetWare 2.*x* be capable of running NetWare 4. The process involves upgrading the file system to NetWare 3.1*x* format and then upgrading to NetWare 4.

search drives

A list of paths that will be searched when you type a command on a workstation attached to the network. These are managed with the MAP command. This is similar to the *path* in the DOS file system.

secondary time server

One of the four types of time servers. Secondary time servers are strictly time consumers; they do not provide time to any servers. They receive time from a *primary* or *single reference server* and provide the time to clients.

security equivalence

In NDS, any situation in which an object or *trustee* receives the same rights given to another *object*. See also *implied equivalence* and *explicit equivalence*.

segment

A portion of a network containing devices that use the same network protocols and are connected by similar wiring. Devices in a segment also use the same external network number.

server

A machine running NetWare acts as a server. The server provides file, printer, and other services to clients.

server-centric

The type of network organization used in NetWare 3.1*x* networks. In this organization, each server keeps its own catalog of users and other resources (the *bindery*). A user who requires access to more than one server must be added to the bindery of each one. NetWare 4 provides a *network-centric* alternative.

server commands

Commands that execute on the server console. For example, the LOAD command is used to load an NLM.

server printer

One of the methods of attaching a printer to the network, and probably the most common. The printer is attached to a printer port on the NetWare server. The port driver, NPRINTER.NLM, drives the printer.

Service Advertising Protocol (SAP)

The *protocol* used for various NetWare 4, as well as 2.*x* and 3.*x*, services. *Single reference time servers* use this protocol to broadcast time information to the entire network at once.

single reference time server

One of the four types of *time servers*. If it's used, the single reference server is the only time provider on the network. All other servers must be configured as secondary time servers. This is the default configuration when NetWare 4 servers are installed.

splitting partitions

The process of creating a new NDS partition. A container object within a current partition is specified, and that object and all objects under it are moved (split) to a new partition.

standards document

A document that describes the naming standards, properties, and values to be used for a network. This is a vital part of NDS planning.

Storage Management Services (SMS)

The NetWare 4 service that allows for backup services. SMS consists of several components, ranging from the *device driver* that handles access to the backup device to the front end.

synchronization

The process NDS uses to ensure that all replicas of a partition contain the same data. Synchronization is handled through replica rings.

Target Service Agent (TSA)

One of the components of the NetWare 4 *Storage Management Services* (*SMS*). The TSA provides an interface to the device that will be backed up. Devices include servers, workstations, and the NDS database. A separate TSA is used for each one.

TCP/IP

A suite of protocols, including Transport Control Protocol (TCP) and Internet Protocol (IP). TCP/IP is supported by NetWare 4 and is typically used for connectivity with UNIX systems and the Internet.

time consumer

A machine that receives time information but does not send time information to any other server. Secondary time servers are time consumers, as are network workstations.

time provider

A type of *time server* that provides the time to other time servers.

time provider group

A group of time servers, usually including a *reference server* and one or more *primary servers*. In a *wide area network* (WAN), you can use separate time provider groups for each location.

time server

A server that performs time synchronization. All NetWare 4 servers are time servers of one type or another. The types of servers include *primary, reference, single reference,* and *secondary.*

time source

See *time provider.*

time synchronization

The process NetWare 4 uses to ensure that all servers are provided with the correct time. Time synchronization is managed through *time servers.*

topology

A type of network connection or cabling system. The term refers to the placement of nodes and wiring on the network. Common topologies include bus, ring, and star.

trustee

Any object that has been given rights to an NDS object or file. Trustee rights can include *explicit, inherited,* and *effective rights.*

trustee rights

Rights given to a trustee (such as a user) for a file in the file system, or for an object in NDS.

typeful naming

The formal method of naming NDS objects, including name types for each portion of the name—for example, .CN=Terry.OU=Mktg.O=QAZ_CO.

typeless naming

The more common method of NDS object naming, which does not include name types—for example, .Terry.Mktg.QAZ.CO. Typeless naming is adequate for most uses within NDS utilities.

Universal Coordinated Time (UTC)

The standard time system NetWare 4 supports. The abbreviation is from the French. UTC was formerly known as GMT (Greenwich Mean Time). The time zone for a NetWare server is defined in terms of difference from UTC; for example, the Mountain time zone is UTC minus seven hours.

User object

In NDS, an object that represents a user on the network. The User object includes properties that identify the user and assign rights to NDS and the file system. You can use a *user template* to create a number of users with similar properties.

user template

In NDS, a special User object that assigns defaults when a new user is created. You can create a user template for each NDS container, and you can change the property values of this object to provide defaults for new users in the container. The user template does not affect existing users.

values

The data that is stored in the *properties* of an NDS object. Properties can have one or more values. Some are required and others are optional.

Virtual Loadable Module (VLM)

One of the components of the *DOS Requester*. The VLM.EXE program loads various VLMs, each for a certain purpose. For example, PRINT.VLM allows redirection of printers. VLMs that are not needed can be unloaded to increase available memory.

volume

A portion of a disk set aside for NetWare files. Volumes can be created within a NetWare partition on the hard disk. The SYS: volume is the first volume created, and is required for all NetWare 4 servers.

wide area network (WAN)

A network that extends across multiple locations. Each location typically has a *local area network* (*LAN*), and the LANs are connected together in a WAN. These networks are typically used for enterprise networking.

wildcard

In the DOS file system, a character that can substitute for one or more unknown characters when typing a command. The DOS wildcards are ?, which represents one character, and *, which represents any number of characters.

workgroup organization

One of the methods of organizing the NDS tree. In this method, workgroups (users who perform similar functions or are participating in the same project) are used to divide the Directory tree. This method is best used in a *hybrid* organization.

workstation

A computer that is connected to the network and has access to a NetWare 4 server. Workstations can be running DOS, Windows, Windows 95, Windows NT, OS/2, or UNIX operating systems. Workstations are also called clients.

workstation printer

A printer that is attached to a workstation on the network. In NetWare 3.1*x*, these were referred to as remote printers and were handled by the RPRINTER.EXE program. In NetWare 4, the NPRINTER.EXE program handles them.

Index